Around the World in 80 Rounds

Around the World in 80 Rounds

*Chasing a Golf Ball
from Tierra del Fuego to
the Land of the Midnight Sun*

David Wood

Foreword by Turk Pipkin

St. Martin's Press 🐾 New York

www.stmartins.com

Design by Level C
Map by David Cain

LIBRARY OF CONGRESS CATALOGING-IN-PUBLICATION DATA

Wood, David.
    Around the world in 80 rounds : chasing a golf ball from Tierra del Fuego to the land of the midnight sun / David Wood ; foreword by Turk Pipkin.—1st ed.
        p. cm.
    ISBN-13: 978-0-312-37577-5
    ISBN-10: 0-312-37577-8
    1. Golf courses—Guidebooks.   2. Golf—Humor.   3. Wood, David—Travel.   I. Title.
II. Title: Around the world in eighty rounds.

GV975.W596 2008
796.35202' 07—dc22   2007042759

First Edition: March 2008

10   9   8   7   6   5   4   3   2   1

For Lisabeth

Contents

Foreword

Jealous. That's what I am. Green with golf envy.

The thing that's driven me to piques of putter petulance is being asked to write an introduction for David Wood's global *tour de golf*, when what I really wanted was to take that year-long golf trip and write the book myself.

But why be petty? After all, David Wood is one of my longest-standing golf buddies, and a passionate devotee of the game and its traditions. He's the kind of guy who chooses public courses over private, links golf over some fancy Trumped masterpiece, and rather than ride in a cart, he prefers to walk with his bag on his shoulder, the same way he learned the game. Most important of all, he relishes that moment on the eighteenth green when he and his playing partners shake hands after a great round of golf.

Why? Because that's the way it ought to be.

Mr. Wood, once a successful comic who appeared on the *David Letterman Show*, began life as a class clown and has grown into a class act.

He is also one of the world's biggest golf nuts. He knows the lore and the legends of the game's storied past, and he can identify current tour players you probably never heard of just by glimpsing their swing from two fairways away.

When the weather is anywhere close to being playable, David Wood plays. When the storms rage or the night shines, he practices his full swing indoors, even it means a few nicks in the ceiling and divots in the carpet. A golfer has to have his priorities.

And so it came as no surprise when Mr. Wood announced he was going to liquidate his assets—ditch the mortgage, the car payment, the job, and all the troubles that come with them—and use the proceeds to make a round-the-world golf pilgrimage.

Why didn't *we* think of that? I mean, what golfer worth his, or her, balls wouldn't want to trade all the troubles of life for the adventure and privilege of teeing it up everywhere from the glacial volcanoes of the Andes to the Arctic Circle in Norway?

And that's not even why I'm jealous.

No. I am demonstrating new shades of golf-writer green because David Wood has undertaken the difficult task of being the Paul Theroux of golf and actually managed to pull it off.

This was no mean feat. His journey didn't begin as some publisher-underwritten fantasy; in fact, there was no guarantee that anyone would know of it but himself. And yet he journeyed up the river to golf's heart of darkness and light. Luckily, he takes us with him.

With a slender travel bag, ten clubs, and a credit card, Mr. Wood travels to the farthest corners of the golf world, playing on fields of snow, deserts of dirt, oceans of sand, and occasionally on fairways of grass. From Mission Hills in China to the Cape of Good Hope, he tees the ball on six continents, and makes friends on all of them.

Legendary golf instructor Harvey Penick said, "If you play golf, you are my friend." David Wood took that famous phrase and proved it true on every corner of the world.

Along the way, he discovers the intrigue of South American dictators and Tibetan revolutionaries, the joy of women caddies and Thai massage, and the gut-wrenching terror of Indian curry and Egyptian falafel.

In a nearly yearlong Homeric odyssey of golf, he plays a thousand holes and very wisely chooses to describe no more than a handful of them. There is more than one kind of score to keep. Why write only about the game, when he can describe the eagerness with which he is welcomed onto the courses he visits and into the lives of the people he meets?.

Don't get me wrong: the descriptions of Ringaringa Heights and Elephant Hills Golf Course are superb, but without a hole played or a shot fired, Mr. Wood's book would remain a fine travel log. It is an eye-opening look at what's good and bad in the world, and how little we Americans know about the other 96 percent of the people who share it with us.

Ultimately, the golf becomes his excuse to see the world, rather than the other way around. And that is exactly as it should be.

The further he journeys, the more he hits his stride, describing a round in the shadow of Great Pyramid of Giza interrupted by the Muslim call to prayer, or strolling solo the streets of Cairo wearing golf shorts and visor under the assumption that being a golf geek exempts you from underlying East-West tensions.

It may be a wide world of golf, but very little of it abides by golf rules. I can't decide if he's lucky to be alive, or if it's his readers who are lucky he survived to tell this tale.

Returning with a passport that must be stamped fully black and stuffed with foreign visas like an old featherie golf ball, Mr. Wood leaves his reader with one underlying thought—that the people he met aren't that different from his friends back home.

So welcome to a world of golf with no rules and no gimmes. All it takes is balls.

—Turk Pipkin

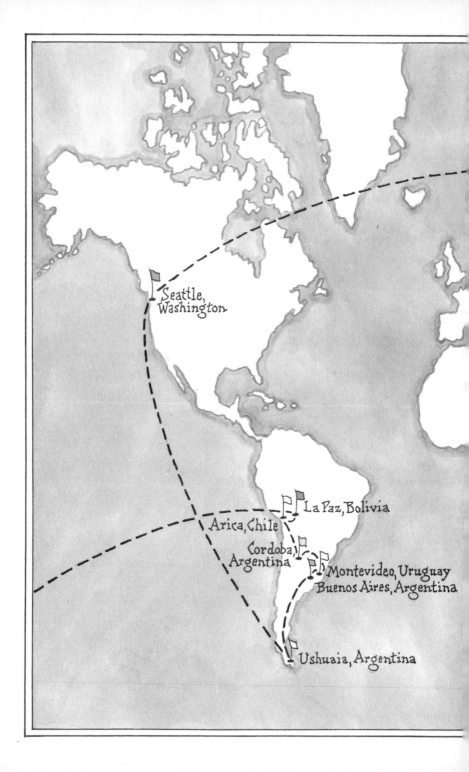

Seattle, Washington

La Paz, Bolivia

Arica, Chile

Cordoba, Argentina

Montevideo, Uruguay
Buenos Aires, Argentina

Ushuaia, Argentina

Tromsø, Norway

Moscow, Russia

Budapest, Hungary

Delhi, India

Kathmandu, Nepal

Kunming, China

Giza, Egypt

Bangalore, India

Hanoi, Vietnam

Chiang Rai, Thailand

Phuket, Thailand

Singapore

Victoria Falls, Zimbabwe

Alice Springs, Australia

Durban, South Africa

Stewart Island, New Zealand

And forsooth, who would not go round the world for less?

—Jules Verne,
Around the World in Eighty Days

Around the World in 80 Rounds

Introduction

West Seattle Golf Course
Seattle, Washington

47.61°N–122.33°W

On the east coast of Scotland in the early 1500s, golf was starting to bloom as brightly as the brilliant burst of luminous yellow gorse that signals the arrival of summer in the Kingdom of Fife. Except for those periodic pesky Viking invasions, there just wasn't a whole lot happening up there on the windswept shores of the North Sea. Several hundred years of sand still had to flow through the hourglass before a Scot could devote every waking moment to the life-or-death Glasgow Celtic versus Glasgow Rangers football (soccer) rivalry as they do today. Life was mundane.

Sure, the sheep had to be tended, but with grass in plentiful supply they didn't roam too far. Shepherding wasn't exactly the most varying of professions. Job-wise, each day was the same as the last, and there wasn't much of a dental plan. How long could one watch one's flock without one's eyes crossing from the tediousness? It was strictly a matter of time before a shepherd grabbed a long stick and whacked a small rock as far as he could out of sheer bloody boredom!

Those early golfers soon learned that hitting a rock off into the sweet Scottish air was more fun than a bowlful of warm haggis. The shepherds started honing their whacking skills, even trying out different sticks to see which was superior in propelling that rock where they wanted it to go. From the beginning, it was obvious this silly endeavor required practice if any degree of proficiency was to be obtained.

It turned out the shaggy fescue covering the wind-formed sand dunes where the sheep liked to hang out was the perfect turf for this new time-killer. The woolly beasts were excellent groundskeepers with their constant munching of the long grass. This was now golf land and the sheep could damn well watch themselves! Bugger off ya furry bastards!

Golf in Scotland became king. Well, "Queen" actually, because their ruler, Mary, Queen of Scots, was such an avid golfer that in 1567 she was roundly criticized for playing the game within a fortnight of the funeral of Lord Darnley, her freshly murdered husband. She surely mourned his loss, but, like all true golfers, her mind soon drifted back to figuring out how to get that ball into that little hole in fewer strokes. While grieving she must have been thinking, "I'll miss my dear husband, but if I would just clear my royal left hip a wee bit faster on the downswing, I could come into the ball more from the inside. . . ."

At roughly the same time in history, on the opposite end of the earth, Ferdinand Magellan, the restless Portuguese explorer, was busy discovering the body of water that would bear his name— the Strait of Magellan. Acting on his crazy notion that the earth could be circumnavigated, Magellan and his Spanish fleet were sailing south along the east coast of South America hoping to find a waterway west to the riches of the Spice Islands. The voyage was constantly under peril. His Spanish crew of two hundred and fifty men didn't take kindly to being bossed around by some pompous dude from Portugal.

After surviving a mutiny and losing one of their five vessels, the unhappy sailing party happened upon an inner passage that separated the little baby toe of the extreme southern tip of South America from the main body of this exotic continent. Magellan called this land *Tierra del Fuego* or "Land of Fires" because of the many bonfires the natives kept blazing to warm them from the Antarctic cold. He found the land bleak and forbidding and chose to quickly sail through. The riches of the Spice Islands were calling!

This long channel across the bottom of South America linked the Atlantic to an immense body of water that Magellan named the "Pacific" for its calmness. The name stuck like a crisply hit pitching wedge. Hopefully, Mary and Ferdinand enjoyed themselves while they could as violent death loomed on their respective scorecards. After only a couple of months on the newly named Pacific, Magellan was killed during an ill-planned attack on the island of Mactan in the Philippines, proving that while the ocean was calm, the people weren't.

Meanwhile, after her husband's funeral, Mary had played her last round of golf. Church elders, the real powers behind the throne, assumed Mary was in on the plot to kill her husband. Mary sought refuge at the court of her cousin, Queen Elizabeth I of England, only to be immediately put in prison. Queen Elizabeth obviously didn't care for golfers, even if they were family. Mary was sentenced to death by beheading. Being a golf nut to the end, with her thin white neck on the chopping block awaiting the sharp blade of the executor's sword, Mary's last thoughts must have drifted to that addictive new game of her homeland: "Perhaps I should go back to the interlock grip. I seem to be missing the fairway to the—" Whack!

My plan was to play the game that fascinated both Mary and me while striving to see the world as Ferdinand had surely hoped to do more of in his short, but adventurous, life. This idea began while I was sitting at my desk at home on the shores of Lake

Washington just outside Seattle. It was a cloudy, gray noon on that typical Pacific Northwest day, and I had on my normal day-time writing attire: red-plaid pajama bottoms, black T-shirt, white golf socks, and my well-worn blue slippers. My uncombed hair stood straight up like a Caucasian Don King. Not a pretty picture, but when you work at home, every day is an extremely casual Friday.

Unable to focus and begin writing a travel article on a recent trip to Italy's wonderful water city of Venice, I had just spent an hour staring blankly at my computer screen. My stupor was getting close to the uncontrolled drooling phase I associate with anyone discussing the merits of term life insurance.

I struggled to stay focused, trying to conjure up in my mind's eye the dreamlike Grand Canal, but as I gazed out onto the gray shimmering surface of Lake Washington from my second-floor office window, all I could think about was the game that took up 99 percent of my nonsexual thoughts—golf.

That day my heart and mind and hormones were in Ireland. Glorious Ireland, where I had recently played golf on the rugged, windswept western coast of that enchanted land. Having just finished writing about that journey, I was sad the piece was over. I loved retracing my steps on the eerie moonscape of Connemara, reliving the majestic splendor of the perfect duneland of the golf mecca of Ballybunion, and basking in the brilliance of what has to be the greatest links-land golf course you never hear about: Carne, in the seaside town of Belmullet hiding up in the isolated north-west corner of the Emerald Isle. Those great golf courses of the world were where I channeled my pent-up energy. I ogle over magazine pictorials of golf courses with the same lustful intensity I used to save for Miss October in *Playboy*. Things change, I guess.

After college, golf had swept me up me as brazenly as Donald Trump's comb-over and became the focus of my adult sporting life. Growing up, I had played most every sport but golf—it was a game that wasn't in my realm of consciousness. Golf was for old rich guys. It was the game of Richard Nixon, for heaven's sake.

Nonetheless, a golfer I became and played the game whenever and wherever I could.

As the years passed, playing in the United States alone wasn't enough to scratch my itch. On a biyearly basis for the past fifteen years, I traveled and played golf over the nooks and crannies of two countries I had grown to adore: Ireland and Scotland. Golf there was windy and rugged and natural. Walking was required; you didn't need some Nixonian golf cart.

I was lucky to have played the more famous courses those two countries offered: The Old Course of St. Andrews, Royal Portrush, Muirfield, Carnoustie, Waterville, Lahinch, Turnberry, and Royal County Down, but I had learned that the real joyous golf experiences often were on courses less well known, such as North Berwick, Crail, Ballyliffin, Rosapenna, Tain, and Machrihanish. The below-the-title-character actors are every bit as interesting as the stars on the movie marquee in the golf world.

I loved slipping into those small towns, playing golf with the regular folks, and just going about my daily business as if I had been living amongst them for my whole life. Of course, we all knew I was just a visitor, but when you mind your own business and let the locals initiate the conversation (and buy them a pint), they let you in on their lives a touch more. Usually after ten pints you were made an honorary member of their clan and were privy to generations of family secrets. I craved the golf and the people in these remote places like a junkie needing a fix.

The more remote and off the beaten path, the more the golf and the lives that surrounded it appealed to me. Sitting at my desk daydreaming of Ireland, I wiped the drool that was now inching toward my keyboard and began wondering where else I could go play golf on this planet of ours. What was even more remote? Having been so consumed with Ireland and Scotland over the years, I was a philistine on the rest of the golfing world.

Instead of working on the article of waterlogged Venice, I started doing Google searches on golf around the world. In the search bar, I typed in the names of countries I thought least likely to have golf.

Nepal immediately came to mind. The search revealed Nepal had two courses. How about Laos? Again, two courses. How about Vietnam? Ten courses! This was getting interesting.

Spending the best part of the afternoon having a blast typing in the name of every country I could think of, I found golf everywhere. Russia, Zimbabwe, India, Chile, Argentina, Uruguay, Indonesia, Malaysia, Egypt—all had golf. I became more intrigued to see if I could find the most remote courses of our world. Where was the northernmost golf? Having no idea, I guessed it would be somewhere in Iceland. I did another Google search.

It turns out several places claim their course to be at the top of the golfing world. Fairbanks, Iceland, Finland, Canada, and Greenland all make that boast. My old tattered *National Geographic Map of the World* proved the winner is Tromsö, Norway, sitting at just under 70 degrees north of the equator and rightfully holding this claim as the northernmost golf course in the world. What must Tromsö golf be like? Is this snow golf? Igloos with Laplanders serving whale blubber at the turn? I wanted to find out.

Next, I found the earth's southernmost course. The winner hands-down was the Ushuaia Golf Club in Ushuaia, Argentina, at 54.8 degrees south. I found Ushuaia on my map way down at the bottom of South America—just a speck on the globe and the southernmost city in the world with golf. The next bit of land straight south was Antarctica. What must that be like? Were there penguins on the course? Floating iceberg par-threes? All of a sudden, a plan started forming in my restless, goofy brain.

This had the makings of an intriguing golf adventure. What if some idiot was to travel from the world's southernmost course to its northernmost? From Ushuaia, Argentina to Tromsö, Norway— now that would be a golf trip! What if that same idiot decided to play in as many obscure countries and courses en route as he could? And what if that person was a forty-seven-year-old bachelor with no real commitments or anything else to hold him back?

What about financing this costly endeavor? Well, suppose said idiot sold his condo, his only tangible asset (besides his trusty old

Mizuno MS-7 irons) to fund this adventure? Who needed a home anyway? Who needed monthly bills? Who needed financial security? I felt sure I knew the perfect idiot to do something crazy like this. Me.

I'd long wanted to emulate travel writer Paul Theroux, my literary hero, who took his sharp focus and literary insight to exotic locales like Katmandu or Patagonia or Cairo. For years I read and reread Mr. Theroux's *The Great Railway Bazaar* or *The Pillars of Hercules* or *The Old Patagonian Express* and yearned to take adventurous journeys as he had done boarding trains and rickety buses and seeing the world up close and personal. The only difference was I wanted to golf while there.

Simply put, I wanted more worldly experiences. I felt like a baby in my knowledge of the world. It was embarrassing not to be able to talk about Hong Kong, Bangkok, or Auckland from firsthand experience. I had never seen Sydney's Opera House, the Kremlin, or the Sphinx except on television or in books. This was all about to change.

So there I was: a bachelor, a writer, a former stand-up comedian who has never held a steady job. I was pretty much unemployable in anything that required any real skill. There was nothing holding me back from a long journey around the world. So what if my Roth IRA was in such bad shape I was probably going to become an expert on the nutritional qualities of cat food in my later years. I'll manage.

I was curious about golfers in far-off lands. Did they love watching Tiger Woods's awesome combination of technically brilliant golf swing and unrelenting will to succeed like I did? I was curious, also, about foreign golf talk. Do they say, "I'm on the dance floor!" in Hindi when they hit their approach shot onto the green? Do they say, "Hit it Alice!" when they leave a putt woefully short of the hole? Do they know that the correct phrase is *Hit it Aliss!* and refers to Peter Aliss, the witty ABC and BBC television commentator and former member of the British Ryder Cup team? The phrase was born when Mr. Aliss famously hit a crucial putt short of the hole in a tight Ryder Cup match against the Americans in the 1950s and isn't a slur on Alice, wherever she might be. That poor woman has suffered mightily in this case of mistaken identity by scores of awful putters missing putts all over the world! These are the life-and-golf questions that aroused my curiosity.

Do they care about golf and love the game the way I do? Do they treasure the tradition, manners, and orderliness of the ancient game? Do they love the fact that golf is a game where one can't hide behind teammates—good or bad—and there's no one to blame but yourself? Like me, do they feel that golf is best when inclusive and public and not just a rich man's private game? Do they feel there's nothing better than carrying your bag and walking the course rather than taking a ridiculous golf cart? Do they love playing the game with their buddies on a cheerful Saturday morning as I did weekly with my pals at the municipal West Seattle Golf Course, or going out alone at the end of the day to see how many holes you could get in before night falls? I planned to find out.

In a whirlwind two months, I had sold my condo, become inoculated against the terrifying diseases of the world, put my meager furniture and belongings in storage, and started my quest from Ushuaia to Tromsö. I had my passport, a small laptop computer for writing, my credit cards, and my yellow card listing all my vaccines. Everything I owned was either in my golf travel bag or in storage. For the first time in my adult life I didn't have a telephone, television, house payment, electric bills, or monthly concerns. I had the money I had made from the equity of selling my former residence. I was homeless, jobless, completely free of the usual mundane tasks of life, and if truth be told, the happiest I had felt in a long time. I was a touch nervous, but excited about the unknown. Who knew what the coming year out in the world would bring?

I didn't give myself too much time to question the sanity of my actions. I just decided to keep my eye on that little white ball as I traveled completely around the big blue one and hoped the Golf Gods would watch over me.

1

Ushuaia Golf Club
Ushuaia, Argentina

54.49°S–68.19°W

Four centuries plus after Mary's last game, my bus bounced along the rocky dirt road that parallels Magellan's discovered channel as I was on my way to Ushuaia, Argentina, the home of the world's southernmost golf course. Ushuaia was the first goal of my around-the-world golfing quest.

It had been a long slog of travel from Seattle to get to within spitting distance from Ushuaia. Zigzagging across both Americas, I had flown ten thousand air miles south from the Pacific Northwest to Santiago, which sits midway down the shaft of the one-iron–shaped Chile.

I had spent five days in Santiago acclimating myself to South America and enjoying the robust, but terribly smoggy, capital city. I met with travel agents trying to find the best methods to get around overland. The common consensus was the overnight sleeper bus— the *salon de cama*. I had hoped to take trains, my favorite mode of transportation, but rail travel is sadly on a severe decline in those parts. While sipping Chilean coffee in Santiago's charming sidewalk bistros, I came up with an outline of an itinerary for the South American portion of my quest.

My plan of attack to explore golf in South America was to make my way to Ushuaia first and play the world's most southern course (once the snow cleared). Next was a trip to golf-rich Buenos Aires with a side excursion to Uruguay. While doing my hasty research in Seattle, I had read that there was a terrific course in Montevideo designed by the Michelangelo of golf-course architecture, Dr. Alister MacKenzie. Along with numerous golf-course masterpieces built in the 1920s and 1930s, MacKenzie has golf's greatest design on his vaulted résumé—Cypress Point on California's splendid Monterey Peninsula. An Alister MacKenzie–designed course in Uruguay? If true, it would be like finding an unknown Picasso hanging next to the velvet Elvis on the wall of a double-wide in an Arkansas trailer park. This I wanted to see. Finally, my plans were: back to Chile for the northern half of the one-iron and then top it off with a journey to Bolivia's La Paz and a visit to their nosebleed-high course. It was a rough outline and that's all I wanted—just me, my golf clubs, my Dramamine, and my map.

My only other obligation was the promise I had made to my sister that I would find out whether or not the water swirls the other way around in the toilet when flushed in the Southern Hemisphere. She was under the belief that it flows in the opposite direction below the equator. Living in Minnesota, and the mother of my two beautiful teenage nieces, she probably wanted something clever to impress her friends and loved ones on those bitter-cold Minnesota nights in January.

While in Santiago, I had also attempted to use the small bits of Spanish I had hurriedly crammed into my head. Back in Seattle, I bought a self-learning cassette-tape course of elementary Spanish and tried to give myself a crash course in *Español*. Up until then, the most complex phrase I knew was *tacos al carbon*. Having decided to take this trip only two months prior, there obviously wasn't the time to learn Spanish as thoroughly as I would have liked. Especially since Santiago seems to be the wild-dog center of the universe with packs of ferocious canines trotting around in roving gangs most every block, the phrase that would really could have come in handy was:¿ *Perdóname, cuándo fue la última vez que ese gruñiendo, destraillido Doberman tuyo mató y comió un viajero norteamericano?* ("Excuse me, when was the last time that growling, unleashed Doberman of yours killed and ate a North American traveler?")

Traveling south from Santiago my next destination was Valdivia. I went to the main bus depot to find my *salon de cama*. When a South American takes a bus trip, every member of his or her family comes to see them off. Grandparents, parents, brothers, sisters, and third cousins twice removed all come along for moral support. I saw this ritual repeated over and over again in the continent's bus terminals. On the platform next to me stood a thirtysomething gentleman from Santiago who was waiting for the same bus as I was. He was accompanied by eleven relatives to see him off. Thinking perhaps he was moving away from home and wouldn't be seeing his loved ones for a long time, I asked him if he was leaving Santiago for an extended time. "No, I'm going to Valdivia on business. I take this trip twice a month. I'll be back in two days." I was going around the world for a year and no relatives back in the U.S. saw it necessary to go see me off.

The overnight ride to Valdivia cost me twenty-nine dollars and served two purposes—it got me hundreds of miles closer to Ushuaia and was a cheap place to bunk. Our double-decker bus arrived, and I began the Chilean leg of my quest for Ushuaia.

From Santiago, it was ten hours overnight to the delightful river city of Valdivia—where I stayed for a couple of days as Chile was celebrating its independence day. Their holiday is similar to our Fourth of July except they don't get drunk and blow their fingers off with fireworks like we do. They get drunk and blow off their entire limbs. What people in Chile consider fireworks, we consider major artillery fire. There were explosions throughout the night that shook my hotel room. I wondered if a war had broken out instead of a celebration.

Moving on from Valdivia, I took a four-hour ride to the dour Chilean port city of Puerto Montt. From there, I immediately boarded another flight and flew three hours due south to another of Chile's outposts—Punta Arenas, which unhappily boasts of having the world's largest hole in the ozone hovering over its exposed head. From there, I boarded another passenger bus to travel fifteen hours overland across the archipelagos of southern Chile and Argentina to Patagonia and then down into Tierra del Fuego and Ushuaia sitting on the basement floor of the continent.

Entering Tierra del Fuego, I could feel the edge of the golfing world was near. The pale blue horizon looked more atmospheric than sky, as if the blue molecules were sparse and a well-struck golf shot could pierce the fragile veil and soar directly into deep space. The middle of the earth seemed to hog all the oxygen and only threw us the scraps as the latitudes became smaller in circumference. If you set a globe of the earth on the ground like a golf ball, Ushuaia would be smack-dab on the grass alongside frigid Antarctica. These were areas where people visited to watch penguins frolic, not to play golf.

I had spent the previous night in a tiny hotel room in Punta Arenas—a city of 121,000. Scottish and British immigrants flocked there in the later 1800s to seek their fortunes in the wool and gold booms of the time. With the harsh winds and barren landscape, the Scots would have felt right at home.

Punta Arenas sits on the Strait of Magellan, and was a perfect locale as a trading city for the Southern Hemisphere. Before the Panama Canal, it was also a crucial refueling station for ships circling South America. Great fortunes were made in the boom, and opulent mansions built at the turn of the twentieth century stand as testament to that wealth today. Most of these homes have lost their luster, but were indeed grander than one would expect given their location on the earth.

I had phoned ahead from Puerto Montt to book this hotel on the advice of my guidebook. Calling my room small wouldn't have been doing it justice. Actually, calling the accommodation a "hotel room" was a bit of a stretch: it was a broom closet with a bed. Being claustrophobic, I went down to the front desk to see if a larger room could be found. I had no desire to sleep in a coffin until I no longer had any say in the matter. "No, Senor Wood, you're in our deluxe room," the innkeeper insisted.

Accepting my fate, I went back to my casket-sized room. I had to slow dance with my golf travel bag to get back into the teeny space. I could lie in bed, stretch out both arms and touch the opposing walls. The bathroom sink was so close I didn't even have to get out of bed to brush my teeth before nodding off.

Waking up surprisingly rested and ready for the final leg to Ushuaia, I woke early with the excitement that this was the day I would venture to the very end of South America. The weather was brisk as snow was in the forecast. Wisely, I put on my silk long underwear just in case the bus was cold.

My hotel was only one block from the bus depot. I showed up bright and early, clean, packed, warm, and fully prepared for the day of travel. Then all hell broke loose. I discovered they didn't take credit cards for the bus ticket. I had no Chilean pesos left. I had tried to play it smart financially by spending all my Chilean pesos as I would be in Argentina the following evening. My guidebook had warned that changing money between the two countries was a risk as one rarely accepts the currency of the other. Thinking I was being a clever traveler, I spent every last cent of my Chilean pesos the night before on a wonderful seafood dinner and bought provisions for the long day of bus travel set to begin at seven the next morning. Clever traveler, I wasn't.

People in Chile were among the nicest, kindest, most helpful people I was to meet in my travels, but the "gentleman" at the bus counter wasn't one of them. We weren't communicating well, and he was one of the few people who didn't take kindly to my terrible Spanish. I think the only English words he knew were: "No Visa!"

The bus was leaving in twenty minutes. I sprinted down the streets of Punta Arenas looking for a cash machine at seven in the morning. The central part of town, where the banks were, was about eight blocks away. I was running as fast as a forty-seven-year-old man can run a with a fifty-pound fully packed golf travel bag, my sole piece of luggage, in tow.

ATM after ATM was either out of order or, because of the early hour, locked up tighter than the Unabomber. It was at that moment I began to realize that my decision to wear the long underwear was starting to be an incredibly bad one, as sweat was pouring off me like an embezzler during a company audit. I only had about five minutes until the bus was to leave when I remembered that I had some U.S. dollars tucked away in my golf bag "in case of emergency." The next bus to Ushuaia wasn't for three days. This was an emergency! I knew that the only way I was getting on that bus was if the guy at the bus station would take dollars. I ran back to the depot, pulled out some cash, and asked the evil bastard at the counter if he would accept U.S. currency.

It turned out that the only other English words he knew were: "No U.S. money!"

I was defeated. Ushuaia would have to wait, and so would I. It was at this point the Chilean Satan behind the counter laughed, pulled out a calculator, converted dollars into pesos, and wrote down on a piece of paper that for twenty-two U.S. dollars the ticket was mine. I don't know if he felt sorry for me, or if a spark of humanity had entered his dark soul, but he sold me the ticket. He was chuckling and speaking in Spanish to a friend of his who was standing beside the counter. I was sure they were laughing at my sweaty expense.

Now that I had the hard-won ticket in my hand, I looked him directly in the eye and said in perfect Spanish: "I hope you develop the worst case of hemorrhoids in the history of the world!"

Well, actually, I certainly couldn't have managed a Spanish phrase that complex. I meekly said "Gracias," and boarded the bus to Ushuaia.

Calming down from my altercation at the bus depot in Punta Arenas, my sweat-soaked long johns started to dry. I settled in for the long bus ride to Ushuaia as I reflected on how far golf had traveled from its birthplace in Scotland to one of the earth's bookends there in Tierra del Fuego.

It is said that at its zenith at the turn of the twentieth century, the sun never set on the British Empire. The sun also never set on the world of golf. By 1900, those seafaring wanderers and invaders from those rather small islands in the North Atlantic controlled 20 percent of the world's land mass and over 400 million people born without that stiff upper lip. No matter where they decided to plant their Union Jack on the globe, even in lands that had the audacity to already have had their own flag, they took everything England with them and tried to turn these foreign locales into replicas of Liverpool or Cardiff-by-the-Sea or Ipswich. They brought along their warm beer, stern military rule, strict boarding schools, corporal punishment, horrible cuisine, dainty afternoon tea, and inflicted all of this mess onto their realm. Thankfully, they also brought along something positive as well: the game of their homeland—golf.

From my seat in the back of the bus to Ushuaia, I thought on how strange this land must have appeared to Magellan in 1520. With little imprint from the hand of man, it couldn't have changed much from then to now. There's ample room for millions of new golf courses. This is land to get lost in. If I was ever in the federal witness protection program, I would have them send me to Patagonia—even the Gambino crime family couldn't find you down there.

Actually, the area could use a mob family in the cement business, because the long road to Ushuaia would benefit from pavement. The ride was rough. Every fifteen minutes or so, we'd hit a small boulder in the road that would send me bouncing up toward the bus ceiling like I was sitting in James Bond's Aston Martin passenger ejector seat. It's a wonder we didn't break an axle. My intestines were tossed like a chef salad for fifteen bone-jarring hours on that teeth-chattering ride.

As our bus crossed the Strait of Magellan on a rusty old ferry, I met two couples who were traveling together. A foursome of doctors, Josef and Renee were from the Bay Area of California while Callam and Sara were from Cupar, Scotland—which is just outside St. Andrews. Josef and Callam had met and become friends during medical internships in New Zealand.

We shared our travel stories. They got me all excited with tales of the golf bounty of New Zealand, which has more golf per capita than any country on earth. It had been awhile since I had spoken with people fluent in English, and it was fun to converse without using my Spanish-English dictionary for every other word. They were lively, well-traveled, and adventurous.

When I had bought the bus ticket from Punta Arenas, I assumed that it went all the way to Ushuaia. This turned out not to be the case and was my second stupid mistake of the day. The bus only went as far as Rio Grande, a small town on the Atlantic side of Tierra del Fuego. It was still another four hours to Ushuaia. I had the feeling I was going to be stranded because not only didn't I have Chilean money, I didn't have any Argentine pesos—there hadn't been an opportunity to get them. Rio Grande, bleak and forlorn, didn't appear ATM friendly either.

My new friends came to my rescue. Callam spoke Spanish confidently, and being the doctor he is, he took control and found a van that was leaving for Ushuaia in twenty minutes. He must have sensed my hopelessness because he bought a ticket for me along with his group. I gratefully promised him quick repayment upon arriving in Ushuaia. Having the unlikely but good fortune to meet a Scot fluent in Spanish was the first of many lucky travel situations I would encounter in the coming eleven months. The Golf Gods were watching over me so far, despite my ineptitude.

We shared the van with a young Chinese spiked-haired back-packing couple who looked more rock and roll than Chairman Mao. They too were lively and fun and while they didn't speak much English—they certainly knew more than I did Chinese. They taught me some simple Chinese phrases that I forgot as quickly as I learned them—I was still trying to get a grip on *Español*.

En route to Ushuaia, the landscape started to become extremely mountainous as snowflakes started to fall. A day that had begun with me running like a madman all over Punta Arenas seeking a cash machine had morphed into this merry band of diverse wanderers motoring up the steep incline that would eventually lead down toward the bottom of the earth.

When I first encountered Ushuaia during my Google search for the southernmost golf course in the world, I pictured an abandoned snowy outpost with more penguins than inhabitants. How wrong that impression was. Ushuaia is a thriving community of 64,000 nestled alongside the gloriously blue Beagle Channel, named for Charles Darwin's ship—the HMS *Beagle*—that the naturalist used to sail on his two-month survey of South America. The channel is surrounded by the snowy peaks of the Fuegan Andes, which soar majestically up from the peaceful harbor.

I found my hotel just off the town center, the Hostal Del Bosque, checked in, and found an invitingly cozy room that had a radiator hissing warmth to beat the cold and snowfall outside. I got out of my long johns—they'd done yeoman's work that day.

Ushuaia had me immediately charmed. There was a prosperous feel to the city floating through the brisk air and falling snow as I walked around to de-bus my legs. I walked past several restaurants and bars full of late-night diners and folks gabbing and laughing and looking as if the end of the world is the only place to be. Ushuaia seemed like an energetic Italian ski village that just happens to be at the southernmost extremity of an entirely different hemisphere. The locals spoke Spanish in rapid-fire bursts that seemed more *Italiano* than *Español*.

Not only do Ushuaians talk like Italians, you quickly learn they also drive like Italians, which means traffic rules are merely suggestions. Ushuaia is small. You can walk from one end of town to the other in ten minutes, but cars were zipping around like in the chase scene from *The French Connection*. The local rule is you go as fast as you can whenever and wherever you want. This wouldn't have been so bad, but there are no stop or yield signs in the entire town. Plus the main part of the village is on a steep slope, so cars are careening downhill like gas-fueled toboggans.

In the mornings while killing time waiting for the weather to turn, I would sit and read my newspaper by the window in a corner coffee shop watching near-miss after near-miss as cars buzzed up and down the hills. It was insane! As near as I could figure, the first car to the intersection had the right of way, and if you weren't there first, you better be wearing your seat belt and a crash helmet.

It took several days for golf weather to finally emerge. My fourth morning in Ushuaia, I opened the blinds on my hotel window and sunlight flooded my room. The snow had finally stopped! There was a thin layer of white frosting on the cars parked on the street, but the bright sunlight gave me hope. I decided to go for it. It turns out I would be the first player to start the new golf season at the world's southernmost golf course.

Passersby gave me strange looks as I waited for a taxi with a golf bag slung over my shoulder in front of the hotel. People heading out for a day on the snowy slopes surrounding Ushuaia were walking by with skis and snowboards that seemed more appropriate. I hailed a cab that was thundering down the street toward the demolition derby of downtown Ushuaia.

The cabdriver and I had a lively conversation on the three-mile trip to the course, which is located just west of the town. Actually, he was having a lively conversation; I couldn't understand a word he said. I had learned that even though I never actually understood 99.9 percent of anything anyone ever said to me in South America, if I just smiled and said, "Sí," things usually went along pretty well. For all I knew, the taxi driver could have been asking me if I had eaten a feta cheese and hamster omelet for breakfast while wearing a tutu, and I would have just smiled and said, "Sí."

We reached the Ushuaia Golf Course; things didn't look promising.

Resting in a river valley at the base of several dramatic peaks, the nine-hole course looked unplayable with a blanket of white hiding the green playground underneath. The snow obscured the tees and greens as well as the contours of the land. It looked like a white winter pasture from my Minnesota youth.

There was a local gentleman who had also driven out to the course; apparently he felt there was a chance of golf as well after their long hard winter. He had parked in front of the wooden farmhouse that serves as the clubhouse. The small shack gave the impression of having been boarded up for the winter.

The local was a fellow golf addict, who I could tell wanted to play as badly as I did. A junkie knows a junkie. The sun was starting to peek through the mountains and some green bits of fairway were starting to show through the white frosting.

In Spanish, I think he asked me if I had clubs. I smiled, and said, "*Sí*." For the first time on my trip as far I knew, my answer matched the question. I assumed he told the cabbie that he would give me a ride back to town as I got my clubs out of the trunk. The cabbie muttered something about "*muy loco*" as I paid the fare. He raced back to the joy of possible multicar collisions in town.

The setting of the Ushuaia Golf Course is one of the more dramatic a golfer will find. Five glacial Fuegan Andes mountains soar to the heavens surrounding the Pipo River valley where the course resides, as the nine holes of golf transverse a serpentine river that is really more a creek. There are old railroad tracks from the early 1900s that parallel the right side of the first fairway. Because of its remoteness, Ushuaia was first settled as a notorious penal colony in 1902. Initially, the prison housed political prisoners and later, criminals with violent offenses. The Argentine judicial system in Buenos Aires probably had no clue they were sending the convicts to somewhere so idyllic. They just knew it was the end of the world and as far away as criminals could be sent in Argentina.

The prisoners were trained out to this river valley to work, chopping down trees for firewood and gathering building materials for the growing town of Ushuaia. The bucolic spot must have been a welcome relief from the direness of their tiny prison cells. Their backbreaking labor had cleared the land for golf decades later.

There was a glorious silence in the golfing valley. Gliding hawks were swooping along the steep slopes of the mountains like graceful kites. The narrow river meandering across the course had broken the dams of ice that held back its flow and was now cheerily bubbling along to its next destination, the Beagle Channel. After a long, brutal winter, spring was finally waking up and getting out of bed after a deep slumber. I was happy to be there.

My golfing partner was Raul, a retired businessman form Buenos Aires, who had decided to settle down in the beautiful scenery of Tierra del Fuego. The Ushuaia Golf Club, a compact three thousand yards, gave him a place to scratch his golfing itch, weather permitting. Wisely, he took out an orange golf ball on the first tee. I'm not one for playing anything but a gleaming white Titleist, but I was jealous of his brightly colored ball. I looked down the field of white that was the first fairway of the short three-hundred-yard par-four and knew he was going to have a better chance of finding his ball than I was. We both hit decent drives, given the circumstances and volume of clothing layers we wore to fight the cold, which had to be near the freezing mark. Off we went.

Raul knew less English than I knew Spanish, if that was possible. In his late sixties, he still possessed robust health and I could tell he had always enjoyed the outdoors.

We had a blast playing winter golf. We laughed often because of the absurdity of what we were doing as we whacked the ball around the slushy course. Initially, there was so much snow it was difficult to tell where the greens were hiding, but my new wingman Raul guided me as he'd shout from across the fairway, *"Por allá!"* and pointed me toward the spots where my shots were supposed to go.

After an hour, the sun had finally risen higher than the glacial peaks that horseshoe the valley and started to melt the snow on our second nine. Finally able to shed a couple of layers of clothing and free up our swings a bit, we marched happily along communicating in the only language we had in common: golf.

Raul had played golf since he was teenager. I would later learn that Argentina—especially Buenos Aires—has a long golfing history dating back to the start of the twentieth century. Raul, strong and burly, possessed a powerful athletic swing and a handicap of thirteen compared to my seven. I was glad we weren't playing for pesos. There is nothing more dangerous on a golf course than a thirteen handicap with a well-timed swing. That's a license to print money.

Though twenty years older, Raul hit the ball every bit as far as I did, and on the par-five sixth his ball sailed twenty yards past what I thought had been a well-hit drive of my own. Raul knew he had caught one on the screws. His sly smile and twinkling eyes told me he had tried to better my tee-ball. I had ample opportunity to compliment him with *"Bueno!"* after all his excellent shots—which were occurring with a far greater frequency than mine were.

A euphoric feeling of accomplishment fell over me after completing my round in Ushuaia. Raul and I shook hands on the final green after playing the loop twice; two cold but happy golfing warriors playing the game we love. We hadn't kept score or even worried about putting out on some of the greens because the course was in such bad shape from the long winter and recent snow, but that was hardly a concern. Today was the start of the four short months of golf there at 54.8 degrees below the equator before the Arctic cold would return with a frosty vengeance. It was golf at its fundamental best—two new friends out smacking a ball around a field, enjoying the fresh air and carrying on in the tradition of those bored shepherds five hundred years ago in the Kingdom of Fife. I laughed to myself that I had gone from daydreaming in my old office in Seattle two months ago to playing golf at the southernmost course in the world. I had reached my first goal of this crazy adventure and would now start making my way slowly around the world to Tromsö.

As Raul and I had walked up the final fairway I could see puffs of smoke wafting out the stone chimney of the little wooden clubhouse. It looked cozy and inviting with the hope of something warm to drink after we had finished the last. It was exactly the way the southernmost golf course in the world should be—cold and rough around the edges. If only Mary and Ferdinand were there to see it as well. They could have joined up with Raul and me. We would have been a hell of a foursome.

2

Campo Publico de Golf
Juan B. Segura
Buenos Aires, Argentina

34.21°S–58.30°W

Having had the crazy idea to get to the bottom of the golfing world and actually to have achieved it was gratifying. It's not like I had climbed Mount Everest without oxygen or discovered how to turn salt water into petroleum, but it had taken a great deal of effort to get all the way down there south of the Strait of Magellan, a few miles from Cape Horn, just to play a round of golf. It wasn't quite the end of the world, but it's where you hopped on an ice cutter to get there.

I wandered into the small wooden clubhouse to heat up and check it out. Converted from an old farmhouse, the brown weather-beaten building was a cozy one-story affair with a small kitchen and a main room big enough for five tables. The welcoming fireplace was blazing. There were pictures on the wall showing the history of the course since it opened in 1992. The pictures were mostly of the beloved Argentine golfer Roberto De Vicenzo, who played the inaugural round in Ushuaia.

De Vicenzo is revered in his home country as a great gentleman and ambassador for the game of golf. He gained worldwide sympathy for his role in one of the greatest blunders in golf history.

In the 1968 Masters at Augusta National, De Vicenzo, the reigning British Open champion, fired a closing round sixty-five to tie Bob Goalby for the lead, forcing a two-man play-off for the championship. However, there was a problem brewing. After De Vicenzo had holed out on the final hole, the crowd surrounding the eighteenth green had broken out into a spontaneous rendition of "Happy Birthday" for the gregarious Argentine who had turned forty-five that day. De Vicenzo, a sensitive man, was emotionally touched by the tribute and fought back tears as he went into the scoring tent to sign his scorecard and make his round official.

In professional golf, you keep the score for the other golfer in your group. De Vicenzo's playing partner, Tommy Aaron, had written down a score of four for De Vicenzo on the par-four seventeenth, but he had actually made a birdie three. Because of his emotional state from the singing crowd and the excitement of playing so well on the final day of a major championship, De Vicenzo didn't realize the mistake and signed the incorrect scorecard, which disqualified him from the tournament. That simple error of arithmetic, an archaic rule of the game, cost him the chance to win a second major and don the prestigious green jacket awarded to the winner.

After being informed of the fatal mistake, his distraught reply in his accented English became famous: "What a stupid I am, what a stupid!"

De Vicenzo's grace and sportsmanship after this famous gaffe earned him a spot in hearts of golf fans around the world. He blamed no one but himself and was a far bigger man than I would have been. I would have screamed and yelled and ordered a mob hit on the tournament officials from a hired assassin. Unlike mine, De Vicenzos' natural grace was abundantly evident, plus he had shown his fellow golfers back in Argentina that they could compete on the world stage. De Vicenzo opened the door for *El Gato*.

El Gato is the nickname of the affable world-class Argentine golfer, Eduardo Romero, who followed in De Vicenzo's admirable footsteps. I have long been intrigued by Romero. Born in 1954 to a family of modest means, Romero has taken on the best golfers on earth since he turned professional in 1982. With my vivid imagination, I always thought his nickname of *El Gato* ("the Cat") was coined from Romero's ability to stalk his opponents on the golf course, delivering a fatal strike as he birdied the last hole to snatch victory from the teeth of his vulnerable prey at the end of the hunt. His ever-present grin hid his uncanny ability to strike the jugular of his unwitting foe at precisely the right moment.

There are surely golfers who felt that way playing against the gifted *El Gato*, but the nickname actually comes from his love of hanging out in the trees and rooftops in his hometown of Córdoba in central Argentina as a small boy. Asked where her grandson was, his grandmother exclaimed, "He's always up in the trees and roofs like a cat!" *El Gato* seems too nice a guy to be a killer anyway.

Romero crossed my radar for the first time when I was getting ready to play the Old Course in St. Andrews, the birthplace of golf, on a gray cloudy Scottish day in April of 1991. That was the first time I had ever laid eyes on the wondrous old windy links. The Old Course starts right in the center of the historic town. You walk down the lively streets of the bustling burg toward the sea, turn the final corner past the old stone buildings that grandly line the narrow lane that leads to Scores Street and voilà—there it is! The ancient links of St. Andrews right before your eyes!

My first glimpse must have been like Neil Armstrong's as he stepped onto the moon. The Old Course that day had a lunar gray-matted finish with rippling bumps, knobs, and hollows spreading down the shared first and eighteenth fairways like covers on an unmade bed. It looked made of turf from another time on land that had stories to tell. It dared you to seek its secrets at your peril. It was enticingly sinister.

Many people come away from their initial sighting of the Old Course disappointed by the ruggedness and lack of emerald green associated with the American notion of a well-manicured golf course. How wrong they are. For me, it was love at first sight!

Except for the modern monstrosity of the Old Course Hotel, which lurks obscenely alongside the famed seventeenth hole, there was no definition to the horizon other than the moon-dusted, volatile terrain leading you out of town as you hit your little white ball through the wind gusts off the near North Sea. You and your ball march out toward the estuary that serves as the course boundary to the north. The holes are situated end to end. You walk directly out of town on the outward half and then turn around at the estuary and walk back in toward the lovely spires and towers of the *Auld Grey Toon*. With four other courses flanking the Old, it looks as if you could play golf there forever. A happier prospect I couldn't fathom.

Traveling in Scotland for the first time with my golf writer pal, Turk Pipkin, we had entered the daily lottery of tee times the previous day and—glory of glories—had been given one. Bursting with excitement, I had gone down to the practice putting green just off the first tee in front of the citadel of the golfing world— the Royal and Ancient Clubhouse. It was still four hours before I would hit my first shot, but I wanted to practice putting and simply wallow in the ambience of the epicenter of the game I love. It was going to take a full four hours for me just to calm down enough to make a decent swing. I was going to play the Old!

St. Andrews is a true public course on public land. This democracy adds to its greatness. In addition to the playing of golf, the sporting turf is a shared walkway for citizens taking their daily constitutional in the healthy seaside air. Scanning the area, people were playing golf, walking their dogs, and simply enjoying the recreational use of a jubilant piece of land. There was nowhere on the earth I would rather be.

In between sighs of joy, I was putting by myself on the small practice green just behind the green caddie shack that abuts the first tee. I noticed a slightly built, sweet-looking, gray-haired lady standing at the green rail that separates the sidewalk from the green. She was watching me putt. In St. Andrews, the locals are keen on the game and take interest in visitors playing their beloved links. They are the wisest golf crowd in the world. When I barely missed a twenty-foot practice putt, my sole spectator smiled shyly and said to me, "I thought you may have hit it a wee bit too hard."

I complimented her on her accurate assessment of my nervous putting stroke and we started chatting. She had been a golfer, as was her dear late husband. She had learned golf from her father as a young girl there in St. Andrews and grew up loving to play the game. I asked her if she still played. She replied that, owing to her frailty, she no longer played, but still enjoyed watching others during her daily walk. The talking filibuster that I am, I monopolized her ears for some time with an excited chatter about my tee time four hours' hence. She smiled gently and said she knew just how I felt. "My husband used to get so excited before his game he'd forget to tie his golf shoes," she giggled shyly.

She knew golf. I asked her who her favorite golfer was. I expected her to name a Scot like Colin Montgomery or perhaps England's Nick Faldo—a golfer of a more local variety. Smiling coyly with her blue eyes twinkling, she said, "I simply adore *El Gato!*"

Finding it so charming that a golfer from Argentina had captured the golfing heart of a sweet little lady on the other side of the world, I started to follow Romero's career. He became one of those golfers whose score I always looked up in the newspaper summaries of tournaments around the world. His constant good play always brought a smile to my face as well as memories of playing St. Andrews for the first time with the kind, cheerful old lady taking a break from her walk to watch me putt.

Before visiting Argentina, my knowledge of the country was a series of half-baked stereotypes at best. From afar, all I sensed was chaos. Argentina was monthly military coups d'états, disappearing political prisoners, rioting soccer fans, Evita Perón on the Presidential Palace balcony (or was that Madonna playing her in the film version?). The country was a Marx Brothers movie with the Three Stooges running the government: a land of fiscal insanity with runaway inflation. You needed a complete set of Samsonite luggage packed to the gills full of pesos to buy a single cup of coffee. There was that bizarre war with England over the bleak Falkland Islands, which seemed to be nothing more than a Club Med for sheep. Argentina was the carnival fun house of countries.

Ushuaia allowed the scales to fall from my eyes on Argentina. The physical beauty of Ushuaia coupled with the prevailing feel of good humor flowing through the mountain air whet my appetite for more of South America's second biggest country. There is a definite live-for-today, put-off-everything-until-mañana attitude that was appealing down there at the bottom of the continent. Argentineans leave the macro version of living for everyone else in the world to worry about. While probably not the best course of action for long-range fiscal planning or political stability, it is nonetheless an excellent method of killing the day. Mañana meshed well with my current lifestyle—wake up, find a cup of coffee and a newspaper, go looking around and perhaps play golf. How could you not love a country where procrastination was a lifestyle? It was one language I was fluent in.

My next travel goal was Buenos Aires. There was no direct overland route to the Argentine capital, so I bought a ticket on Aerolinas Argentinas for the three-hour flight north. At the Ushuaia airport, I had bought a copy of the *International Herald Tribune*—a worldwide English newspaper. I scanned the stories: the invasion of Iraq, Tony Blair's battles in the House of Commons, sports and financial results from the world's markets, *Dilbert*, *Doonesbury*, and my daily horoscope, which said that today was a good day to stay home under the covers. It was too late for that.

I kept scanning the paper for anything on South America. The only mention was a one-paragraph blurb on a violent uprising in Bolivia. One paragraph for an entire continent!

I had been monitoring the political clash in Bolivia since arriving in Chile. Seventy-five people had just been killed in a riot in La Paz. Bolivia is the poorest country on the continent, and the citizens were upset that the revenue from their country's vast mineral and oil riches didn't trickle down to them. In Bolivia, the average GNP per person is less than nine hundred dollars a year.

Because of the escalating violence, the U.S. State Department had issued a travel warning for Bolivia. I was hoping to end the South American leg of my trip there, golfing at the highest golf course in the world, but was getting uneasy with the daily news that seemed to worsen. I decided to continue monitoring the situation in the coming weeks. If things got dicey there I could always leave for New Zealand sooner.

Buenos Aires was another case of love at first sight for me as I taxied in from the airport to my hotel just off the Avenue de Colon. The city is enchantingly beautiful. Elegant flourishing parks, grand old-world European architecture, beautiful people wearing the latest fashions—the experience is an intoxicating cocktail of unforgettable sights and sounds and smells. Every block seemed a fully fleshed-out three-act play with wonderful outdoor cafés for the break at intermission. All that's required from the visitor is to stay awake and watch. In Buenos Aires, that's not hard to accomplish.

It also didn't take me long when walking the busy streets to notice how beautiful the women were. As a forty-seven-year-old semiprofessional admirer of the opposite sex, it didn't take long to realize: *Hey, something's going on here!* You can't walk more than a block or so without seeing a shoo-in winner for the Miss Universe pageant. It was extraordinary! Open-mouthed drooling isn't attractive on a middle-aged man wearing a golf visor.

In order to stop ogling, I decided instead to go looking for the public golf course that I'd been told was smack-dab in the center of Buenos Aires. I had read the course was in the Palermo section of the city in that neighborhood's vast urban green space that rivals New York City's Central Park in size and usage—it teems with activity. I asked person after person out on their Sunday stroll if they knew where the golf course might be, but no one had ever even heard of it. After three hours searching in vain and many miles of hoofing it, I finally gave up for the time being. Perhaps it didn't exist. Exhausted, I stopped for a bite to eat just across the street from the northern end of the park. After I had eaten, I thought I'd give it one more shot and asked the waiter if he knew where the course was. He said it was another five kilometers up the road away from the park, but his information sounded dodgy.

Defeated, I decided to give up. I looked at my map to get my bearings, and started walking over to Avenue del Libertador that would return me to my hotel. By chance, I looked to my left and— there was a golf course! No doubt about it! Greens, flags, bunkers— if there's one thing I know it's a golf course when I see one. It was right in the middle of the park. How could no one have known? Was my Spanish really that bad? With a renewed burst of energy and wanting to play golf, I hurried back to my room, retrieved my ten traveling companions and caught a cab to go back to the course for a whack at golf, Buenos Aires style.

Golf first came to Buenos Aires and South America via those travel-ing Scots and Brits who were out and about building railroads, bridges, and monopolies in the eighteenth and nineteenth cen-turies. In 1879, roughly the same time golf was introduced in North America, a Scot named Henry Smith arrived at the port of Buenos Aires with a golf bag on his shoulder. The customs official obviously had never seen odd-looking implements such as golf clubs before and thought the wooden sticks and heads of iron were weapons and decided to confiscate them. The Scotsman was as fluent as I am in Spanish, but wasn't about to part with his beloved golf clubs. Mr. Smith showed the official that they weren't weapons by demon-strating how they were swung, and, of course, showed the per-plexed official they didn't have a rifle barrel or even the sharp edge of a knife. As golfers have known throughout the ages, the only danger inflicted from these weapons is to your own sense of pride.

One hundred and twenty-four years later, me and my sticks were there at the Campo Publico de Golf Juan B. Segura. The mu-nicipal course, one of only two public courses in the entire coun-try, is completely surrounded by the high-rise apartment buildings of the upwardly mobile neighborhoods bordering the huge park. The course and the large green space are a soothing respite from the urban havoc and fast-paced bustle of the city. The contrast of the upscale neighborhood's bricks and mortar towering skyward alongside a golfing ground abundant with thriving leafy trees gave the course a special feel—it was golf in a locale where you wouldn't have expected it. I couldn't ever remember playing golf right in the middle of a flourishing major city before—especially one as robust and vibrant as Buenos Aires.

Campo Publico de Golf Juan B. Segura was my kind of golfing place with all the characteristics of a public golf course: there was a grumpy starter doling out tee times, golfers dressed to play an outdoor game rather than about to pose for an *Architectural Digest* photo op, and it was cheap to play. The green fee was twenty pesos, which was less than seven dollars. That was the golf my trip was all about. I'm a sucker for a good public golf course with low rates.

There were only two other golfers going out to play when I arrived—Daniel, a Buenos Aires lawyer, and his wife, Mariana. Both spoke excellent English and we chatted on the tee of the par-four first. Daniel took me aside and explained that Mariana was a novice at the game and wouldn't feel comfortable with a stranger watching her swing, so he asked me if I'd like to go ahead of them. It was a kind gesture, but I was getting used to the politeness of South Americans. Off I went like a kid riding a new bike.

Campo Publico de Golf Juan B. Segura was a challenging and mature golf course with grand, bushy elms flanked by groves of poplars and multitudes of birds flitting around a series of small lakes that frame the greens and fairways. I often judge a course by the wildlife in residence—the more the better, to my way of thinking. Birds are a great indicator that the course isn't tricking Mother Nature with scores of pesticides and chemicals. The more natural and environmentally friendly, the more I enjoy the course. I think that's why I adore the natural links golf of Scotland and Ireland so much. They let nature be nature.

Having left Mariana and Daniel in my wake, I never saw another golfer and had the place to myself. The course was an excellent test of golf. At over 7,100 yards in length, it wasn't a pushover;

in fact, it was difficult with a high level of proficiency required to make pars. I was playing erratically—no, make that downright awful. I'm a golfer who needs to practice constantly to be any good at all, and I hadn't practiced since leaving Seattle. Between the numerous ponds and perimeter trees guarding the otherwise flat golfing playground, there were plenty of hazards and my ball found all of them as I sliced and duck-hooked with wild abandon. My errant shots found the water on the first, eighth, eleventh, and fourteenth holes—and not the edge of the water either, but the center of the *agua* complete with a gentle splash like an Olympic diver performing a perfect ten. I kept hitting bad shot after bad shot with supernatural precision. In Ushuaia, Raul had taught me to yell: *"Mono!"* if my ball was headed for the trees. *Mono* is Spanish for "monkey" and golfers want the *mono* in the tree to throw the ball back into the short grass of the fairway. I yelled *"Mono!"* countless times as my misbehaving drives screamed toward the trees with such violent velocity the *monos* were probably taking cover for their lives. I never saw any actual monkeys; if they were there they didn't feel it necessary to toss my ball back into the fairway.

However, while my play was miserable, my golfing attitude was changing there in South America as I became more like the locals who accepted the hard facts of life with nothing more than a rueful smile and a shrug. Besides, what did ten double-bogeys and probably as many balls lost in the drink matter when you have a Miss Universe on every block?

This laissez-faire golfing attitude was new to me. I wasn't fretting about my lack of skill or beating myself up as this type of play would usually do to me, putting me in a mental funk. When my skill of the game I adore leaves on a sabbatical, I usually mope like a jilted lover, but not that day. I just walked after my poorly executed shot, found it, and hit it poorly one more time. Not wanting to count that high, nor wanting proof of my ugly and rapidly climbing score that would have been a major day of trading on the floor of the Dow, I tossed the scorecard in a wastebasket near the oblong-shaped fourteenth green and continued my merry trek to look for my wayward ball in the trees or bushes. Bad golf or not, the real thrill was the realization of "Hey, I'm playing golf smack-dab in the middle of Buenos Aires!" Perhaps, I'll play better mañana.

Golfwise, after playing Campo Publico de Golf Juan B. Segura, I had hit the jackpot in Buenos Aires. Since arriving in South America, I had been e-mailing Mark Lawrie, the executive director of the Argentine Association of Golf (AAG) for ideas on where to play when I arrived in his home city. Mark's Scottish ancestors had immigrated to Argentina from Edinburgh, and while he speaks English as if he went to Oxford, he's as Argentine as the tango. Working in and around the world of sport has been his vocation, and it suits him well.

The history of golf in Argentina parallels that of the U.S. The game has flourished in both for the past 120 years. In its long, proud golf history, Bobby Jones, Tiger Woods, Byron Nelson, Gene Sarazen, Jimmy Demaret, Jack Nicklaus, Henry Cotton, Paul Runyan, Sam Snead, Arnold Palmer, Seve Ballesteros, Jose Maria Olazabal, Mark O'Meara, Sergio Garcia, and Tom Watson have all made the trek to play there. The Argentine Open is the seventh oldest golf tournament in the world, and is run by Lawrie and the AAG While not quite as popular as soccer, golf is well established in this sporting country.

Lawrie's organization also heads the Argentine National Amateur Golf team, which represents the country in tournaments around the world. That team, several members of which I would meet and play with while there, was preparing for an upcoming world amateur tournament in South Africa. I was hanging with the elite of golf on the continent. Lawrie and his boss, Romulo Zenboren, are members of the Royal and Ancient of St. Andrews, which is the governing body of the world of golf. They, on the other hand, were hanging with a guy with no home, three Polo shirts, and ten golf clubs in a skinny golf bag on my traveling squad.

When I first met Mark Lawrie in person, I sat in his modern high-rise office in downtown Buenos Aires explaining my around-the-world golf-seeking mission. Mr. Lawrie was impressed by my crazy adventure. Opening his schedule book, he said my arrival had coincided with a rare break in his busy calendar—he wanted to play some golf himself.

"These are the courses you must play," Mark said as he handed me a piece of paper with the Buenos Aires Golf Club, Olivos Golf Club, and the Hurlingham Club written on it. "These are three of the finest courses on the continent. I think you'll enjoy them," he said, smiling. Life was getting good.

Mark then asked if I had a rental car. I explained I was hoofing it and taking public transportation when necessary. Mark replied, "I think you'll need a car and driver. Some of these courses are a bit of a drive from the city center. I'll make arrangements to have you picked up at your hotel." He said this in a way that suggested it was wise to accept his generous idea, which, of course, I did at once. My own personal driver—I liked the sound of that. Life was getting even better.

Golf is far more popular in Argentina than in any other South American country. They have over 260 courses and roughly sixty-five thousand golfers—thousands more than any other country on the continent. I asked Mark why golf was more prevalent in Argentina. He answered, "For golf to be widespread, you have to have a country with a large middle class, and we have that here."

Most countries in South America have two classes: the very wealthy and the extremely poor. Argentina had those as well, but the ups and downs of their economy had nonetheless allowed a middle class to grow and stabilize between these two extremes. The Argentine love of sports was due to their ability to have free time and money to play. Leisure time from work, if you have a job, is a rare commodity in South America.

While life was grand, with a personal driver, a VIP golf partner, and plenty of courses to play, unfortunately, my golf game was getting worse. My game was sick, pale, dreadful, unwell, diseased, disordered, fevered, ailing, and just plain god-awful. Where did it go? How could something I enjoy so much leave me powerless to impose my will on that little stationary white ball? I speak so highly of golf. Why me? If the state of my game was a prizefight, the crowd would have been yelling at the referee to end the bloodshed. It was ugly.

After years of fairly decent play as a single-digit handicapper, I was hacking the ball around like an absolute beginner. These evil spells had reared their grotesque heads before, but not when playing some of the best courses in the world. My game usually rose to the occasion and acquitted itself at least well enough to give the illusion that I could play a great course. There were no illusions—Elvis had left the arena! I sucked raw eggs. These were first-rate, world-class golf courses Mr. Lawrie had kindly got me on, and my poor play was embarrassing.

My first shot in Mark's company was the worst. I was on the first tee of the Buenos Aires Golf Club, an ultraexclusive club just outside the broad city limits of Buenos Aires. Alberto, my driver (I like saying that), had picked me up downtown at the Goya Hotel where I had been happily living in three-star luxury for twenty-one dollars a night including continental *desayuno* in the morning.

After thirty minutes of driving through urban sprawl, we arrived at the Buenos Aires Golf Club, with armed guards at the entrance. The surly soldier impeding our entry was clad for war in battle fatigues complete with helmet and rifle. Unhappy that we were trying to enter the grounds through his post, he wasn't going to let us pass. Alberto and he began speaking in heated Spanish and, since the guard was the one with gun, he was winning the debate. Luckily, Mr. Lawrie happened to drive in at the same time and was known by the guard so we were, reluctantly, let in. I turned back to see the guard's reaction as we drove into the property. He kept his evil eye on us until we left his sight.

I was surprised by the vehemence of the guard—he was protecting the golf course as if he would gladly lay down his life rather than let the wrong person in. If they have to protect whatever or whomever is inside the gates that strongly, in my view, someone is up to no good. Ill-gotten gains have a way of making those less moneyed angry; at least that's the way it works with me.

Perhaps it was because this was the playground of the superrich there at the Buenos Aires Golf Club, and the super-poor weren't happy with the one-sided arrangement. All I knew was that they weren't going to accidentally let a pauper with only ten clubs into their exclusive establishment without a bit of a fracas.

After Mark and I had put our golf shoes on in the ornate, library-quiet, wood-paneled locker room, we made our way to the first tee. The club's owner was getting ready to tee-off with two of the best polo players in the world (so I was told). Polo is another major sport in Argentina. I had no clue who the players were, but they did have the confident demeanor of world-class athletes. Since Mark and I were a twosome, we were allowed to tee-off first, so we wouldn't be held up by the group of three.

With the millionaire owner, the two world-class polo players, and the executive director of Argentine golf watching, I have to admit I was nervous. I was fully aware of the current state of my game and this was a big-time golf course. In its life span of ten years, the course has seen the cream of the golfing world. The club hosted the World Team Championship of Golf in 2000, won by Tiger Woods and David Duval. Tiger's pal Mark O'Meara won the Argentine Open here in 1994. Now they hosted me.

As a guest, it was my honor. Pulling out my driver, I teed my ball up and took a deep breath that did nothing to calm my nerves as I lined up to attempt my initial shot down the stout dogleg left of the par-four first hole. Trying to focus on the task at hand, I addressed the ball, swung the club, and almost completely whiffed it! Somehow I had barely hit the very top of the ball and it scurried like a frightened squirrel into the deep brush that was only ten yards in front of the tee-box. It was the single worst shot I could ever remember hitting since I had first taken up the game as a teenager. My face was as red as the shirts that Tiger wears each and every closing round of a tournament. The idea of being a good golfer was as far away as Tromsö, Norway. I tried to laugh off the inept opening shot, but it wasn't to be the only one that day. It was just the start of a flood of awful golf on my part.

I wish I could say that I remembered the Buenos Aires Golf Club in great detail, because I faintly recall the look and feel of some-where special to play as the muscular holes form a triangle around several large bodies of the water in the middle of the layout. The course was big-time golf in every aspect-clever design, championship length, high degree of difficulty and was named the "Best South American Course" by *Golf Digest* in 2000. I was plowing up the well-groomed bent-grass turf like a gopher on amphetamines. Bad shot followed bad shot. There weren't enough *monos* in the world to throw back all those horrific shots! I was so busy trying to find my ball I hardly had a look at the fairways and greens, but can report that the rough is penal and no place to play from. Mark (who played well) kindly helped me search for my frequent offline shots that flew deep into the wild wheatgrasses flanking the fairways. I appreciated his reassuring condolences on my erratic play, however, my game stunk. Where does it go? My new mañana attitude was being severely tested.

After the round we went into the grand clubhouse for some lunch. While Mark went into the locker room, I hung out in the bar and started chatting with a gentleman who asked me how I had played. I went into my sad song of horrible tee-balls, wildly off-target irons shots, bladed chips, not to mention my nervous putting stroke. The man appeared to be in his sixties, but had the look of a Las Vegas lounge singer. His hair was dyed jet-black and his teeth were bleached so white I could almost see myself in the enamel. He had the open-collar Tony Soprano wiseguy look with a gold chain shining in the gap. He looked like an older Wayne Newton.

He said he too had played that day and we discussed the many merits of the fine course. It was a pleasant conversation, one I have had countless times in clubhouses with strangers commiserating on this goofy, elusive game. Mark returned and the gentleman and I said our "good-byes" and "nice chatting with you"s as we shook hands.

Mark laughed as the lounge singer left and said, "Do you know who that is?"

Just as I was about to tell him my theory that the guy was the Argentine Wayne Newton, Mark said, "That's Carlos Menem, the former president of Argentina!" Who knew?

Menem was the president of Argentina from 1989 to 1999 and is known for his flamboyant lifestyle as well as the scandals and controversies that marked his run in office. What I found the most impressive is that at sixty-eight years of age he married the former Miss Universe from Chile, Cecilia Bolocco, who is thirty-five years younger than he. I wondered where I could get my hair dyed and teeth bleached and several million dollars.

Menem is a notorious figure in these parts and has been accused of lining his own pockets with millions of pesos from what many have called "shady dealings." He had the country's constitution altered so he could run for another term of office and became the poster boy for the crooked South American leaders that have kept the bulk of the continent's people well immersed in poverty. When I would bring up that chance meeting with their former president, Argentineans would always say the same thing: "I hope you washed your hands and counted your fingers." He was forced to leave the country after my visit, and, as of this writing, lives in exile in Santiago with his beauty queen wife. If you are forced to live in exile, it doesn't hurt to have a former Miss Universe by your side. Hell, I'd have her wear the Miss Universe sash and tiara every waking minute.

3

Club de Golf del Uruguay
Montevideo, Uruguay

34.51°S–56.10°W

After a grand week in Buenos Aires, I boarded the *Buquebus*, a large, modern passenger ferry resembling a baby cruise ship, for the three-hour crossing of the horseshoe-shaped Rio de la Plata to Montevideo. On this foggy gray Sunday morning the weather had turned to rain following a week of warm sunshine. The idea of crossing this wide expanse of water in a bit of a storm was appealing to me—it gave a banal, pedestrian ride a hint of adventure.

On our way to Uruguay, the sun had broken through the clouds as we entered the harbor of Montevideo. The word *Montevideo* comes from the Portuguese phrase *monte vide eu*, which means, "I see a hill." Had I been Portuguese, I too would have said *monte vide eu* because Montevideo is indeed situated on the side of a gently sloping hill that meanders slowly down to the river. There is a laid-back atmosphere to the place that was welcoming after the constant buzz of Buenos Aires. It was a small-city feel, more Spokane than Seattle.

Of all the countries in which I planned to play golf, Uruguay had intrigued me the most. When I was back in Seattle doing my Internet searches on world golf, I had discovered that Uruguay boasts the distinction of a course designed by Alister MacKenzie—the greatest course designer the game has known. This had stunned me—an Alister MacKenzie golf course in Uruguay? How could that be?

Dr. MacKenzie had been all the rage of the golfing world in the first third of the twentieth century, and used his widespread notoriety to travel the world. Oh, what fun it must have been to be Alister MacKenzie in the 1920s! Having gained fame for his revolutionary natural designs, Dr. MacKenzie, a trained physician who drifted out of the medical world to build golf courses, had assembled a worldwide résumé like no other in the profession of golf-course architecture. From his home country of England to points beyond, including Scotland, Ireland, the new world of America, New Zealand, and Australia, MacKenzie left a trail of golfing gems in his brilliantly creative wake. MacKenzie was the Picasso of his trade, and on his palette were the finest pieces of golfing turf the world had to offer. What more could a golf-course designer want?

In those Roaring Twenties Lahinch in Ireland; Australia's Royal Melbourne, New South Wales, and Royal Adelaide; California's Pasatiempo; and New Zealand's Titirangi were all glittering examples in the sparkling galaxy of his works. MacKenzie's masterpiece, Cypress Point, golf's Sistine Chapel on the Monterey Peninsula in California, had been completed in 1928. Offers for his time and services poured in from all over the globe, and the golfing world was his oyster.

After designing Cypress Point, MacKenzie took his genius touch to South America. In 1930, with the Great Depression gathering strength, MacKenzie was asked to travel to the economic-boom land of Argentina to bring golf to the Jockey Club in San Isidro—the most chic suburb of Buenos Aires. He traveled to Argentina via steamer through the Panama Canal, and designed what were to become the Red and Blue courses of the Jockey Club while he basked in the high life of Buenos Aires society.

Even in the 1920s, Montevideo had long suffered in the shadow of fashionable Buenos Aires. Not wanting to be outdone, the Club de Golf del Uruguay sent their vice president, Jose Pedro Urioste, to ask MacKenzie if he would visit their course to see if he might be interested in turning their existing nine holes into the full complement of eighteen. They figured, MacKenzie's in our neck of the woods, so let's go ask!

MacKenzie agreed to visit, and immediately was taken with the property. He is said to have felt the Club de Golf del Uruguay sat on one of the finest pieces of golfing land he had ever seen. Coming from a man who had worked on the wild western coast of Ireland as well as the dramatic clash of land and sea of California's Monterey Peninsula, this was high praise indeed. Uruguay was about to enter the world of first-class golf.

With downtown Montevideo grandly in view, the Club de Golf sits on a promontory standing sentinel over a picturesque beach on the long, gradual harbor of the Rio de la Plata. Because the bluff slopes toward the river, it affords grand water views from numerous points. MacKenzie felt he had the chance to build something special. He was paid one thousand dollars for the job, a king's ransom at the time, and completed the design in 1930. His original plan hangs at a place of honor inside the charming, low-key clubhouse. The eighteen new holes he created smack of his genius.

After Cypress Point and St. Andrews, I can think of nowhere else I would rather play than the Club de Golf del Uruguay. The wonderful setting looking out over the vast river, combined with the easygoing atmosphere around the clubhouse, forms an ideal location to play the Scottish game.

I had taken a taxi to the course on a warm, sunny Monday. The armed guards at the gate waved us right through—a welcoming sign. It turns out that on Mondays anyone who shows up to play gets to do so for free. Free golf on an Alister MacKenzie course for anybody! Were they teasing me? Were they playing a joke on this goofy traveling stranger? Nope, free it was.

Though the price was right, there was only one other golfer

hanging around to play when I arrived: a local medical student named Frederico, who I took to be around twenty-five. Frederico took a break from his studies every Monday to play golf there. Though he spoke excellent English, he apologized that he wasn't more fluent in my native tongue. The locals I encountered always apologized for their lack of English, but they usually spoke it as well as I did. I was the one who should have been apologetic, which I usually was, and would utter one of the few phrases I had down pat to explain my uneven Spanish: *"Lo siento."* I'm sorry.

Frederico was good company and possessed a fluid golf swing that was syrupy smooth. He was much more mature at his age than I was; no, I take that back. He's more mature than me now. He was calm and reasonable with a touch of humor—all the attributes that would make him a successful doctor. We discussed golf, which he had been playing there since he was a small boy. We chatted about the beautiful women in this region of the world. He was polite and good-looking, so I'm sure he had no trouble in that area. Neither one of us was keeping score; we were just hitting the ball and chatting during the walk between shots. It's my favorite way to play.

I started to relax and enjoy the beauty of this extremely pleasant golfing park. Old, sturdy oaks line the lush, rippling green fairways and severely mounded putting greens—a MacKenzie trademark. The holes are never less than excellent and the sixteenth, a short slightly uphill dogleg left, is known as one of the great short par-fours in the world. Though built on the side of a cliff, all the slopes are gradual and you never feel as if you are trudging uphill. You happily golf your ball in the warm sunshine as you share the grounds with several varieties of birds joyfully swooping and darting around the plethora of trees. The course didn't possess one ounce of pretension—which, I like to think, is how MacKenzie would have preferred it. It is golf simply for fun and enjoyment as you play a gem designed by the greatest architect the game of golf has known. What a discovery to find a course that wonderful in Uruguay of all places—it was what my trip was all about. I could have kept playing forever on that glorious spring afternoon in the Southern Hemisphere.

Lo and behold, I even began playing decently—at least my shots were in the same universe as golf, as my ball behaved itself and avoided landing in one of MacKenzie's ubiquitous sharp-edged bunkers flanking the undulating putting surfaces. I even made a curling downhill twenty-foot putt on the par-four eighteenth green for a birdie and received a hearty *"Bueno!"* from Frederico. Oh, how I adore this maddening game!

It was a glorious day. Having the chance to play a MacKenzie course doesn't come often to a public golfer like myself, and I relished the opportunity. I loved the free-for-all-comers policy on Mondays—the game blossoms when it includes all walks of life. I could go on and on trumpeting the glories of the Club de Golf del Uruguay.

There is a regal atmosphere to a MacKenzie golf course that upgrades the foolish endeavor of trying your best to put a little ball in a little hole into a noble enterprise. With the grand blue Rio de la Plata flowing out to join forces with the mighty Atlantic on my left and the stylish old colonial buildings of Montevideo grandly in view off to my right, I gladly played the game I love between the two. Thanks, doc!

4

Córdoba Golf Club
Córdoba, Argentina

31.22°S–64.15°W

In the back of my mind, two travel fears had been running amok like children hopped-up on chocolate. The first was the worsening political situation in Bolivia. The recent violent uprisings against the government had been bloody, with seventy-five people killed in one clash. In the past month, the unfed but fed-up peasants had staged a nationwide strike that paralyzed the government and forced the resignation of President Gonzalo Sánchez de Lozada. Sánchez de Lozada had installed a pro-U.S. free-market economy, but the peasants watched as oil flowed out of their country without any of the promised "trickle-down" revenues flowing back to them. It's a common tale in the political history of South America.

Bolivians are the poorest people on a continent well-versed in the subject of poverty. They had finally had enough of the one-sided economy. The protesters set up improvised roadblocks with boulders and pyres of burning tires, making travel into and out of the country difficult. The U.S. State Department was urging its citizens not to travel to Bolivia, and strongly suggested those U.S. citizens currently there leave immediately. Fortunately, nothing was said about any idiots wanting to play golf there. I took their lack of specificity as a blessing to go there and find golf.

The second fear scampering around my golf-addled brain was the mighty Andes standing in the way of where I intended to travel. Against my better judgment, I decided to travel up and over them via bus like an ant crawling over a picnic table. I wanted to see the countryside of north-central Argentina up close, plus, I wanted to see the Atacama Desert of northern Chile—the driest place on earth. The Atacama has had no rain in recorded history. Because of this lack of moisture there are few clouds hiding the heavens, so the Atacama Desert has the clearest night sky in the world. The prospect of seeing the lights of the universe spread out as brightly and brilliantly as I would probably ever see them in my lifetime seemed worth the bother of facing my fear of heights. But, I was pensive to say the least. My goal was to travel from Montevideo to Córdoba and Salta, two spirited cities in central Argentina, and then across the Andes to Arica, Chile, through the Atacama.

Arica's exotic golf course had drawn my attention from a continent away. Back in Seattle, I had seen a picture of the course in a *National Geographic* article on the Atacama Desert. The Arica Golf Course didn't sport a blade of grass—it was as bald as Andre Agassi's scalp. From the pictures, the thought occurred to me: to have golf on barren land where not even grass could grow required golfers who really wanted to play the game despite the lack of frivolous flora. The course is said to be the driest on earth and that alone had clinched it—Arica was on my itinerary.

My first overnight bus ride in Chile that took me from Santiago to Valdivia had been, by far and away, the most luxurious I would take in South America. That ride, with huge reclining seats, headphones, soft pillows, warm blankets, and food service was a fluke. I never had another bus ride even half that comfortable. It was fifteen hours of torture as I took the overnight ride to Córdoba.

The bus was drafty and frigid. The temperature cooled dramatically at night as the elevation slowly increased while we motored into hilly central Argentina. Across the aisle from me, a grandmotherly older lady had fallen asleep and was snoring like a drunken lumberjack after a three-day bender. Her mouth was gaped open wider than a golf hole. She couldn't have weighed more than one hundred pounds, but a large walrus in heat would have nothing on her vocally. Adding to this cacophony, a horribly violent Chinese movie in English with Spanish subtitles was playing on the video screen overhead. A typical line of dialogue was, "Where's my money, asshole?" *Casablanca* it wasn't.

I looked around to see if anybody else was disturbed by the blue dialogue, but they either didn't understand English or were too tired to care. The ear-bleeding volume of the movie was louder than a Megadeth concert. I was the lucky passenger with the seat directly under the speaker. The cold, the snoring foghorn of a granny and the loud blasts of cinematic gunfire and gangster swearing made for a long night.

The next morning we finally arrived in Córdoba, a bustling university town founded in 1573, but my bag didn't. I didn't think it was possible to lose a bag traveling on a bus. Did it get out along the way and start hitchhiking? In Montevideo, I had checked the bag in at the bus depot and it had been tagged exactly as an airline bag would be. The clerk who took my sole luggage item told me it would be stowed under the bus and could be picked up in Córdoba. I guess my clubs wanted to stay in Montevideo near that glorious MacKenzie course. After that dreadful ride, I can't say as I blame them.

I wasn't worried about losing my clothes, but the loss of my beloved Mizuno irons and my not-quite-as-beloved-but-still-very-dear Titleist three-wood and driver and Ping putter would be a drag. My trusty irons were twenty-five years old and were, by far, my longest relationship. I reported the loss to a harried lady at the Córdoba bus depot who looked as if she had worked the graveyard shift and had slept the same amount as I had—nada. "We'll find them, Senor Wood," she said wearily. Too tired to put up a fuss, I simply walked away and hoped she was right.

Needing sleep, I got a taxi and went in search of lodging. The hotel I had prebooked on the Internet was awful—it was small and dirty and looked as if it was the type of establishment where people checked in by the hour.

With the blessing of the great exchange rate of the dollar to the peso, I went looking for somewhere better. I found the local tourism office, and they called over to the Panarama Hotel—a comfortable, sleekly modern four-star affair. The hotel abutted downtown Córdoba and was a perfect location from which to explore the city. The hotel had worldwide cable television, air-conditioning, and room service. More importantly, I wasn't going to have to share the room with any freeloading arthropods. This magnificent room was twenty-six dollars per night. Argentina has to be the greatest travel bargain in the world.

Though anxious about my lost luggage and tired from my lack of sleep, I decided to stay awake as long as I could and went strolling around the attractive university town. Córdoba sits on the banks of the Rio Primo at the foothills of the Sierra Chica, which begins the long gradual climb west to the imposing Andes. With soft, rolling landscape bathed in golden sunlight, and the wonderfully fragrant jacaranda and *lapacho* trees in full blossom, Córdoba is a soothing destination. The alluring downtown is a labyrinth of plazas and colonial architecture dotted with welcoming restaurants and bars. No one was in a hurry to get anywhere—it was a place where one strolled leisurely, and because the weather was stiflingly hot during the middle of the day, everything closed down for siesta in the afternoons. I could feel my blood pressure dropping by the second. A siesta was in the cards for me. The lovely pedestrian-only streets and fragrant scenery caressed my worries away.

In a moment, I had forgotten all about my lost luggage. When I returned to my hotel, I learned that my bags had arrived on a later bus from Montevideo and were at the depot waiting for me. Sweet!

I was overjoyed that my golf clubs, my loyal traveling companions, had been located because Mark Lawrie said the Córdoba Golf Club was one of the best courses in Argentina. I was also intrigued by the course because it was the home course of *El Gato*. Romero had grown up working as a caddie at the course. His dad had been a caddie there as well, and later became a teacher of golf for the poorer locals who wanted to learn the game of the wealthy. He obviously taught his son well. A poor boy who liked to hang out in the trees and rooftops of Córdoba became one of the best golfers on the planet. I had hoped to perhaps meet him while in Córdoba, but I was told he was away playing a tournament in Europe. I would have enjoyed meeting *El Gato* on his home turf.

Settling in nicely in Córdoba, I spent my mornings wandering around the charming squares of downtown and visiting the beautiful Catholic churches that dot every block. Golf and religion have a lot in common. Both seem quite willing to forgive your transgressions and allow for the start of a new life the next day, as long as a bit of penance is involved. The credo is much the same for both: tomorrow I'll be better.

After strolling for a few hours, I would find a pleasant outdoor café with a table in the shade of a flowered tree and sip coffee, read newspapers, and catch up on my notes. After a pleasant morning, I usually wandered back to my hotel, grabbed my sticks, and headed to the Córdoba Golf Club. Life didn't suck.

With a grand, but comfortable, white Spanish-style clubhouse perched on a hill overlooking the course, the Córdoba Golf Club has seen the best of South American golf pass under its red-slated roof. Built in the 1920s, the pictures on walls of the club recall a splendid history of great players who had tried their hand at taming the excellent 6,800-yard layout. Tom Watson, Lanny Wadkins, and Nick Faldo have played there. With gentle sloping hills and elusive tricky greens, it's all the golf a player of any caliber will ever need. The course record is sixty-one, by the great Roberto De Vicenzo on April 11, 1979. His scorecard from that day is framed on the wall, and oh, how I wish it were mine.

I copied down his scores in my notebook. Front nine: 3-4-3-3-2-3-3-3-3 for 27 on the first nine. Back nine: 2-5-5-4-4-4-3-3-4 for 34 and a total of sixty-one strokes! As we amateur golfers usually have fives, sixes, and sevens dominating our own scorecards, I marveled at all the twos, threes, and fours. I too have shot a sixty-one, but only because it started raining and I walked in after twelve holes.

The club was friendly and I was meeting other golfers every day who wanted to play golf with the visiting gringo. The second day I went to the golf club, a young, good-looking golfer named Martin Monguzzi asked if I would like to join him for a round. Martin was decked out like a professional golfer, and as he took practice swings on the first tee I could see he had the swing of one as well. Martin is one of the top amateur players in Argentina and his dream is to play on the PGA tour in America. He was good company and spoke English well, plus it was fun to see him play the game at such a high level. His booming drive split the fairway of the 400-yard first hole and was seventy yards past mine. I felt like an old man.

The course was another first-rater, but Martin handled its difficulty with ease. He birdied several holes on the front nine as well as the brutally hard 480-yard par-four eleventh with three wonderfully struck shots as he skillfully avoided a grove of cork trees on the left and the out-of-bounds fence on the right. I did neither. We weren't in the same league golfwise. I'd give up a couple of internal organs in a heartbeat to hit a golf ball that well. After we had holed out on the wonderful eighteenth green sitting just beyond a treacherous ball-eating pond in the shadow of the elegant clubhouse, Martin said, "You must come over to my house to meet my father. We live just across the street from the eleventh hole." It was an offer I gladly accepted.

Martin's father, Roberto, had been one of the best golfers in South America as a young man. Born into a sporting family, Roberto took to golf as a teenager and had quickly excelled at the difficult game. We sat in his comfortable living room, which offers a splendid view of the golf course and clubhouse across the street, as he took out scrapbooks that told the tales of his golfing career. He showed me pictures of tournaments in South America playing against the likes of Jack Nicklaus, Gary Player, and Tony Jacklin. He won scores of tournaments as an amateur. His mentor and buddy, Roberto De Vicenzo, thought his young friend's game was accomplished enough for the world stage, and De Vicenzo suggested he make the long trip to Scotland to try and qualify for the British Open in 1969 that was being held at Carnoustie. Carnoustie is about a one-hour drive north from St. Andrews and sits seaside just past the Firth of Tay.

Carnoustie is one badass golf course. Many think it's the most difficult championship layout in golf. While not a championship golfer myself, I agree. With gorse rough so thick you rarely find your wayward-struck ball, granite-hard putting surfaces unwilling to accept your iron shots, and bunkers so cavernous you need a road map to get out of them, Carnoustie is harder than taking the SAT test in Mandarin. Despite having played it several times over the years, it always beat me up like a high school bully wanting my milk money. Carnoustie is cruel, mean, and intimidating and always makes me think croquet might be better suited for my meager skills. Yet, after I repair my bruised golfing ego, I always go back to chasing that little white ball on my elusive quest. Some people never learn.

Roberto, an amateur, did indeed make the trip to Scotland, and qualified for the British Open at Montifieth Golf Links, an excellent no-nonsense test of golf just down the road from mighty Carnoustie. Montifieth and neighboring Panmure are those types of lesser-known but truly great golf courses that tourists visiting Scotland seldom play. They should.

Roberto had never ventured out of Argentina, let alone played in an event of this magnitude. On the unforgiving Carnoustie, Roberto played well and made the cut—which is no easy task in a major, especially for an amateur playing in his debut. He discovered that his game, developed at the Córdoba Golf Club, matched up against the best players in the world. Roberto held his own for the four rounds of the championship, finishing in the top third. A glorious debut! At that point, Roberto decided he was going to turn professional and play golf for a living. He was young, handsome, and ready to conquer the golfing world after the Open at Carnoustie. Roberto Monguzzi was the heir apparent to the great Roberto De Vicenzo.

Not long after his triumphant return to Argentina from Scotland, Monguzzi was driving to Buenos Aires from Córdoba on
family business. He was driving alone on the hilly two-lane road
linking the two cities and saw an oncoming car in his own lane up
ahead that was passing two slower trucks. He moved over to the far
right side of his own lane thinking there was plenty of room, but
the onrushing speeding car sideswiped his as they passed and his
vehicle careened violently off the road. The accident shattered his
right leg and Roberto was knocked unconscious. When he awoke
several days later in the hospital, the prognosis wasn't good. The
lower part of his leg was so severely injured that the doctors
wanted to amputate it at the upper thigh to save at least some of
the appendage. Roberto's father asked the doctors to wait another
day to see if the leg might be saved intact. Luckily, that is indeed
what happened, but Roberto's dream of professional golf was over.

In his sixties now, Roberto doesn't hold any bitterness about his
stroke of bad luck. He told me, "I have a beautiful wife and great
sons who care about me. I still love to play golf and do so most
every day. After my accident, I could never again play like I knew
I could." Yet he treasured a love of the game. He invited me to
play with him the following morning.

Roberto is strong and fit and looks as if he could play on the
Champions Tour, until he starts to walk with a noticeable limp.
The accident left him with limited use of his right knee and he
can't use the power of his legs to hit the ball with any force. As
good golfers know—it's all in the legs. He still scores well because
of his expertise around the greens with a wonderful short game.
When he holds a golf club, it looks as if he had been born with
one in his hands.

The morning of our golf outing dawned bright and sunny as did
most every day of my Córdoba stay. I was happy to have heard
Roberto's story and have the chance to play a round of golf with
him. He has a sharp eye for the game and gave me little tips that
helped me improve immediately as we played the gently rolling but
demandingly long course. "Suave," he would say, trying to get me to

swing smoother as he demonstrated the fluid motion of his own. "*Suave*, David, *suave!*" With his encouragement and gentle coaxing, I finally began playing decently as I was actually making more pars than not.

We finished the ninth hole and were walking to the tenth tee-box that was right in view of the clubhouse to begin our second nine when Roberto said to me, "There's Eduardo Romero!" I quickly turned to look, and there standing on the first tee, getting ready to play the course he grew up on, was the great *El Gato*. He had that suntanned sheen of a successful professional golfer who makes his living outdoors and was resplendent in his Calloway-logoed azure blue golf shirt, pressed black pants, and glossy white golf shoes. He could just have easily been on the first tee of the opening round of the Masters as on his home course. I was shocked speechless.

Roberto kindly introduced me to Romero, who has a constant mischievous grin as if he were about to spring a practical joke any second. He asked me what I was doing there in Argentina, and I told him of my around-the-world adventure and how I had come to play golf in Córdoba because it was his home course. Speaking a mile a minute, I told him about the little old lady who adored him in St. Andrews. He loved the story. "No kidding? I'm her favorite golfer!" he exclaimed as he beamed his big smile, which grew even wider.

He inquired where I was going next on my journey and I replied that Salta was my destination. Romero said, "That's where I had my first job as a club pro. I'll call up there and make sure they take care of you." He immediately pulled out his cell phone to call the course.

After a few minutes of spirited banter with whoever was on the other line, Romero put the phone away, smiled once again, and said, "Mr. Wood, you're all set up in Salta. They're expecting you."

You've gotta love *El Gato*.

5

Arica Golf Club
Arica, Chile

18.29°S–70.20°W

After another cold and drafty overnight bus ride, my clubs and I reached the mountainous Argentine colonial city of Salta and immediately I felt the dizzying effects of the altitude. Salta sits at 4000 feet above sea level. I had a slight headache and my breathing was as labored as a pregnant woman in her eighth month hiking up the Matterhorn. This didn't bode well for the next leg of my journey over the Andes at 15,000 feet. Another night of no sleep on the bus hadn't helped. Adding to the mix, a mysterious fellow bus traveler had introduced himself during the overnight ride.

Our bus had stopped for coffee at two in the morning in Santiago del Estero, which was roughly halfway between Salta and Córdoba. The night air in the mountains was crystal clear and chilly, with millions of stars glittering across a vast southern sky blacker than ink. Like all bus depots in South America, this one was teeming with people in the middle of the night. Argentineans are as nocturnal as bats.

I had spied the other Westerner, traveling alone, a few rows up from me. These drafty buses were mostly used by locals, and gringos were a curiosity even to another gringo like me. During the rest stop, I gave in and was having a coffee despite the late hour. Caffeine in the middle of the night isn't usual for me, but if I was going to freeze to death on a bus ride, I wanted to be awake for my final moments.

The other gringo came up and introduced himself to me. His name was John, and though he was British by birth, he said he lived on a coffee plantation he owned in Kenya. "It's a mess in Kenya right now," he warned me, ominously, as if it was our next stop.

John looked to be sixty with a silver mane of wild hair and the white bushy eyebrows of a mad scientist. His dark eyes were a touch fierce and he had the serious air of a university professor, or, perhaps, a hit man. We chatted about the cold. Although I enjoyed speaking with someone whose first language was English, my new traveling companion turned out to be more than I had bargained for.

John said that his wife had died recently and he was traveling around South America with his daughter, who was currently in Buenos Aires with her boyfriend. He continued on, informing me that he and his daughter were both involved with finding and freeing political prisoners in Chile and Argentina. Both countries have long histories of people disappearing without a trace. John said there were still hundreds of innocent people being held against their will for speaking out against various corrupt South American regimes. Just as we were called back to the bus he added, "I'm not well liked by the government here in Argentina." We agreed to meet for breakfast upon arrival in Salta. His story intrigued me.

It was seven in the morning as we pulled into Salta. South American cities can be slow to wake, but Salta was humming with activity at this early hour—there was an Andean festival that week and the busy town center was packed with mountain folks who had made the pilgrimage to the market town. Normally, I would have found all the excitement of the town thrilling, but all I wanted to do was lie down and sleep. I was reeling and lightheaded and needed a room. However, that was a problem because of the festival. I hadn't made hotel arrangements and everything was booked. My guidebook had said that finding lodging in Salta was never a concern. I beg to differ.

Dragging my golf bag around from hotel to hotel, I was turned away each time as every room was booked. It was at times like that I cursed myself for bringing my golf clubs—it was a chore lugging them around. Finally, I talked a hotel clerk into letting me store my bag behind his desk for a few pesos while I tried to find accommodations. Plus, I was due to meet John for breakfast in a few minutes.

"I have a bit of a problem, old boy," John said, eyeing me as I plunked down gratefully into a chair at the outdoor café where we had agreed to meet. "I seem to have left my passport and wallet in my daughter's hotel room back in Buenos Aires. I don't have a penny to my name. I can't believe I did something so stupid!" he lamented.

During my midnight coffee break, John had told me that he was coming to Salta for just a few hours to pick up some legal documents for a case and was hoping to take a bus directly back to Buenos Aires if everything went smoothly.

I was happy to reply, "Don't worry, breakfast is on me."

Grateful to be sitting down and speaking English, I turned what was left of my attention to my mysterious guest. For the next hour he filled me full of stories of being a witness against South American governments in trials to free political prisoners, as well as horror stories of torture and murder inflicted on dissenters by the brutal leaders of Argentina and Chile. My head was spinning from the altitude as well as this onslaught of tales of the unfortunate *desaparecidos*. Finally, he said, "Old boy. I was wondering if you might bail me out of my pickle by lending me some pesos."

Despite my altitude-riddled mind-set, it had occurred to me that perhaps his story was complete bullshit, and he had found an easy mark in me. Though in my mind's eye I thought I looked cool and worldly to outsiders, the truth is I probably looked like a sap. Any idiot lugging around golf clubs at the base of the Andes can't be the brightest bulb on the tree.

I considered his plea. If it was indeed a true story, the guy was in a jam, but there was part of me that was appropriately apprehensive.

I was on a budget and watching my money carefully and I didn't want to be a fool. "How much do you need? One hundred pesos?" I asked. This was about thirty dollars.

"No, that won't be enough. Three hundred pesos should do the trick," John answered. "Once I get back to my daughter, I can have the money sent to you wherever you would like."

Doing the math in my head, I figured it was two days by bus to Buenos Aires and he would probably have to spend a night in a hotel along the way. Three hundred pesos was one hundred U.S. dollars, at least double what I was currently spending a day. It certainly wasn't an outlandish request. I decided to believe him. If he was ripping me off, at least he had spent a couple of hours doing it, plus it gave me a story to tell. After all, he had been entertaining.

"I'll give you the money. I don't want to be paid back, but I do want you to match the hundred dollars and give it to someone in need." If he was a con man, at least I had tried to put a touch of guilt into his conniving head and turn him loose on his own karma.

He smiled and replied, "Very good, old man. I'll make sure it goes to someone truly in need. You have my word." I gave him the money, we shook hands, and in a matter of a few minutes he said good-bye and disappeared, like a ghost, into the horde of locals on the crowded narrow sidewalk.

After my not-so-satisfying train wreck of a sleepless bus ride, altitude headache, and possible con-artist breakfast, I was not in the mood to hang around Salta's crowds. I could feel bad on a bus just as easily as in a hotel room, which I wasn't even sure could be procured anyway. Stopping briefly to collect my golf bag, I moved on to the bus depot to see about a ticket to San Pedro, a small Chilean outpost in the middle of the Atacama. Luck was with me. The bus was leaving at ten that morning and would arrive in the early evening. At least I would get to see the Andes and the Atacama in the daylight.

From the station, I called the Salta golf course that Eduardo Romero had set me up at, to explain that I wasn't going to visit and express my thanks nonetheless. The friendly gentleman on the other end said, "Next time you come this way, we'd love to have you visit, Mr. Wood. Any friend of Eduardo's is a friend of ours!"

I had the feeling the Andes weren't going to be as nearly as accommodating. They had me worried. I had read tales of altitude sickness where people's eyes started bleeding due to the lack of oxygen. Cerebral edema is no picnic. My imagination was running wild as I knew for sure that my eyes were going to burst into a river of red spewing out of my two sockets. It was going to be tough trying to impress any senoritas I might meet en route with blood pouring out of my eyeballs.

The symptoms of altitude sickness include nausea, headaches, and hallucinations—how's that for a triple threat? As prevention, about the only thing the traveler can do is to drink plenty of water, because the body loses moisture as your heart pumps harder and faster the higher you ascend. There was a store at the depot. I bought out the entire stock of bottled water. A small army could travel for several weeks in the Sahara on the ration I had allotted myself, but I wasn't taking any chances. Although the bus was crowded, I had two seats to myself. The extra room was welcome; I needed it for all the water traveling with me.

Not only were visions of me without any vision dancing through my sleep-deprived brain, but also, as long as I can remember, I've been scared of heights. I don't like being on airplanes, elevators, escalators, ladders—basically anything that goes up. I get queasy when I stand on a dining room chair to change a lightbulb. Having had this fear my whole life, I wanted to finally come to grips with it. In many ways, this trip was about confronting my myriad of fears. I took a big gulp of water. Okay, I was as ready as I was ever going to be. Bring it on!

Almost immediately after taking off, the bus started a steep ascent, which I thought was good. Let's get the climbing part out of the way early. The road was paved for the first hour, but then it turned into gravel and narrowed from two lanes to no wider than your average golf-course cart path. The front of the bus was pitched several yards above the back where I sat. It was the effect of a roller-coaster car climbing to the top of the ride before the wild plunge down, but this climb went on for hours. I was busy chugging water like a camel at an oasis.

We had started the journey in mid-morning. I looked at my watch. It was now four in the afternoon and we were still going up the steep mountains. I felt okay, although I was getting up to pee every fifteen minutes because of my incredible fluid intake. I was using the onboard bathroom at least five times more than the rest of the twenty or so passengers combined.

I was proud of myself, because I still felt okay and the views were amazing as we climbed up to the heavens. Fighting my fear of heights, I was actually looking down at where we had been because the gravel road was a series of switchbacks, and at this altitude there wasn't any vegetation to block the view. I never dreamed I would ever be on a dirt road at this elevation—at least not in this lifetime. Every once in a while I would look up ahead and see a car or truck higher up the mountain ahead of us, and would think that couldn't possibly be our road way up there. No way! How could vehicles travel on a slope that steep? Of course, it was our path too.

We passed a car on the side of the road that was obviously having engine problems. The hood was up and the driver was peering at the engine like a fortune-teller gazing at a magic ball. I couldn't think of a worse place on the planet to have car problems. "Hello AAA? I'm going to need a tow truck. My location? Oh, I'm at fourteen-thousand feet in the Andes."

We finally reached a flat stretch and I thought, "Cool! I made it! I beat the Andes!" I was elated as we drove horizontally for about half an hour. I had survived! I wasn't ill and felt a touch euphoric to have faced my fear of heights head-on.

Yet, this glory was fleeting. I looked ahead and saw Mount Everest, Jr., directly in our path. The realization came to me that for the past several hours, we'd only been on the bunny hill. Up we went.

My head was starting to hurt a touch, and it was definitely harder to breathe, but I was hanging in there. We went up the final peak, and the bus was damn near vertical as the driver downshifted to fight the steep incline. The engine roared, we climbed and climbed, and, at last, reached the top. It was now six in the evening but still light out as the pale blue of the atmosphere and our bus were now eye to eye. I was sitting in the sky!

The bus was due to arrive in San Pedro at seven that evening, which I thought was odd. We were still at 15,000 feet, and I knew from my guidebook that San Pedro de Atacama was around 7,000 feet above sea level. It was six o'clock. We couldn't possibly drop that fast in an hour. We didn't. We dropped that fast in forty-five minutes as the roller-coaster bus had reached the pinnacle and started hurtling down.

Almost immediately as the bus descended, I could feel the vise grip that had just begun to wrap itself around my head start to tighten. The inside of my head started pounding as if my brain cells were throwing themselves against my skull trying to break through and escape. "We need oxygen!" they screamed. I knew right away I was in trouble. It turns out with altitude sickness it's not the "up" part that gets you, it's that tricky "down" part they don't tell you about. Bastards!

If you've never had altitude sickness, it feels like you've died, crawled out of your grave, then were hit by a truck, and then again by a bigger truck. I kept it together on the bus as best I could, but my altitude sickness was getting worse by the second. Every inch of me was screaming, "I'm going to be sick!"

We reached San Pedro and for the first time that day, I realized that I hadn't booked a hotel room there either.

San Pedro de Atacama is a tiny village, and by tiny, I mean there weren't many buildings and I was taller than all of them. It's basically a group of adobe huts in the middle of nowhere. It's not often in life that I can stand flat-footed, look down, and say, "I think you need to retile your roof." I was trapped in Pueblo Barbie's Dream Town.

After I weaved my way off the bus, a local approached me to see if I needed a ride into town. I had no clue where I was and was too sick to care. The driver put my bag in the back of his truck, and drove me about twenty yards into the town from the bus station. By the way, I should clarify that the local "station" was merely a trash can with *Autobús* spray-painted on it.

We stopped at hotel after hotel (and by *hotel*, I mean "hut"), but everything was booked. My world was spinning out of control as I prayed I wouldn't throw up all over this guy's clean truck. I was thankful that the gentleman who was helping me wasn't a robber— I would have been easy prey in my weakened state. My head was pounding like it had never done before in my life. Actually, it was comical to be driving around a town this small. We would get back into the truck for the next ten-yard drive to another sold-out hotel. Were the Shriners in town?

About ready to give up and go die in the mountain desert like an Inca warrior, I found a hotel that had an opening. I staggered in to look at the tiny room. It was hobbit size and reminded me of a coffin. I didn't see a bathroom. I pulled out one of the few Spanish phrases I had down pat: "*¿Dónde esta el baño?*" Where's the bathroom?

The old lady pointed out the window to a bucket and garden hose in the tiny courtyard. No way! If I was going to die, which I was getting more and more convinced would be soon, it sure as hell wasn't going to be at the Dogpatch Hotel. I was also becoming more certain that, given my current condition, adequate plumbing was going to be a survival necessity.

We got back into the truck and I asked the driver where the best hotel in town was. I was thinking, *I have money, I'll pay whatever! Damn the cost!*

The Spanish driver didn't fully comprehend what I was saying, so I asked him, "*¿Querido hosteria?*" This hit a nerve with him.

"*¿Querido hosteria?*" he repeated.

"*Sí! Sí!* Fine hotel!" I shouted.

He drove me another fifty yards to the best place in town (twenty-eight dollars a night), where luckily they had a cancellation. Thank god! I made it to the room just in time and dove onto the bed fully clothed. I couldn't have gone another step. My world was spinning like I was the lone sock in a dryer. I didn't even have the strength to take off my shoes. I grabbed onto the bed and held on for dear life. My brain was on fire.

As sick as I was, I was still determined to see the sky above the Atacama. That's why I had faced my fear of heights and gone there in the first place. I woke up at three in the morning and my head felt like someone was smashing it with a sledgehammer. Despite the beating my temples were suffering, one thought dominated all others: I was here to see that Atacama sky and I was going to do it! I crawled on all fours to the door of my room, which opened to an outside courtyard. I was so weak it took all my energy to open the door. There was no way I could even get close to standing erect without having to dive instantly back onto the bed. I flipped over like a turtle on its back, and using my legs, I scooted my head and shoulders outside into the courtyard. The rest of me was still in my room. There, with nothing blocking my view, I looked directly up to the heavens and the clearest night sky in the world.

Even in my terrible condition, the billions of stars illuminating the sky were amazing. Entire whorls of whole galaxies and constellations mixed with brilliant clusters of light that were brighter than flawless diamonds in a spotlight. The night shine was so illuminating it seemed you could read by starlight. It was glorious! The sheer magnitude and vastness of the universe didn't seem possible. With that many possibilities, there had to be other intelligent life out there waiting to communicate with us on this lonely water-dominated planet. Did they play golf out there?

I wanted to just lie there peacefully and sleep under all the brilliance. The glory of the universe cured my sickness as if my illness wanted to stretch out alongside me and gaze up as well. It was awesome! I didn't know this kind of look at the heavens was even possible as I lay there mesmerized, waiting for the stars to speak to me. All of a sudden my headache said, "That's enough, star boy!" and started the pounding of the drums. I plummeted back to earth, sick and spinning out of control once again.

That was the sickest I have ever been in my life.

Awakening the next morning, while weak, I felt okay. It seemed a miracle. I thought about the stars and wondered if that had been a dream. The pounding and nausea had run their course. My headache was gone. It didn't seem possible that I could have been that sick and now felt okay. It was almost a cruel Andes joke. I cleaned up and went to breakfast but could only manage some tea and crackers. At least I was back among the living.

The hard part of the Andes was over for this leg of the journey and I enjoyed seeing the full scope of the dry Atacama as I bused on to Arica, Chile. The Atacama is known by climatologists as absolute desert—you don't see a cactus, a blade of grass, or even a lizard scurrying across the road. With no moisture, nothing rots; if something dies in the desert, it becomes an artifact for eternity.

Mile after mile of brown gave way to pastel salt flats stretching to the horizon, looking smooth enough that ice-skating seemed a possibility. It was silent and beautiful and worth the bother of all that sickness. Glad to be alive, I took it all in, happy to be a simple traveler going to a new town to play golf. Arica didn't let me down.

The town of Arica sits at the very northern tip of the extra-long stiff-shafted one-iron of Chile. It is wedged between the Atacama and the dust bowl that is southern Peru. As the border point for Peru and oceanfront for northern Chile, Arica is trying hard to become a resort town, but that's going to be a tough sell. The town is anything but attractive and unless you were there for golf, as I was, I couldn't imagine staying for any length of time. It was a boomtown with no reason for the boom.

I taxied out to the course and met a couple of golfers who were going out to play. Being Chilean, they were welcoming and politely asked if I would care to join. Of course, I gladly accepted. The Arica Golf Course was about to change my thinking of the game.

In all the years that I have seriously tortured myself with the foolhardy endeavor of trying to put a golf ball into a little round hole, I have considered grass to be a necessary requirement of the game. Just like oil needs vinegar, peanut butter needs jelly, and Brooks needs Dunn, I figured golf needed grass. Golfers know grass. I may not know the difference between Bach and Mozart, but I sure as hell know the difference between bent grass and Bermuda. The Arica Golf Course proves grass isn't all it's cracked up to be.

Thirty years ago, some Arica folks got together and decided that they weren't going to let a little problem like no grass stop them from playing the world's oldest game. They built the Club de Golf Río Lluta, a 6,570-yard course that is as enjoyable a golfing experience as I have ever had. By the way, in Spanish the word *río* means "river." The *Río* Lluta is a river in the same way that McDonald's is a health food restaurant. Perhaps, it's just wishful thinking.

The first look at the course there is one of the strangest a golfer will ever see. From the clubhouse perched on a hill overlooking the entire course, all you see is brown and more brown. The only thing breaking up this color scheme is a series of white painted lines that serve as the boundary definitions of the eighteen fairways. It looks like eighteen crime-scene chalked outlines of murdered giants who have been carted off to the morgue. You then start to notice circular pools of black periodically spaced around the dirt hills. It takes a second or two to realize that these are the "greens."

Just because there's nothing but dirt, don't think there aren't hazards. They have created water from stones. When you hit your ball wayward into an area with sporadically placed blue-painted rocks, you're in a water hazard! The locals have a sense of humor: in some of these water hazards they've put shark fins rising up out of this sea of dirt just to let you know that you're indeed in golfing peril. You can walk on the water to retrieve your ball, but that's all you can do. You must play your ball like it's in the bottom of the Pacific Ocean. Get it out of the drink and take your penalty. Areas with green-painted rocks are considered the rough, and your ball can be played as it lies, but think twice about hitting it if your ball is resting near one of these green mini-boulders—it can't be moved. You swing at your own risk, to your health and that of your club.

This is a course where hitting the fairway is a premium. Each golfer carries a one-foot square piece of Astroturf you can hit your ball off of, if your shot has landed between the chalked boundaries for that hole. You have a much better chance of reaching the green from your piece of synthetic turf than trying to hit it directly off the unforgiving brown hardpan. The greens are mixture of dirt and used motor oil that has been sifted together and are as messy as they sound.

Each player also is given a flat wooden rake that is used to smooth the black ground between your ball and the hole before putting. Once smoothed, the greens roll remarkably true.

By the way, the local golfers are very serious. There are no gimme putts there; you keep putting until your ball is in the bottom of the cup, and the golfer who had the least number of strokes has the honor on the next tee, thank you very much. Dirt or no, these golfers played the game the way it should be played. They were my kind of golfers.

As if all of this isn't unique enough, after all the players have holed out, one player takes a wooden pole with iron-mesh netting attached to the bottom that sits behind each green, and drags the putting surface clean of the footprints that were just created so the golfers in the next group will have a smooth surface for their shots. It's hard to put backspin on a well-struck iron when it lands in Bigfoot's shoe print!

What a pleasure it was to find golf like this in that converted wasteland. Though there are only thirty golfers in the area, they are as keen on golf as any place I've ever been. The spirit of the game is as alive there in the Atacama as it is in St. Andrews, Dornoch, or Pebble Beach. I finished the round a wee bit dirtier than usual, and weeks later I would still find Atacaman sand that had crept into my golf bag, but I'd go back to the Arica Golf Club in a heartbeat. Grass is overrated.

6

La Paz Golf Club
La Paz, Bolivia

16.10°S–67.43°W

I made the decision to not fret about the current violence in Bolivia and hope my good fortune continued. My next locale was La Paz. I had bought a ticket to La Paz on Chile Bus not realizing until I mentioned the name of the company to the front-desk clerk at my Arica hotel that a Chile Bus had been shot at a few days earlier en route to La Paz. In fact, the very bus I was to be on was the one that had received the un-friendly fire—the bullet hole was just over the front driver's-side wheel well. The bus company had taken a can of white paint and painted over everywhere on the vehicle that had the word *Chile* on it. I hoped this clever disguise would fool the snipers.

It turns out that Chile and Bolivia, like Tiger and Phil, aren't fond of each other. The land on which Arica resides has long been a sen-sitive issue between the two countries. Bolivia and Paraguay are the only two landlocked countries on the continent. The lack of a port city has put them both at the bottom of the economic heap. Several wars have been fought over this land around Arica, and since Chile won the last bout in the late 1800s, the ocean turf belongs to them.

The bus ride to La Paz was scheduled for eight hours, but it took us almost double that because of the roadblocks of burning tires and huge boulders that the protesting peasants had put on the main highway into La Paz. They were telling the government that commerce can't enter or leave the country without going through them. I can personally attest that it was quite a good argument. Their plan was working. The new government was promising immediate reform, but I had the feeling the peasants would believe it when they saw it. It was an old song and dance performed by the haves for the have-nots.

While unfired-upon by bullets, our bus was constantly diverted into backcountry roads that were bone-jarringly rugged. These were roads built for donkeys, not a large coach. Many of the road blocks were manned with men holding rifles and wearing red handkerchiefs over their faces. The masks showed the seriousness of the confrontation and spooked me. It occurred to me that perhaps our State Department was smarter than I thought. What the hell was I doing there? Oh yeah, I remember: golf.

It was another long, gradual climb up the Andes to La Paz. The world's highest capital city at 15,000 feet, La Paz has almost two million inhabitants fighting for those scarce molecules of oxygen. The bus was crammed full of Bolivian families. These were small mountain people with colorful shawls and bowler hats on the women, and most of the men wore small, jaunty fedoras. The sporty headgear made me like the people instantly; it seemed strangely defiant. Though we were on the bus for hours, it was silent—these weren't chatty folk. I'm willing to bet a small fortune that I was the only one on the bus going to La Paz to play golf.

Glimpsing the mountainside metropolis of La Paz for the first time was unlike viewing any city I'd ever seen. The city clings precariously to a steep canyon on the side of a mountain that cascades four miles from top to bottom. Two million people live rim to rim sticking to the ledge like Spiderman on the side of the Empire State Building. This is a city where falling out of bed is a real possibility. If one building at the top started to tumble, it looks as if the whole city would crumble like a house of cards. In La Paz you're walking either uphill or downhill. There's not a level lie in the city limits.

Our bus entered La Paz from the very top of the city and we started spiraling downhill to get into the city center. I won't bore you with the gory details, but the descent sent me into another severe bout of altitude sickness. To get to my hotel from the bus depot, the taxi I was in traveled vertically for one mile straight down. The road was a black diamond ski run that, had I been skiing, would have had me snowplowing with all my might. My head wanted to explode immediately—I knew the symptoms.

Between my illness and the fact that I didn't know the denominations of the Bolivian currency yet, I accidentally paid the driver ten times the amount I should have when we reached my hotel. He didn't speak English. I should have known: when I handed him a wad of cash, his eyes nearly popped out of his head and he ran back to his cab and quickly sped away. I was so dizzy I couldn't do the long division correctly. I lopped off three zeros when it should have been four.

I don't recall checking in to the hotel. I do know that I barely made it to my room and had to stay in bed for two days to recover from my second bout of altitude sickness. How in the hell do people mountain climb? I have no clue. I can't even do it on a bus.

After a bedridden couple of days recovering, I started walking the mountain city to check it out and build up my lung power in the thin air. Despite the huffing and puffing I had to endure to walk even a few blocks, I found the bustling city and its hardworking citizens appealing. Though the people are poor, it isn't for lack of trying. These are industrious people who are busy morning to night hawking goods or shelling corn or clearing rocks. No one was idle or begging. All they wanted was a piece of that skinny Bolivian economic pie. I saw one enterprising old man who had a box of Band-Aids and was eagerly trying to sell them one at a time to passersby. I guess he was hoping for a big day of open wounds.

Finally acclimated to the altitude, I took a taxi to the La Paz Golf Club to play the world's highest golf course. There is controversy on which golf course actually sits at the highest elevation of the earth. British engineers built several rudimentary courses as they traveled the Andes, including the nine-hole Tuctu Golf Club in Peru at 14,335 feet above sea level. The course was abandoned in the late 1900s and is unrecognizable as a course from the overgrowth of grasses and weeds there today. There are courses out in the world that are only golf in the broadest sense of what constitutes an actual golf course. In Pakistan, there's said to be a course with holes laid out over rocks and terrain on which the game can't be played as it historically has. Explorers hit golf shots on the North and South Pole to flags or holes placed in the ice and snow. Astronaut Alan Shepard hit a golf shot on the moon, but despite this, it can't be argued there is golf there. My quest was for golf courses that were ongoing functional places where golfers played the game in a style and manner of the ancient game played over the links of St. Andrews. To me, anything else was a novelty and didn't count. At 10,880 feet, the La Paz Golf Club in now thought to be the world's highest and is very much open for play.

Though hardly level, the La Paz Golf Club rests on the only fairly level spot of land I came across in La Paz. The course sits at the southern end of the city and abuts the dramatic Valle de la Luna (Valley of the Moon), which isn't a valley at all. It's a badlands of hills and rocks eroded into bizarre shapes and deep gullies that does indeed look lunar. As my taxi traversed the series of steep switchbacks leading to the course, I saw neither a blade of grass nor any ground even capable of sprouting life, let alone enough elbow room to strike a golf ball.

We passed through one of the armed-guarded gates protecting the entrance, which are ubiquitous in South American golf, and entered the surprisingly lush, amazingly green La Paz Golf Club. As we pulled up to the clubhouse, a dozen caddies had made a mad dash to help me with my bag and perhaps secure a gig for the day. There was only one other car in the parking lot, so the chance of earning pesos that day was going to be tough. The winning caddie was Gonzalo Reynaldo Ballion, a twenty-five-year-old golf fanatic with a shy, quiet manner like most Bolivians. Gonzalo was slight in build and though he looked hardly old enough to shave, he was married with two children. He was trying to learn English, and as we went around the course, he kept me busy quizzing him on the days of the week and counting to ten in my native tongue. He had me do the same in Spanish as he, in turn, quizzed me; but he was learning at a much quicker pace than I was.

The first hole, a testing 406-yard par-four, climbs to a small, oval green that is the highest point of the course at 10,964 feet. Though the slope is gradual, I huffed and puffed as I walked to my ball on the green. After you catch your breath at the summit of the second tee-box, the course then plays downhill all the way to the excellent 167-yard par-three fourteenth, which has a captivating view of the volatile topography of the Valle de la Luna. With the gnarled nooks and crannies of the canyon looking as if Salvador Dalí had a hand in the design, it has to be the harshest and most surreal-looking out-of-bounds in the game.

Being surrounded by the biscuit-brown fissures of the Valle de la Luna makes the green turf and shady oaks lining the fairways stand out all the more. The course is an Andean oasis for the haves of La Paz, as 120 members golf there on a steady basis. Playing to 6,600 yards from the tips, but with scarce molecules of oxygen to impede the flight of your shots, a golfer can drive their ball distances though the thin air that allows them to be Tiger Woods, as least for one day.

The course is an excellent championship layout, which was in much better condition than I would have ever thought possible in poverty-stricken Bolivia. Most of the groundskeeping duties are done without the benefit of machinery. Gonzalo and I shared several tee-boxes with groups of ten or so Bolivian ladies sitting in semicircles and weeding crabgrass by hand nearby. The women all wore the flowing multicolored skirts commonplace there, as well as the brown derby hat that sits jauntily askew on the noggin of most every South American Indian woman you see. These hats, similar to a Charlie Chaplin bowler, are worn at a funny angle like a teacup sitting on the roof of an A-frame home. Though appearing to teeter precariously, I had the feeling a tornado couldn't knock those hats off their heads.

There was only one other golfer playing while I was there; I joined up with him for the back nine. Alex Morales, a local golf lover who learned the game while he attended college in England, is a professor in business management at a local university. He surprised me when he said, "I'm all for the current demonstrations. The way this government goes about its business just isn't fair to its citizens." We strolled along playing our shots and chatting as I asked him about the turmoil. "We simply have too many poor people!" he said.

I told Alex about Mark Lawrie's theory that golf is a great economic indicator for the financial well-being of a country. The more golf courses a country has, the more likely it possesses a large middle class, with not only the money needed for the expensive equipment and green fees, but also the personal freedom required to play the time-killing sport. Bolivia has three golf courses and virtually no middle class. He agreed, saying, "I hope the next time you come back to visit us here in Bolivia we have golf everywhere!" I hope so as well.

Gonzalo had been a great companion as well as caddie, and by the end of the round he knew the days of the week in English better than I did. He was excellent at his job and I gave him a tip I knew was more than triple what he expected. For the second time in La Paz, someone's eyes popped out as I handed them cash. The first was a rip-off; the second I was happy to have caused.

After two months of exciting travel, good and bad rounds of golf, and facing a few of my personal demons, it was time for New Zealand and Australia. I had met my starting goal of playing at the southernmost course in the world. I had tried to tame the Andes, but certainly wasn't the first to fail miserably in that foolish quest.

I only missed one goal in South America. After two months in the Southern Hemisphere, I still had no clue if the water swirled the opposite way around as it went down the toilet. In all the excitement, I forgot to look.

7

Ringaringa Heights Golf Club Stewart Island, New Zealand

53°S–168.06°E

What is it about New Zealand? Once I started thinking of destinations for my journey, New Zealand held a lock on the pole position by several car lengths. Thinking of New Zealand, I'd get weak-kneed and tongue-tied as if I'd opened my front door to find Ashley Judd standing there wearing nothing but a deliciously evil smile and holding a bottle of champagne and two flutes. New Zealand was a spot in the world I yearned to see, although I wasn't exactly sure why. This feeling of wonderment wasn't exclusive to me, for when I'd bring up my plan to go to New Zealand, folks would gush and exclaim: "It's my dream to go there!" It was mine as well.

The remoteness of New Zealand adds to its mystery. As the southern boundary of the twenty-five-thousand-plus isles of Oceania dotting the South Pacific as far north as Hawaii, New Zealand is comprised mainly of two large islands with the uninspired names of *North* and *South*. With all their magical beauty, I would have dubbed the northern island *Sophia* and the southern one *Loren*, but I don't think the locals would have gone for anything quite that racy. That's not the New Zealand way, mate. Many small, scarcely inhabited islands are also included in the territory of New Zealand, with the largest being Stewart Island, twenty miles south across the sea from Loren (just kidding—South New Zealand).

My flight landed in Auckland after eleven hours of flying across the Pacific from Santiago. We arrived at four in the morning. As I walked down the Jetway, groggy and bleary-eyed from the early hour and the long flight, a smiling gentleman under a big WELCOME TO NEW ZEALAND sign was handing out free coffee to the new arrivals to his country. "Welcome, mate!" he said as handed me a hot cup of coffee. I had never been offered a free cup of coffee upon entering a country—it was a lovely touch. Exactly as those curious, seafaring Polynesians must have felt nineteen hundred years ago on their initial landing, I liked it there already.

While traveling from hotel room to hotel room in South America, I had had the idea of checking into renting a camper van to get around New Zealand. Having had my fill of buses and tiring of hotels, I wanted privacy. Renting a camper van solved several personal dilemmas. My shelter and transportation would be taken care of and wouldn't require constant searches and rebuilding of the nest. A glorious vision of pulling into golf courses and camping in their parking lots while waiting to play danced in my mind. And my home would be constantly set up and waiting for me as the homing-pigeon side of me demanded. No unpacking was required. My nest would always be there, patiently waiting for me to roost.

I arrived at the camper-van rental location by taxi and met the owner, Michael, who had recently bought the business; today was the first day of his endeavor. Around thirty years old and full of good cheer, Michael had plunked down his life savings on this business and had left the world of banking where he had been, as he so delicately put it, "Bored out of my friggin' mind." He had traded in a suit and tie for a blue T-shirt and white pants that were either very long shorts or long pants that had shrunk drastically.

He was the epitome of New Zealand casual. Michael was a golfer himself, and was excited about the prospect of my trip. "We have a ton of golf here, mate," he said enthusiastically. Lucky me: he had saved a brand-new gleaming-white Fiat Ducato camper van for the "Yank." It had a king-size bed, stereo, microwave oven, stove, re-frigerator, and bathroom with a shower. It was far nicer than I had imagined it would be when I first thought of the idea in South America.

Michael spent a good half an hour explaining how everything worked, but as I have done my whole life when being told any-thing worth knowing, I nodded in agreement as it went in one ear and out the other. All I wanted was to get out on the open road of New Zealand.

I had asked Michael where a good spot on the ocean might be to camp out, with a golf course nearby. He congenially replied, "Muriwai Beach is about two hours north. There's a nice camp-ground by the sea and a lovely links course there as well. Sounds like your cup of tea, mate." Indeed it was.

As it turns out, two hours was about all I could have driven, be-cause I was so tired from the flight and time change. Having crossed the international date line, there was a sixteen-hour time difference from Santiago. I didn't like that I had skipped a whole day of my life. What if that now-missing day was to be the first time I was to shoot even par for eighteen holes or win the lotto or have Hugh Hefner call me and tell me he'd like me to move into the Playboy Mansion rent-free so I could take a couple of bunnies off his hands? All sorts of great things could have happened on that missing day, which had vanished into the geographical ether.

I stopped at a supermarket on the way to the campground and loaded up on provisions. Getting off the highway at the Muriwai Beach exit, a long, winding road through dense forest, I tooled up and down the twists and turns to the campground at the water's edge. It was exactly what I was seeking, with sand dunes the only barrier between the campgrounds and the sea.

The campground was empty except for a couple of my fellow

RV brethren. We parked well away from each other—there was plenty of room along the sandy seashore. I chose the highest ground that looked out to the sea and plugged into the electrical socket of RV site number twelve—my new home. I made my bed and opened the window slightly to get a full ration of the salty ocean air, and for the next fifteen hours, I slept as peacefully and as long as I ever had in my life.

I awoke the next morning to warm sunshine and the cawing of seagulls that were busy hovering in the breezy ocean air. I have no idea what seagulls actually do on a daily basis, but it does seem as if *hovering* is a big part of their job description. Having been so tired the day before, I hadn't checked out my surroundings well; I had just gone into my deep slumber. As I lay in bed looking out the back window of the camper, I could see a yellow flag fluttering in the sea breeze no more than fifty yards from where I was parked. It was the flag on the green of a golf course. When Michael had said there was a links golf course near the campground, he wasn't kidding. It was just a flip of a sand wedge from where I was parked. Perfect.

Not having paid better attention to Michael's demonstration on how everything worked in my camper van proved to be a mistake but one I was used to, because somehow I never know how anything works right off the bat. It requires all my concentration for the simplest of mechanical tasks. After an hour I finally figured how to turn on the gas for my stove. Though a chimp from the wilds of Africa could have probably figured it out in half the amount of time.

After breakfast I wandered over to the Muriwai Golf Club to try and get a game.

The Muriwai Golf Club was the type of course I loved finding—talk about preaching to the choir. The course was as Scottish as bagpipes. First off, it was a true links course. For those of you who have made it this far in my journey but aren't big golfers, a links course is a golf layout built on the thin strip of sandy soil that links the ocean to the inland. Over time, the winds off the ocean create plateaus and hollows through the dunes and form natural prospects for fairways and greens and tees. True links golf rarely has water hazards other than the sea itself. It is usually treeless, with yellow flowered gorse the vegetation of choice. Depending on its direction or force, the wind can be your friend or foe. Links golf is the sport at its fundamental best—a seaside trek chasing a little white ball through the sand dunes formed over the centuries. Oh, I love it so.

Though just a few days removed from the dizzying heights of the Andes, I was now blissfully seaside, playing golf in New Zealand on a warm sunny day over a course I immediately loved. It was a Monday, and though the sun was out in full force as a warm breeze blew in off the sea, the course was mostly vacant. There wasn't anyone to play with, which wasn't a concern; I just wanted to hit the ball around the links and enjoy my first day of golf in the paradise of New Zealand.

Way out on the course, I did finally see a gentleman out playing alone over on an adjoining fairway. He was driving a motor scooter from shot to shot as he pulled his golf clubs behind him on a trolley that he had jury-rigged to the back. It was a novel contraption if I'd ever seen one, and one I'd certainly never seen on a course. This hybrid was so unique and ingenious it made me laugh. I'm not one for golf carts, but had to admit to liking his motorized setup—it looked like fun, plus he could go much faster than a golf cart. He was the Road Warrior of golf.

The Golf Warrior waved to me and I returned his friendly gesture. He was as curious about a stranger on his course as I was about him. He cruised over to me and skidded to a stop inches from my golf bag. I think he said his name was Ned, but I couldn't quite catch it as the whine of his motor mixed with the roar of the wind off the ocean. By now, I could see that he was elderly and so frail that I wondered how he could muster the energy to swing a golf club, let alone keep the scooter upright. Better yet, he wore thick Coke-bottle glasses that turned his eyes into giant black orbs blinking through all the magnification like a mosquito caught under a microscope. It was a touch unsettling. Now he looked more like the Golf Terrier than the Road Warrior.

I also couldn't understand a word he was saying. I hadn't had much dealing with New Zealanders yet, but had begun to notice they had a slight tendency to mumble.

"Good morning, sir. Lovely day, isn't it," I said, bravely, to the fellow.

"Mumble mumble mumble mumble," he replied as I watched his gigantic eyes blinking under his glasses as if he was outside in the sun for the first time in twenty years.

"How are you hitting them today?" I tried, hopefully.

"Mumble mumble mumble bloody mumble mumble golf," he laughed as he answered. I got two words figured out that time. He continued on, "Mumble mumble goddamn mumble!" He ended with a big belly laugh, as his eyes grew larger with the merriment.

I laughed as well, as I nodded and pretended to know what he was saying. He seemed pleasant and cheerful, but his enormous eyes seemed to keep expanding into large pools of visceral motor oil. I had to turn away from his gaze because I was afraid his pupils might overtake his entire head. Perhaps he was an alien sent to earth to play golf and hypnotize strangers one at a time with his amazing peepers before dragging them behind his scooter, back to the mother ship. Maybe I had somehow called him from outer space that night in the Andes when I'd been spinning up amongst the stars. They knew I knew there was golf out there, and he was here to silence me. Having gotten so much sleep, my wild imagination was rested and ready to ramble. I somehow snapped out of it as he finished, "Mumble!"

"That's quite a vehicle you have there." I stated confidently.

He laughed again and replied, "Mumble mumble mumble."

Then he leaned forward, suddenly just a friendly old golf fanatic once again, and we shook hands as if we had just had the most enlightening of conversations.

"Hit 'em well," I said, as he gunned the engine and mumbled something else to me before motoring back to his ball. I made a mental note to have my eyes examined at the very first opportunity.

After playing, I went into the small, but well-stocked pro shop and chatted with the gentleman behind the counter. It was a slow business day for him: my camper was the only car in the parking lot. He asked me how I liked the course and I told him about my love of links golf. "Ah, links golf is the only way to play the game, isn't it," he sighed happily. "Where are you going next?"

I told him I didn't know yet, which was true, as I had nothing planned for New Zealand other than to see as much of it as I could and play golf as it presented itself. I regaled him with tales of my around-the-world golf trip so far.

"Go up the road an hour or so to Mangawhai Heads and talk to the professional at the golf club there," he replied, after I had whiled enough of his time away with story after story of my (to me) fantastic voyage. "He's a great chap named Ted McDougall. He's the one you want to speak with. He knows everything about golf in New Zealand."

It sounded like as a good a plan as any and I appreciated the tip. "I'll do it, thanks," I said.

As of yet, I was in no hurry to leave my Eden of a campground, especially since it had a wonderful links course just outside my camper door. I spent a few days there taking daily runs on the beach and playing golf in the afternoons. I figured out how all the gadgets worked in my new home—the lights and water heater and microwave. I never did figure out how to get outside from the back cabin once I had locked myself in for the night. I tried and tried to open the side door from the inside, but finally gave up and for the next month I crawled out over the driver's seat. It was no big deal—my lifetime of mechanical ineptitude has made me impervious to such inconveniences.

It was another lovely day as I motored up State Highway One through towns with names like Leigh and Waipu and Wellsford, each as gleaming and spotless as the last. It was the middle of November and spring had arrived full throttle with the picturesque towns basking in the sunlight. The bursting brightness of the towns and proverbial good weather of New Zealand matched my jolly mood.

Reaching Mangawhai Heads, I pulled into the parking lot of the Mangawhai Golf Club. Still unsure of handling my gigantic camper van around parked cars and through tight spaces, I parked as far away from the other dozen or so cars as I could. The car park looked out over the invitingly vibrant green golf course, which, I had the feeling, would prove to be a pleasure to play. The red flags on the greens near the low-key white clubhouse fluttered in the sea air. I took a long, relaxed breath as I looked over the peaceful playground, and then I sauntered into the clubhouse, found the pro shop downstairs, and met E. J. "Ted" McDougall.

Ted McDougall, now in his later sixties, is a substantial bear of a man. Many folks refer to him affectionately as "Big Ted." His hands are as large as a first baseman's mitt, and though he has gained a few extra pounds over the years, he wore the ease and confidence of an athlete who has known success like a pro.

Scottish by birth, Ted was born in Lochee, Scotland during the onset of World War II and learned to play golf at Pitlochry—a charming inland course in the Perthshire Highlands of golf's birth-place. When Ted was fourteen, his father followed the lead of relatives and moved the clan to New Zealand for hope of a better life. Being a member of the British Commonwealth, sparsely populated New Zealand was seeking citizens in the 1950s and those who took the chance and made the journey found a welcoming land of sunshine and prosperity. It was an easier climate both economically and weather-wise. I was to meet many people in New Zealand who had taken this major gamble with their futures and moved to the opposite end of the earth sight unseen. To a person, they couldn't believe how fortunate they were to find these islands tucked away in the South Pacific. The immigrants I met had never looked back. New Zealand was the Promised Land.

Being the good Scottish lad he was, Ted keenly took to golf and became one of the more famous amateur golfers in his new homeland. He represented New Zealand seven times in the prestigious Eisenhower Trophies—a worldwide team championship featuring the finest amateurs in the game. In this international competition, Ted teed it up amongst the likes of Ben Crenshaw, Curtis Strange, Bruce Devlin, and Peter Oosterhuis—world-class golfers all.

In 1970, Ted and his mates finished second to a mighty American team led by Tom Kite and Lanny Wadkins. To give you an idea of how good Ted was, in 1968, in eighty-four rounds of competitive tournament golf, his scoring average for the year was 69.85 strokes per round. In today's big-money world of professional golf, that stroke average would mean hundreds of thousands of dollars! In a land full of excellent golfers, Ted won two New Zealand Amateurs thirteen years apart with his first win in 1957. In 1983 he lost in the finals in what would have been his third title, again separated by thirteen years. Ted played top-flight golf for almost forty years.

Except for Bob Charles, who was the only New Zealand golfer to win a major championship, with his 1963 British Open victory at Royal Lytham until Michael Campbell's come-from-behind victory to win the 2005 United States Open, most golfers from New Zealand didn't take the plunge into the ranks of the touring professional world of golf. With New Zealand being one of the more isolated spots on the globe, it wasn't exactly an easy matter to travel to tournaments around the world and be a successful family man. With a wife and kids to feed, Ted gave up professional golf and went into business to provide for his family. From everything his golfing contemporaries told me about his golfing prowess, Ted could have been a fine world-class professional.

With the kids grown, Ted is back in golf: he is the head professional and runs the busy pro shop there at the Mangawhai Golf Club. I explained my mission to him and he said straight away, "Good on ya, mate! Let's get you sorted out on where to play in New Zealand." I knew I was in good hands.

Ted had me pull up a chair behind his counter. While performing the duties of collecting greens fees, booking tee-times, and selling everything from ball markers to candy bars as golfers wandered through, Ted filled me full of stories of golf in New Zealand. He apparently keeps a running commentary going as he goes about running the shop and giving lessons to golfers eager for his locally legendary wisdom. My favorite line happened when a gentleman came in to select one golf ball, from a basket of singles by the cash register, for his round. Ted smiled and teased, "One ball! Oh, you must be quite a good golfer!"

Ted and I chatted for several hours. Ted said that going up to the northernmost course in New Zealand was a must. As should be patently obvious by now, I have a lust for courses off the beaten path. Like me, Ted is fond of links golf, having learned the game on those types of courses as a youngster in Scotland. New Zealand, all coastline and seascapes, has a bounty of seaside courses. "There's a lovely links course called Kaitaia that you must play. When you get there ask for a guy by the name of 'Irish.' I think you'll get on well with him."

Before I left, Ted handed me a stack of his business cards and told me to present one when introducing myself at the various courses he suggested I try and play. "Most folks in golf know me," he said, in what turned out to be quite an understatement. Because the gregarious Ted is so well-thought-of in his adopted land, all I had to do at any course I visited was present myself, say I was a friend of Ted's, show them Ted's business card, and I was treated like golfing royalty. All of this because of a chance encounter with a gentleman behind the counter of the pro shop at the Muriwai Golf Club had suggested I look Ted up. I followed Ted's advice to a tee. The influence of the Golf Gods seemed to be strong in New Zealand.

I drove four hours north to Kaitaia, and immediately went to the golf course. Set against one of the more beautiful beaches in the world, the Kaitaia Golf Course is golf at its pure democratic best. There's no person who accepts your money at the clubhouse. You pay the visitor's greens fee of twelve dollars by dropping an envelope with the cash into the "honor box" and go play—no fuss, no

muss. I asked a gentleman who had kindly showed me this payment procedure if he knew where I might find a fellow by the
name of "Irish." The gentleman pointed to a figure out on the
rugged practice range in front of clubhouse and said with a strong
New Zealand lilt, "They-ah he aiz."

I turned and saw a skinny, grinning gentleman in a wide-
brimmed floppy hat giving a golf lesson to a local Maori teenager.
It was pure luck that Irish was there. He's not employed by the
club to give lessons. When locals ask for help learning the game,
he shows up at the course to teach them for free. Irish donates his
time, energy, and all the golf equipment that he can muster. He
even has a class of over thirty Maori kids that he tutors on the
game, and they react to him like he's the pied piper from Ireland.
With his baggy shorts, floppy hat, and three days' growth of whis-
kers, he looks like a cross between a leprechaun and the guy who
drives the stagecoach in old Western movies. When I went over
and introduced myself, Irish decided to take himself and his pupil
out on the course to play golf with me. He said cheerily, "We'll
have a hit with ya, mate."

We played golf over the seaside swales of the friendly links
while chatting and hitting it off grandly as we all enjoyed the sea
breeze and glorious sunshine at the top of New Zealand. The sea
vista there at the start of Ninety Mile Beach, as the gentle surf laps
up on the broad, white sandy shore, seems to stretch north all the
way to the horizon. It is a uniquely beautiful spot for golf. Like
that idyllic setting, Irish's golf style is distinctive as well. To get
every ounce of power out of his slight frame, on most every swing,
he takes a violent lash at the ball like a man killing a rattlesnake
with a hoe. To get extra distance, when teeing-up his ball before
hitting his driver, Irish uses a homemade device: a ten-inch piece
of wood wrapped with what looks to be two feet of duct tape with
a normal tee stuck to the top to create a launching pad to cradle
his ball. His ball then hovers grandly well above what anyone in
the golf world would consider "teeing your ball high." Then, he
takes such a tremendous wallop at the precariously teetering ball

that his indestructible tee is often twenty yards down the fairways as well. As I had the feeling he does with most every aspect of his life, Irish does things his own way.

It turns out that Irish, who I took to be in his mid-fifties (he won't reveal his real name or age) is Steve Williams's best friend and housemate there in Kaitaia. For you nongolfers, Steve Williams is Tiger Woods' caddie, and is actually the highest paid sports person in New Zealand, where he lives when not on the PGA Tour with Tiger. Irish and Williams started caddying together thirty-plus years ago on the Australian Golf Tour. Deciding to seek fortune toting golf bags, they took their act on the road to Asia, Europe, and every golf tour they could find. They were hardworking and professional, and that put them atop the ranks of their trade. They have been best friends since they first met.

Irish had left the homeland for which he's named (he grew up just south of Dublin) when he was a teenager bent on deciding to go see the world and make his own way. While in Australia, he was asked to caddie by a friend of his, and he found his calling: "I loved it! It was like getting paid to be a backpacker."

Irish is now retired from the grind of world travel and professional caddying. As we sat in the backyard of his house looking out over the beach and having drinks, I asked him why and his reply was simply, "I'm too old, mate."

When playing golf earlier that day, my new best buddy had asked me where I was staying in Kaitaia. I had indicated that I was staying at the local campground in my camper van. "I know where you're staying tonight, and it's not at a campground," was his reply. That's how I ended up staying at the house that Irish and Steve Williams share on the most beautiful beachfront one could possibly imagine.

The roomy wood-beamed house sits about thirty yards back from some smallish sand dunes that lead down to the flat, smooth beach. The sky and ocean are constantly changing colors with various shades of blue, gray, and green offering the best of their respective shades to this kaleidoscope of natural wonder of northern

New Zealand. It's breathtaking. As I sat out on Irish's backyard patio, I couldn't imagine a more beautiful ocean vista or a more peaceful place to watch time go by. After traveling the world caddying for Nick Faldo, Bernhard Langer, Carlos Franco, and scores of other golfers, Irish has found his spot on the earth there on that beautiful beach at the top of New Zealand. I envy him. Who can fault me?

Not to complain, but as I made my way south from Kaitaia, there was almost too much golf in New Zealand. It pained me that I was missing so many wonderful courses, as I simply couldn't play them all. Following Ted McDougall's advice, I had started at the geographical top of New Zealand and made my way down the country, playing one excellent golf course after another. Traveling south on the North Island, I pulled my camper van into course after course on Ted's list: Kauri Cliffs, Mangawhai, Whangarei, Ngamutu Links, Wanganui, Wairakei, Belmont Links, and Paraparaumu, and played the game I love the way I love to play it. There were dozens and dozens of other excellent courses I could have played as well, but not if I wanted to get all the way around the world in a year. I would just have come back in the future—a prospect that made me smile in sheer anticipation. Any future visit back to New Zealand would have to include the Paraparaumu Golf Links, my favorite course in New Zealand, hands-down.

At the time of this writing, Paraparaumu was ranked as the ninety-ninth best course in the world. The fact that it was ninety-ninth out of the top one hundred intrigued me.

Every year when the rankings come out for the "One Hundred Top Golf Courses" in the world, it's never a surprise which courses are in the top ten. Just like Sweden and Venezuela in the Miss Universe pageant, the top two spots are annually reserved for Cypress Point in California and New Jersey's Pine Valley. They tend to switch positions every couple of years, but I think that's more to do with the vintage of the port served to the judges after a round than the condition of their pristine magnificent layouts. The next few spots are usually a game of musical chairs between the Old Course, Pebble Beach, Muirfield (Scotland), Augusta National, and

Shinnecock. The mighty Royals of Ireland and Australia—Portrush, County Down, and Melbourne—along with the new kid on the block, Sand Hills—Ben Crenshaw's homage to Scottish links golf in Nebraska of all places—are in the mix for positions seven through ten. The loser sinks to that dreaded eleventh spot. Having the pleasure of playing Paraparaumu, it occurred to me that obtaining that ninety-ninth spot is infinitely more difficult to obtain than the rarefied air of the select ten.

Think about it. When you're number ninety-nine, you're in a precarious position in the world of golf courses—only two spots from not making the cut in that lofty group. Each year the latest golfing creations from the golf architectural greats like Tom Fazio, Jack Nicklaus, or Tom Doak, as well as every other golf architect du jour, are nipping at your heels. Every billionaire who hoodwinks a zoning commission to buy an unbelievably gorgeous piece of land and then goes to their ATM for millions more to create a new golfing playground for their cronies wants your spot. The thousands of courses that think they possess top-one-hundred qualities have their beady little eyes on you. Courses that were once in the top one hundred, but were bounced out like a deadbeat drunk at closing time, want your spot at the bar. When you're number ninety-nine there's a target on your back. It's like Norm of the television show *Cheers* said to Sam Malone as he walked to his usual bar stool after a long day: "You ever feel like the world's a dog, and you're wearing Milk-Bone underwear?" That's how number ninety-nine must feel!

Paraparaumu Beach Golf Club is a classic straight-ahead, no gimmicks, what you see is what you get, links-style course sitting just a wee bit inland from the Tasman Sea on the western coast of New Zealand's North Island. This is golf the way God sitting up there at the ultimate nineteenth hole intended it to be: hard, fast fairways with bumps, knobs, and hollows; greens that are nestled in windswept sand dunes; and par protected by the natural predator of golfers—wind. There's no billionaire's helicopter pad, as is the current rage at exclusive clubs these days, no armed guards at the gate like South American courses, and you tote your own bag. In a word: ideal.

Through not long, by modern standards, at just over 6,600 yards with a par of seventy-one, it's all the golf you want. The holes are never less than very good, and two can be considered great. The club nominated the par-four seventeenth for the survey of *Golf* magazine's "100 Best Holes in Golf." At 440 yards, you have to hit a long drive between two dunes flanking both sides of the fairway. If this mission was completed successfully, your only hope of hitting and staying on the green is a high left-to-righter that brings into play an evil greenside bunker lurking thuggishly short right of the green. Any shot struck to the center or left of the putting surface is laughingly bounced off the green down into a deep swale that semicircles that elusive target.

For my money, at 443 yards, the par-four thirteenth is even better. Like the wonderful Foxy, that infamous par-four fourteenth at Royal Dornoch in Scotland, there's no bunker on the hole to ruin your hope of par. It's all laid out naturally, right before your eyes. You simply have to stand on the tee and hit a long, perfect right-to-left tee-shot that avoids the shaggy-grassed dunes that await anything not simply well hit. Your second shot requires a precisely struck left-to-right long iron or fairway wood from a probable uneven lie to a narrow but deep green that slopes from back to front. Good luck! Any shot landing short will roll back toward you, with the only positive being you don't have to walk as far to hit your difficult third. This is a classic par-four where bogey is not a bad score, and a par has you moonwalking to the next tee.

Oh, they all want your spot, number ninety-nine. They'll say you're not long enough, you're out of date, you're too easy for the modern player. You'll lure them out with easy daydreams of shooting a fifty-nine, but then the wind will blow, your bunkers will lurk, and the scores will soar. I'm rooting for you, number ninety-nine—you're exactly what we need more of in this wonderful game of golf: a true and honest test.

I became a friend of the general manager of Paraparaumu, a genial Irish chap named Dermot Whelan who is a lover of travel and golf and, had he not had the responsibilities of running the thriving club of eight hundred and fifty members at Paraparaumu, he'd be out on the road with me. There's an adventurous soul hidden beneath his unassuming business suit and tie. Dermot came to New Zealand in 1976 and, like most everyone else who made that plunge, he liked what he saw and decided to stay. Dermot has a guest cottage in front of the beach house that he shares with his lovely girlfriend, Lynn, and that's where I stayed during my time in Paraparaumu. I had never experienced such kindness from complete strangers as I did in New Zealand.

New Zealand had me hopelessly smitten. Its scenic wonders, the friendliness of its people, and the abundance of its golf courses had aroused in me a love like only a fourteen-year-old schoolboy with a Dallas Cowboys cheerleader for a substitute teacher could know. All of this adoration on my part stemmed merely from my journeys around the North Island, having still yet to visit the larger South Island, which everyone kept telling me was even more scenically spectacular. Skepticism would wash over me upon hearing this claim. How could anywhere be more beautiful than what I had seen so far? The North Island was all dreamy beaches giving way to glorious multicolored ocean sunsets, lush green rolling pastures with cows contently grazing on picture-perfect farms, and golf courses as natural and beautiful to the eye as any to be found in the world. The South Island was better than this? Yeah, right! Next, you're going to tell me Ringo was the Beatle with all the talent. Yet, after now having seen the South Island, I can certainly say that calling it *merely beautiful* is like calling Angelina Jolie *kinda cute*.

Though, I must confess: the South Island didn't bowl me over at first. It was a cold and gloomy day, with rain pelting the *Interislander* ferry as it pulled out of the dock in Wellington for the three-hour ride across the Cook Strait.

After docking in the nondescript port town of Picton, I drove an hour to Nelson on the upper northwest coast of the South Island for the night. Though only a hundred miles as the crow flies from the North Island, as I entered the city limits of Nelson I thought I had somehow taken a wrong turn from the ferry and driven to somewhere in the middle of England. I was to learn that the major difference between the two main islands is that the South has much more of a British bent than the Maori-influenced North Island.

In Nelson, between the dozens of fish-and-chips shops, corner pubs, and pallid town folks, I kept double-checking my map to reassure myself I hadn't somehow time traveled to the Midlands or Nottingham. I was further convinced I might be in the United Kingdom when, after coming up with the correct change as payment for a cup of coffee at a tea shop, the girl behind the counter said, "That's brilliant!"

You can't travel anywhere where a large influx of Brits live without hearing the word *brilliant* used for the most menial of completed tasks. This use of the word *brilliant* may be why the British Empire is not what it used to be. I have been told in the Gatwick Airport in London I was "brilliant" by a waitperson after I had ordered a toasted ham and cheese sandwich while waiting for my flight to Edinburgh. I've been called "brilliant" for handing a lady a twenty-pound note for a golf hat while in the Royal County Down pro shop in Northern Ireland. Countless bartenders have called me "brilliant" for ordering a Guinness as I have traveled the remnants of the once-great realm.

How did the most mundane aspects of British life get to be termed *brilliant*? It's not like the British haven't had actual brilliance in their midst. Winston Churchill was brilliant. William Shakespeare was brilliant. Oscar Wilde was brilliant. Even Nick Faldo has been brilliant at times. Reaching into one's pocket and pulling out a two-pound coin for a cup of coffee puts me even with Koko the talking gorilla, but certainly does not make me *brilliant*. I just think they need to raise the bar a touch. That's all I'm saying.

My next travel goal was to get to Stewart Island, which lies fifteen miles straight south across the Foveaux Strait from Invercargill, the southernmost town on the South Island. Stewart Island had me interested because it was remote and had the second-southernmost golf course in the world. I figured any idiot could visit the southernmost course in the world, but to visit the two southernmost courses required a special stupidity; and, once again, I knew the right guy for the job.

On my way to Stewart Island, I drove for ten lovely hours through the scenic wonderment to the town of Queenstown, which was named for Queen Victoria. I don't know if you have ever seen a picture of Queen Victoria, but she looked a wee bit like a monkfish with a tiara. Thankfully, the town takes after her in name only. Against a backdrop of an achingly majestic lazuline sky and a mesmerizing lake so richly blue it has to be seen to be believed, the town is encircled by a range of breathtaking jagged snowcapped peaks actually called "the Remarkables." When you choose to name a group of mountains the Remarkables, they better be something special—and no problems there, mate.

The base of the awe-inspiring Remarkables gives way to Lake Wakatipu on whose shores the town rests peacefully. The mesmerizing water is what other lakes in their wildest dreams would hope to look like. And whatever blue that amazing water is, it sure isn't in the box of sixty-four crayons. This is blue to the tenth power. And to put a cherry on top of that awesome sundae, there is a wooded peninsula that juts out into this heavenly body of water and upon it sits a great golf course. Are they kidding? What are they trying to do, kill me with joy? Have I died and, through some error of sin record-keeping, actually found myself in golfing heaven? Don't tease me, Golf Gods! I rubbed my eyes, shook my head violently back and forth like Daffy Duck, and slowly reopened my eyes. It was true! Kelvin Heights Golf Course sits like Excalibur in Avalon, surrounded by the mystical results of what nature can conjure up with some volcanic land, a touch of water, and a couple of million years.

It was difficult to play Kelvin Heights because I would find myself gazing out at the whitecaps on the lake and the surrounding

snowy peaks of the Remarkables with a line of silvery drool suspended from my chin. The constantly agitating wind brought, as
the Scottish say, "the horses out" in the waves, as foamy white
manes billowed on the gorgeous aqua-blue crests. Though not in
the same league as Cypress Point, technically, as a golf course,
Kelvin Heights was nonetheless equal in its physical setting. Only a
small handful of courses in the world are surrounded by beauty this
awesome.

At several spots, the course goes right to the edge of the lake. I
found myself mesmerized for long spells of time as I stood at the
shore, taking in the grand glory of Mother Earth. I was, once
again, the only golfer on the course; the wind was too strong for a
sane person to be out there. Luckily, I wasn't holding up other
golfers as I tried to get my mind around this beautiful spot on the
globe. I have a message for whatever divine force was responsible
for this kaleidoscope of natural wonder: If you're going to make
something this pretty—at least sign your work!

After Queenstown, I was again heading to one of the ends of
the earth—the bottom of New Zealand. The land became dis-
tinctly more barren and the few trees that dotted the countryside
were bent at the waist from the steady wind. The sheep still had
on their wildly wooly winter coats and needed that extra warmth
to fight off the cold wind blustering and blowing from the south.
The bottom of the South Island was settled by golfing Scots who
came for the whaling industry of the 1800s. They must have felt
right at home with the constant chill and harsh landscape. They
had traveled to the other side of the world to find the exact same
climate they had fled.

Reaching the bleak, gray port city of Invercargill, I drove down
to the dock to park my camper van for a few days and take the
passenger-only ferry for a thirty-minute cruise across the Foveaux
Strait to the sparsely populated Stewart Island. I was expecting a
bigger boat than the fifty-passenger teakwood ferry.

There were brand-new barf bags on every seat with dozens of
extras all around the cramped passenger cabin, which I took to be

an ominous sign. They were expecting quite a run on barf. There were twenty passengers onboard. Most wore high-tech hiking gear and looked as if they were going to climb the Himalayas rather than trek to a small island on the way to the South Pole. Once again, I was the only passenger lugging golf clubs.

The weather was stormy and the sea wasn't welcoming visitors as the surf sloshed heavily against the sides of the boat while we motored along. The small ferry rode the rough-rolling swells like a surfer paddling back out to sea—it was an up-and-down proposition and it turned out that skipping breakfast had been wise. I could see a little better how the barf-bag business was brisk, but my constant traveling had toughened me up a bit. My own bag went unused, but two traveling college girls from London had turned the color of their foul-weather gear, pea-green, and needed all the bags they could get their young hands on as they continually ran to the bathroom. It would be untruthful for me to say that it wasn't enjoyable to finally not be the sick one.

Stewart Island is often referred to as "the Third Island" of New Zealand, although it is tiny compared to the other two. At merely 270 square miles, the island is only one-twentieth the area of the South Island. The four hundred residents are clustered around the picturesque Half Moon Bay with the remainder of the land secured for nature and wildlife reserves. It's a world unto itself and a place where the cliché "everybody knows everybody else" is as true a statement as can be told.

A round of golf on Stewart Island with a local golfer had been arranged for me by the head of the Island's tourist board whom I'd called explaining my desire to play their course. This serendipity was another prime example of New Zealand's gracious hospitality to me and my quest. Russell Squires, a lobster fisherman, met me at my hotel, and was to be my playing partner for a round of golf that afternoon. As I put my clubs into the back of his pickup, the sun sneaked a peek from behind the solid gray bank of clouds. If we hurried, a round of rain-free golf was possible.

Russell, in his mid-fifties with a gray-speckled black beard, is a shy but funny man with the quiet way of a solitary life spent on the sea. If there was a tense nerve in his body, it didn't present itself in my company. He loves the peaceful life the isolated island offers. Like Irish on Ninety Mile Beach, he too had found his spot on the earth. "The island is peaceful and we're far enough away to keep the loonies at bay," he said, chuckling softly. I could immediately see the appeal of life on the "Third Island." There's no fast lane there, barely any lanes at all, just the steady calm beat of life on the shores of the South Pacific.

The Ringaringa Heights Golf Course is a six-hole affair and as crudely adventurous a course as I have ever played. The only indication that the piece of land could possibly be a golf course was the periodically placed yellow flags on the craggy undulating seaside hills, which told you where the holes on the greens were. The "greens" were "greens" in the broadest scope of the term. The putting surfaces weren't even cut low enough to be called "fairways" on most golf courses. Part of the problem is that because of the constant rain, the island is a petri dish for vegetation. Grass grows as if on steroids. While the bottom of the South Island is barren, Stewart Island is as green and lush as Ireland. This is hardy grass that seems to grow back the minute it is cut. Mowing this course is a Sisyphean task, because once all six holes are cut, you have to get right back on that tractor and do it all again.

Russell and I played the route of six holes three times to complete the eighteen. Playing a six-hole course was a first for me. Enjoying the ruggedness of the course, I wasn't thinking much about my score. I must have been a Scottish shepherd in a previous life, because I really do enjoy primitive golf. After the first six holes, Russell informed me that we were "all square" in our match. I hadn't realized we were playing a match and I saw for the first time that Russell was trying to give the visiting Yank *a proper hiding*, as they say in Scotland. While polite and gracious, New Zealanders take sport very seriously and play hard to win—Kiwis are competitive folks.

While not technically a good golfer, Russell nonetheless had a self-taught game that got the ball into the hole effectively as he knew how to putt over the violent bumps and tufts of wild grass on the greens. He was a worthy opponent. Because the ground was soft from the rain, Russell was wearing his fishing boots while he played and I thought to myself, there was no way I was going to lose a golf match to a guy wearing fishing boots!

The match was tight, but I started hitting a few good shots on the final six holes and ended up shooting an eighty-one to Russell's eighty-eight. He was gracious in defeat and, of course, as a hospitable New Zealander, invited me to his house for a delightful lunch.

What a pleasant day! I hadn't lost my breakfast on the rough ferry ride, played the second-southernmost course in the world, and won a tough golf match against a new golfing friend. What more could a traveling golfer want?

New Zealand is the new standard by which I will always judge the health of a new golfing country. That country teems with places to tee it up and play the ancient game the good old way. New Zealand is my new golf Holy Land. Like a devout Muslim bowing to Mecca, after visiting New Zealand, I pay homage by always sleeping with my feet pointing toward the Paraparaumu Beach Golf Club. It's the least I can do.

8

Alice Springs Golf Club
Alice Springs,
Australia

23.40°S–133.50°E

I *think that kangaroo wants to beat the*
crap out of me!

Getting mugged by a kangaroo—well, two kangaroos actually—
had never once entered my mind until I walked around a grove of
brush separating the fourth green and fifth tee-box of the Golf
Club at Kennedy Bay—a demanding first-rate links course on the
west coast of Australia near Perth. Having never seen kangaroos in
person before, they not only startled me as I had rounded the corner, but I was shocked at their size. Kangaroos were supposed to be
small and cute and cuddly, weren't they? These two specimens
looked like a couple of longshoremen who had been weaned on
doughnuts and beer since they left the pouch. I was surprised they
didn't have tattoos.

It was probably a couple of miles to the clubhouse from out
where I was on the far end of the golf course. The heat of the Australian sun was in its full midday offensive. Wiser golfers had all
played in the cooler morning hours, leaving the course and furnace

heat to just me and the wildlife. There would be no one around to hear my screams once the mugging-by-kangaroo ensued. The roar of the warm wind off the nearby Indian Ocean would stifle any cries for help, anyway. I quickly tried to remember what the procedures were for animal attacks. The only one I could recall was that you're supposed to stand completely still when confronted by a bear in the wild. This was, of course, something I was never going to attempt. If I ever crossed paths with a bear, I planned to run away as fast as I could and hope the bear pulled a hamstring while in pursuit. What were you supposed to do to avoid an attack by kangaroos? Start hopping?

The two menacing kangaroos stood perfectly in place, silently defiant, only five yards from where I was planning to tee-off. They looked in a mood to pick a fight with their gray fur shining in the glaring sun as they stood erect on their muscular hind legs, staring at me like they were a couple of goons from Tony Soprano's gang. They eyeballed me with that "You're a couple of months behind on your loan payment" mobster look.

I teed-off quickly and jogged down the fairway to get away from the ruffians. I continually glanced back over my shoulder to make sure no surprise attacks were in store as I gingerly avoided stepping in the large mounds of ubiquitous kangaroo droppings. They weren't lacking roughage in their diet.

This was my first round of golf in the hot December sun of Australia. My plan for Australia was to travel overland from coast to coast—from Perth back to Sydney—and play golf as the opportunity presented itself. I had long wanted to take the Indian-Pacific rail journey that runs across the country. I hoped to end my visit in Alice Springs in the dead center of the outback. It was an enormous amount of territory to cover: Australia is roughly equal in size to the contiguous continental United States, but the U.S. has almost fifteen times the population. There is plenty of empty room in which to wander Down Under.

Spending all that quality time in the Australian outdoors had one eensy-weensy drawback. Make that trillions of eensy-weensy drawbacks. One of the first things I discovered about Australia is that it is the world headquarters for mosquitoes. From the very first moment when flies-to-be eat through their egg casings and spread their tiny little wings, mosquitoes the world over must dream of joining their seventeen trillion brothers and sisters for a jihad against human flesh on that red continent. I happen to know a bit about mosquitoes, having grown up in Minnesota, where in the summertime they are sometimes mistaken for single-engine aircraft on airport radar. Down there in the outback they aren't nearly as large, but what they lack in stature, they make up for in speed, sheer numbers, and perseverance.

In Australia, "mossies," as they are called (everything in Australia has a nickname), like to fly directly into your ear without slowing down and then try to see if they can get out the other side. They seem to delight in bouncing off your eardrum like it's a trampoline. Once they realize there is a roadblock in there (hopefully), and can't get through, they decide to just hang out in your inner ear, hoping that your skull goes condo and they'll get in on the ground floor. This whole process is not nearly as much fun as it sounds, but it does explain the various funky gyrations you frequently see as Aussies walk down the street attempting to evict the buzzing from their heads.

During my initial Australian round of golf at Kennedy Bay, I was swatting mossies away from my exposed flesh left and right as I tried to navigate my ball around the swales and hollows of the difficult course. Before teeing off at Kennedy Bay, I had asked the young gentleman behind the counter in the pro shop if I could forego the cart and walk the course rather than ride. He gave me a look like I was nuts and said, "No problem, mate. It *is* a mite hot out there. Good luck." His tone suggested I would never be seen alive again.

I set out against the better advice of the native Australian. It was indeed hot, but I actually enjoyed the sweat-inducing walk around the course, especially because it wants so badly to be a great course. Toward that noble quest, there is a replica of the infamous St. Andrews Hell Bunker on the par-five fifth, and the par-three sixteenth is a poor man's "Postage Stamp" clone of the glorious eighth hole at Prestwick in Scotland. Normally, I don't care for gimmicks on golf courses, but at least the designers have tried to mimic two of the greatest holes in the game.

The Golf Club at Kennedy Bay is an arduous course. Playing to over 7,000 yards with deep penal Scottish bunkers protecting the greens, the tough layout was more than a challenge for a golfer of my modest abilities. The course would be hard enough to conquer without the constant wind that dries the greens to as hard as linoleum, but that doesn't happen there in southwest Australia as gales of hot afternoon air blowing inland off the Indian Ocean roar across the links. Every shot I attempted seemed to be against the violent breeze. On the par-four first hole I hit what I thought was a perfect five-iron for my second shot only to find out that wind had knocked it out of the air as if it were made of cotton. My ball was twenty yards short of the putting surface. This was going to be a tough round of golf! Giving it my all, I had played well and I have never been more proud of shooting an eighty-six as I was that day. Out on the course it was just me and the kangaroos and they couldn't have cared less about the tough golfing conditions.

I did see one other person out on the course—a groundskeeper who was watering the fourteenth green with a hose to protect the closely mown grass from the savage afternoon heat. My attempts to chat him up were unsuccessful. Aussies don't always respond to "Hello" or "How are you today?" There doesn't seem to be much middle ground: Australians are either as friendly as a candidate running for office or rudely silent. Though I was no more than a few yards from where the groundskeeper stood, I clearly must have been invisible as he stoically watched the stream of water fall onto the parched earth and didn't respond to anything I said. The kangaroos had at least blinked a couple of times.

Unlike the unloquacious help, the course turned out to be excellent and one of the more testing I have ever played. Along with Michael Coate, who designed the bulk of the layout, the code-signer on the scorecard is Ian Baker-Finch, the easygoing Australian golfer who, after winning the 1991 British Open and reaching the pinnacle of the game, went into a career tailspin as he suddenly, strangely, couldn't drive his ball in the fairway off the tee to save his life. Golf, even at that high level of proficiency, is a fickle beast. The rapid decline of his once-excellent play found him retired from professional golf just a few years later. It was a sad turn of fortune and I had always rooted for him during his golfing trials and tribulations. Baker-Finch's humor and honesty in dealing with his dramatic decline as well as his charming manner have given him a new career as one of the better golf television announcers.

After playing at Kennedy Bay, I drove one hour north along the coast back to Perth in my rental car. Trying to stay on budget, I had rented the smallest, cheapest car I could find—it had the horsepower of a weed whacker and was about as fast as a mid-range Zamboni. Speeding wasn't going to be a concern, but I was anxious to get back to see the annual Christmas parade being held in downtown Perth that evening.

My lodging was just off downtown and the parade was forming for that night's march right in front of my hotel. Two hundred thousand Perthians lined the downtown streets to watch the annual event. It was a parade like any in North America during this festive holiday season of mid-December, with bands, floats, dignitaries waving from convertibles, and Santa Claus himself sweating like crazy, sporting a burly red wool suit even in the intense summer heat. Santa was going to be losing quite a bit of weight on that hot evening.

The downtown sidewalks were replete with young families and kids holding all the good viewing spots for the parade—they must have secured their vantage points about the same time that I had been threatened by those daunting kangaroos. The crowds of casually attired Aussies were four and five deep as they stood on tiptoes seeking a peek as the marching bands and floats and beauty queens riding in the back of convertibles went by. The whole scene would have been interchangeable with any Christmas parade in our sunbelt—it was as American as Tampa or Phoenix or San Diego.

However, that parade had one contingent marching you wouldn't have seen in America. A group of twelve Aboriginals were also in the parade, with their traditional body paint on their chests and faces, bare feet that looked like they had never worn shoes, and little else except loose, white loincloths. This was my first glimpse at Aboriginals, who were the first visitors to this land over fifty thousand years ago. They had complete run of the place until Captain Cook showed up in the 1700s. His reports home opened the floodgates of European explorers visiting this vast un-populated land on the other side of the world.

I could see the crowd nudging each other and laughing at the motley group of ragtag Aboriginals, but I was mesmerized. Their dark skin appeared almost leathery, which it would have to be to tolerate being in the Australian sun uncovered for any length of time. Their tufts of hair and beards defied gravity and seemed to go off sporadically in any direction those particular strands chose. The marching Aboriginals had skinny legs that were a strange contrast to their thick torsos—the effect was that their top-and-bottom halves seemed to be strangers to each other. Their bodies had a dusty sheen that radiated an aura of a time long past. Nothing about them physically signified they were in the modern world—they looked entirely out of place in the twenty-first century. They seemed to be people who had risen directly out of the land, strikingly *earthlike*, as if they came from the earth itself. They seemed to belong here more than any living beings I had ever seen—I felt like a trespasser; more than just a visitor to their country, I was a stranger in their land. It was a bizarre feeling and as they marched past I felt like I was viewing an X-ray of the history of our planet. I couldn't take my eyes off of them.

Their group had no real form or precision movements like the other well-rehearsed marchers. They just strolled down the street smiling, waving at the crowd, enjoying the occasion and doing their own thing. What I thought was hilariously ironic was that directly behind the Aboriginals in the parade was the lockstepped, bombastic, thoroughly regimented Australian Army marching band. They were blasting the Aboriginals out with that dreadful military march music. In order not to get run over, the outmanned and outgunned Aboriginals were forced to move down the parade route faster than they seemed to want to. I'm no parade chorographer, but I would have at least stuck some clowns on unicycles between them as a buffer. It didn't seem to bother the easygoing Aboriginals, but seemed peculiar to me. It was the entire history of the conquest of Australia in one brief, sad, but comic, moment.

The next day I went to the nearby suburb of Wembley to play golf at the public course of the same name. I had heard in New Zealand that Wembley was the type of course I was seeking—a sturdy test of golf that was also casual and open to the public. That it proved to be. There are two eighteens constantly packed with golfers year-round—every day is a good golfing day in sunny, warm western Australia. During a short friendly chat with the head professional, Robert Farley, I learned that western Australians play a tremendous number of rounds of golf at Wembley yearly. "We did over one hundred and forty thousand rounds of golf at Wembley last year," said Robert. "People in WA love their golf and beer. Or is it the other way around?" He chuckled and suggested I play the "old course" as it's the more difficult of the two eighteens, and also because "it's in good nick at the moment."

Because I was a single, Robert told me to just go the first tee—I wouldn't have any trouble joining a group short of a foursome. I walked out near the first tee-box and was busy putting balls and tees into my pockets, generally getting prepared to play. I glanced around furtively, doubting that any of the cantankerous Aussies would offer me a spot in their group unsolicited. My few dealings around golf in Australia hadn't exactly yielded many sunny dispositions, although Robert in the pro shop had been welcoming. Despite my impressions, in a matter of a couple of minutes, a grinning gentleman about my age came up, introduced himself and asked if I would like to join their threesome for the round. Their fourth hadn't been able to make it. Of course, I was delighted to join them.

The welcoming stranger was Jim Grehan, a friendly Irish expatriate who now considers Australia his homeland. In 1988, with his wife, mother, and five kids in tow, Jim resettled the clan to Australia. They sought sun, adventure, and the possibility of smoother economic times than was possible in the pre–Celtic Tiger dot-com boom of the 1990s in Ireland. Australia was a good fit for the Grehans; Jim and his family immediately took to the casual Aussie life in the warm year-round sunshine. The gamble paid off.

The other two members of Jim's weekly foursome, Graham Ware and Michael Cox, were both recent transplants from South Africa. They took me right into their group by giving me a hard time when I luckily hit a long, straight drive down the tree-lined first fairway of the par-four first. Michael said, "We've got a ringer on our hands, boys." His nice compliment put me at ease with them immediately—they were good guys. That strangers can form fast friendships right from the first tee-box is what I love most about public golf.

In the few days I had been in Australia, I had been having trouble getting the reticent locals into any kind of conversation other than superficial pleasantries, but that wasn't a problem with these chaps. Even better, they had stories of their own to tell as we played our shots through the avenues of stately eucalyptus lining the friendly Wembley Golf Club's 6000-plus yards of solid golfing land.

Graham and Michael had both recently immigrated to Australia to escape the escalating violence in their homeland of South Africa. Graham told a harrowing tale of being held up at gunpoint by a gang of six as he and his wife were pulling into the driveway of their home in Johannesburg. After being robbed and hit with the butt of a gun, Graham had pulled out a pistol from beneath his driver's seat and blasted away like Wyatt Earp at the O.K. Corral as the robbers fled. He said that he had shot a couple of the robbers—one died and the other was seriously wounded. I had never heard a personal story like this and it made me feel all the more anxious about traveling there, because I was planning on going to South Africa later in my trip. Dress slacks, extra socks, and spare T-shirts weren't even in my travel gear, much less cold, hard firepower. No, guns weren't part of my travel pack; in fact, I have never once shot a gun in my entire life. Free throws yes, guns no. Graham related how everyone in South Africa carried guns and that violence was spiraling totally out of control. The robbery had been the last straw for him and his wife. They relocated to Perth, which he said was similar in climate to South Africa, and completely without the violence. "The country has been ruined," he said sadly of South Africa. Perhaps the thoughts of his homeland had put him off as Graham missed an easy three-footer on the eighteenth green that would have won his weekly bets with his pals. However, Jim and Michael didn't seem to mind a bit.

My good fortune continued the next day when I went to play the wonderful Joondalup Country Club just north of Perth. The twenty-seven holes of golf were designed masterfully around a former limestone quarry by Robert Trent Jones, Jr., one of the world's premier golf-course architects. *Joondalup* is an indigenous Aboriginal word for "the place of glistening water." While there was little water that I could see, it was a wonderful property with native bushes and willowy acacia and eucalyptus trees providing shade from the unrelenting sun. It was a fantastic golf course, but unfortunately, as a visitor, I was forced to take a golf cart. For some reason I couldn't figure out, visitors weren't allowed to walk.

Perhaps it was just as well, as the sun blazed intensely and the course was empty. Perhaps the near-desertedness fueled my need for speed. Or, perhaps, I just felt like thumbing my nose at the charade of a healthy individual forced to drive a so-called vehicle that I abhorred and had sworn to never use as long as I could carry myself around on my own two feet. Whatever the cause, I zoomed recklessly around the fairways and played all twenty-seven holes in just under two and a half hours. It was a cross between golf and the Indy 500 as I raced around from shot to shot. To get exercise I would leave the cart on the cart path and run to my ball on the fairway, hit it, and run back to the cart. It was my own version of "cart golf" as I sped around the cliffs and ridges of the old quarry and though I was sweating as if I'd run a marathon by the time I finished the twenty-seven holes in the punishing heat, I loved it.

After my aerobic round of golf, I cleaned up and had lunch with the general manager of the resort, Mark Duder, a gracious and interesting fellow who took a curiosity to my around-the-world golfing quest. "What are your plans for Australia and beyond?" he inquired.

I told him I hoped to take the famous Australian rail journey—the "Indian-Pacific"—as far as Adelaide and then switch trains for Melbourne. After Australia, I continued, my plans were to fly to Singapore and then take a train through Malaysia to Thailand to begin the Asian part of my trek. Mark enthusiastically replied, "The Indian-Pacific is wonderful, I strongly recommend you give it a go."

As an avid world traveler with contacts throughout the golfing world, Mark said easily, "I think I can help you in Singapore. The owner of Joondalup is from Singapore and owns a course there as well. I'll make some arrangement for you." Again, the Golf Gods were watching over me, although I wasn't sure how they could see me from the heavens with all the thick swarms of mossies flying between me and them.

Australia had gotten off to a good start: I was enjoying playing golf and roaming around Perth. Nevertheless, anxious for my great railway journey, I soon went to a travel agent seeking details for the Indian-Pacific. The route, departing for Sydney only twice per week, was heavily booked, but there was an opening on the train leaving the next day.

So, after a sunny five days in Perth, I checked out of my hotel and caught a taxi to the downtown train station. My destination was Melbourne and the journey would require three days and two nights on the Indian-Pacific to Adelaide, followed by a switch of trains and one day of travel to Melbourne. Having splurged for the "Gold Kangaroo" service, which included a first-class compartment and all meals in the dining car, I was ready to relax and see the Australian outback from the comfort of my cozy cabin.

I could have lived happily for the rest of my life on the Indian-Pacific. Just riding the rails between Perth and Melbourne and Sydney, spending my remaining years watching the vast Australian landscape pass by from my cozy cabin. My current possessions easily fit into the small single berth. How much stuff does one really need anyway? All my meals were prepared for me, taken in the regal dining car filled with travelers chatting over tea and world affairs. What could be better? Of course (in my daydream), I'd periodically disembark whenever cleaning or maintenance was required to keep the train running smoothly. Perhaps I'd go play a quick round of golf. But once that whistle blew, I'd be back in my comfortable chair aboard the train as it chugged out of the station once more and made its weekly trip back across the continent.

In Adelaide, I boarded a less glamorous train for my destination of Melbourne. We arrived in early evening and I reluctantly stepped back into the real world. I was getting a bit weary from my first several months of constant wandering. It seemed I needed a break from my break. With Christmas at hand and not wanting to feel like a wanderer over the holidays, I sublet a small, one-bedroom apartment just off downtown Melbourne, not far from the Rod Laver Tennis Arena—the annual site for the Australian Open. My new pad had a full kitchen and cable television and nothing about it read *tourist*. For the next ten days, I was just another person happy to be hanging around.

Like Buenos Aires, Melbourne is a sports-mad city and golf is abundant. I found an enjoyable, easygoing public golf course called Albert Park, one of the earliest courses in Australia, to take care of my daily golfing needs. It was friendly and interesting to play and open to anyone who wanted to tee it up. It was my kind of place. Like I keep telling you, I'm a sucker for good public golf.

However, my main goal was to obtain an opportunity to play Royal Melbourne—an Alister MacKenzie–designed course that is the best of not only Australia, but of the entire Southern

Hemisphere. It is continually ranked in the top ten in the world. Just a short city train ride away from my apartment, I was going to see if I could perhaps obtain an opportunity to play it.

Golf had first come to Melbourne in 1891 at Royal Melbourne, which at the time was simply called the Melbourne Golf Club. In Australian golf, there has been a century-long feud between the Australian Golf Club in Sydney and Royal Melbourne as to which club was founded earlier. The Australian was formed in 1882, but had a six-year span from 1889 to 1895 when it lost its course and wasn't a club. Royal Melbourne's history is continual from 1891, so they feel that they are the oldest in Australia. The Australian Golf Club doesn't buy this "continual argument." The battle is further fueled by the fact that Sydney and Melbourne are bitter rivals as to which is the premier city in the country. Both vehemently boast number-one status, and I never heard a kind word said about one city by a resident from the other. It was the kind of intense dislike usually reserved for neighboring countries with border disputes.

Case in point: one day, on the inner-city train bound for downtown Melbourne, I was chatting with an Aussie-to-the-core elderly gentleman with yellow egg stains from that morning's breakfast on his blue-striped tie. He asked me where I was headed after Melbourne. "I'm going to rent a car and drive to Sydney on New Year's Day," I said innocently.

On hearing the word *Sydney*, a tremendous scowl came over his face as he spat back, "Sydney! You'll not have a good time there!"

While the debate rages on about the oldest golf club, there is no question as to the oldest course in Australia. Bothwell Golf Club, in the midlands of the island of Tasmania, claims not only to be the first course in Australia, but also one of the earliest in the Southern Hemisphere. Its pedigree comes directly from golf's homeland. In 1822, Alexander Reid, a wandering Scotsman, first sailed to Tasmania from his home in Edinburgh and found a land similar in look and feel to his windy rolling-hilled homeland. Tasmania became his adopted home. No one is sure if he brought his clubs along with him initially, but in 1837 he went back to Scotland for two years and in 1839 he returned to Tasmania with his clubs and several featheries (the golf ball of the time). He started the Bothwell Golf Club that very year and golf is played on that very land to this day.

Back at unpretentious Albert Park, I had paired up with Wayne Crook, a local banker with a wry sense of humor, to play golf at the welcoming public course. I had met Wayne in the small clubhouse as I was checking to see about having a go at the course, and we decided to go off as a twosome. With Christmas upon us and business slowing down for the holidays, Wayne had slipped away from his office unannounced for a quick afternoon round. He said, "I just snuck out the back and didn't tell them where I'm going. They'll probably think I'm off to some important business meeting." His secret was safe with me.

We pretty much had the old shady course to ourselves. Both of us tried as hard as we could when hitting our shots to the small oval greens, but we calmly accepted the outcome, good or bad, and continued our conversation as we strolled down the fairway. Wayne, a 22-handicapper, was charming company as we discussed world politics. He thought George Bush wouldn't be reelected (he was), the coming Australian election in which he thought Prime Minister John Howard would be reelected (he was), and the upcoming cricket match between Australia and India that he felt would be won by the Aussies (they did). Neither one of us bothered to keep score as we strolled the easygoing course—it would have just gotten in the way of a good time.

During the round, Wayne not only invited me to play his home course of Waverly out in the west Melbourne suburbs where he lived, but he also had kindly invited me to his family's annual Christmas day picnic at the beach on Port Phillip Bay. I gladly accepted both invitations.

Once the holidays were over, I tried calling Royal Melbourne for several days to see about playing the "members only" course. After several tries, I was told that, due to the lack of play during the holiday season by the members, a spot was open for me on the coming Thursday morning for a greens fee of three hundred dollars. Three hundred dollars for one round of golf! I just wanted to play the course, not make the car payment of someone on the greens committee. It seemed such a ridiculous price, and furthermore, was way out of my budget. Reluctantly, I said, "Thanks, but no thanks." I hate to admit it, but paying that much for a simple round of golf would be eating away at my intestines as I played. Every time I had to write down a bad score on the card, I'd be thinking: "Three hundred dollars to play and I get another double bogey!"

I hung up the phone and an immediate internal argument on whether I should have turned them down started up in my gut. My "cheap" half was debating my "what the hell" half. After several minutes of back-and-forth, the winning argument was: "It's only money, and I may never have the chance to play Royal Melbourne again." I called them back and booked the Thursday time.

I really did want to play the course because Royal Melbourne was the last card needed for my personal royal flush. Having played Royal Portrush and Royal County Down in Ireland, Royal Dornoch and Royal Aberdeen in Scotland, the only club I lacked was Royal Melbourne. "Royal" courses earn their royal stripes by decree from the king or queen of England and are usually courses of the highest caliber. To become a "Royal" usually means members of the royal family have played the course and have found that the course and the club represent their lofty ideals. A formal application for the status is put in to the royal family and then the club waits patiently to see if they made the cut. In 1895, Queen Victoria gave her consent that the Melbourne Golf Club could adopt the "Royal" prefix.

Though annoyed about the green fee, I have to say Royal Melbourne is as good as a golf course gets. It is timeless golf that seems the perfect blend of mankind's ingenuity and nature's invention. The course resides on the so-called "sandbelt" of Melbourne just inland from Port Phillip Bay, of nude-beach fame. As the Scots learned hundreds of years ago, sand-based land is ideal for great golf courses; you could stick Royal Melbourne on the east coast of Fife and it would look like it was there before sheep.

There are two eighteens at Royal Melbourne, but it's the MacKenzie-designed West Course that gets all the attention, and deservedly so. One of Australia's fine golf-course designers, Michael Clayton, has gone so far as to say of the course, "It is one of the two man-made things in Australia of worldwide significance." The glorious Sydney Opera House is the other Australian-built masterpiece Clayton refers to.

As was the case with Cypress Point and the Club de Golf del Uruguay, MacKenzie was presented with a fine piece of property on which to use his camouflage bunkering and wickedly mounded greens. The West Course was designed by MacKenzie during his world tour of the 1920s and he received a fee of one thousand pounds. That fee was a bargain for a course that will always stand the test of time. Darius Oliver, in his book *Australia's Finest Courses*, says it best: "The site remains one of the finest ever found in world golf, full of dramatic undulation, its fertile sandy soil and natural rugged appearance was a gift from the golfing gods." Oliver is spot-on.

Playing with a group of three teenagers—George, Sam, and Andrew—all fine golfers who didn't seem to mind an old coot like me tagging along, I found every hole to be a delightful puzzle that needed to be solved up front if you have any hope of playing it correctly. The puzzle was solved on the par-four first as I got it in the hole in four after a crisp chip with my eight-iron and a one-putt, but a horrific ten on the par-five second as my ball went from bunker to bunker to bunker and preserved Ernie Els's course record of sixty (sixty!) for yet another day. However, it was hard to get upset when you're playing a masterpiece like Royal Melbourne.

Oliver again puts the course in its lofty perspective when he says, "Individually there are at least ten outstanding holes, including six undeniably world class, like the all-carry par-three fifth with its awesome bunkering and slippery raised green pressed against a magnificent scrub covered dune. When MacKenzie first saw this inspired setting he enthusiastically declared that they should be able to make one of the best golf holes in existence." And they did.

Andrew, the best golfer of the three lads, told me a funny story after I had asked him what he thought about Americans as we walked up the glorious eighteenth hole, a 450-yard par-four with more trouble lurking than most golf courses have on all eighteen holes. Andrew had spent a year in Iowa as a high school exchange student. "I told the other kids that back in Australia I rode a kangaroo to school each morning. Not only did they believe me, they all wanted to know the kangaroo's name!"

Rested and refreshed with Royal Melbourne under my belt, it was the first day of the New Year and I was driving my rental car along the southeast coast to Sydney. My plan was to spend a few days driving along the coast and stay at small motels near the sea. Unfortunately, because it was New Year's Day, I found town after town completely booked—no lodging available. The entire population of Australia seemed to have descended to the southeast coast of the country.

In Sydney, I again found a welcoming, unpretentious public course to scratch my golfing itch: Moore Park Golf Course, which was only about five minutes from the city center where my hotel was. Late in the afternoons, the course was usually empty as the heat still hovered in the nineties. I loved playing until the sun hid behind the skyscrapers downtown as the day waned.

One afternoon while playing Moore Park, I met up with a retired policeman out on the course. Playing fast, as I love to do, I had caught up with him on the par-five fifth—a brute of a hole out on the edge of the property—and we starting playing together. Gus said he was eighty (he looked ninety) and had been with the Sydney police force for forty years before retiring to a life of daily golf there at Moore Park. Gus was a walking testament that longevity wasn't always about good habits. For the next two hours he never once didn't have an unfiltered cigarette dangling out the side of his mouth, even when swinging. He would use the other side of his mouth to light a new one just as the dead one was turning to dust. He also kept pulling beers out of his golf bag like clowns getting out of a tiny car—amazingly there was always another one just waiting to be popped open. Every time he started on a new can, he'd get a big smile, take a giant swig and say, "That's just what the doctor ordered!"

He asked me my plans for the rest of Australia. I said I was thinking of going to Alice Springs. He immediately said, "You must give it a go, mate! They're a bit *potty* outback, but they know how to drink! They make me look like a sheila." I found that hard to believe.

Alice Springs defines "the middle of nowhere" with hundreds of miles separating it from the nearest communities of any size. Founded in 1870 as a staging point for the overland telegraph, Alice Springs is the true meaning of isolation. Three hours by air from Sydney, "the Alice" rests on the banks of the bone-dry Todd River. It is said that if you see the Todd River flow three times you're a local, but with the riverbed dusty and dry and longing for even a molecule of water, I doubted I would see it flow even once. The entire town looked thirsty and in need of a big swig of water.

The Alice Springs Golf Club was a complete revelation to me. I never expected to find such an excellently maintained course in the harsh outback. However, this lovely course condition wasn't always the case. Golf in Alice Springs dates back to 1933. The rugged original greens consisted of a mixture of oil and sand known as "sand-scrapes" and the fairways were rough-and-tumble over the dry rocky terrain. That is more along the lines of what I had expected to find there, golfwise. This is harsh, dry land that is only perfect for camels (which exist in surprisingly large numbers in the Australian outback). There's little water, it's hotter than Hades, and it just didn't seem like golf country to me. Boy, was I wrong!

First off, Alice Springs Golf Club is a full-on championship golf course redesigned by the renowned Aussie great, Peter Thomson. In 1980, the club had decided to become "fully grassed" and hired Thomson to create a first-rate golfing layout. His work was a resounding success. The course rests against the tabletop mesa of the imposing MacDonnell Mountains that form the scenic boundary of the Alice. The locale is a special one to play the game.

Alice Springs has long been the center of the Aboriginal world and several sacred Aboriginal sites create natural barriers between the well-designed fairways. This respect for the ancient Aboriginal traditions gives the course a timeless feel and created (at least for me) a sense of goodwill for a people that have been so badly treated over time. The course itself can be quite difficult from the back tees, given the sneaky winds whipping through the pass of the MacDonnell Mountains and Thomson's tricky putting surfaces, but golfers of all abilities can enjoy the course—the mark of a great design. I played the excellent course several days in a row with a welcoming, jovial local—Phil Carr—another retired golf-loving policeman who doesn't mind a beer or two or five. Phil loves the remoteness of the Alice. We sat in the clubhouse enjoying a cool drink and the view after a round in the blazing heat—the course's handle of the "world's hottest" golf course is richly deserved. The sun was setting and painting the MacDonnells, off on the horizon beyond the mounds and ripples of the club's fairways, in a wash of nectarine red and soothing gold as Phil said, "I live in the best place on Earth."

The true marvel of the Alice Springs Golf Club is that it is greener than clover. To travel through land as brown as a cocoa bean and then to see this flourishing sea of bright green golfing terrain is almost a miracle. That is my kind of oasis! What makes it stand out even more is that the club connected to the course is one of the best I have found in all my golfing travels. The clubhouse is a whirlwind of activity for all the various groups using the golfing land as well as hosting informal banquets and get-togethers on a daily basis—much like the golf clubs in Scotland and Ireland where the golf clubhouse doubles as the community center. These are social folks out in the hinterlands of Australia—they seem to delight in getting together for most any reason to hoist a few. There is a certain breed of cat that chooses to live outback—they're lively and fiercely independent, but they revel in being part of a community. They'll tell you exactly what they think and they love their golf and beer (Gus was right!) and having a laugh. They have formed a golfing society where friendliness is in ample supply. I couldn't keep up with all the invitations offered to me for rounds of golf or casual dinners at their homes.

This is a club that democratically tries to include anyone who desires to play the game of golf in their town. It's expensive to grow grass that green on the Alice's arid tundra, but the club has kept the prices low and accessible, although it is the only course for hundreds and hundreds of miles. If only all the courses of the world shared that admirable trait! The great spirit of the ancient game is alive and kicking in Alice Springs, in the middle of the desolate Australian outback. Who knew? Now, I do.

9

Laguna National Golf
and Country Club
Singapore

1.18°N–103.55°E

During my final week in Alice Springs, Australia, I discovered that someone had stolen my credit card number (probably when I had been paying a restaurant bill) and was purchasing all the stereo equipment available for sale Down Under.

Luckily, I caught the theft quickly and immediately called customer service back in the States to cancel the card. The bank representative said they were very, very sorry this had happened. Oh, my! Were they, really! She then promised that a brand-new card with a brand-new number would be mailed out and in my very hands within three business days. I nicely, calmly even, explained that I was *in the middle of the Australian outback*, which seemed about a business *year* away from the bank call center in Spokane, Washington.

"You will have it in three days, we promise," the representative cheerfully—persistently—told me. I got the feeling she didn't quite fathom how truly remote Alice Springs is on the earth. Forget about remote from the United States. Alice Springs is remote even in Australia! Providentially, I had some emergency cash tucked secretly away in my golf bag and had already bought an airplane ticket from Sydney to Singapore before this particular fiasco ensued. Oh, and of course, the new credit card never arrived. I wonder if it had anything to do with the fact that I no longer had a permanent address and was roaming the world in search of golf. Not that I would ever admit to actually believing the card would show up. Seeing water flow in the bone-dry Todd River seemed likelier. I placed my odds on Australia and won a bitter victory—my new card never appeared and I continued on to Singapore.

After listening to the "on-hold" music start to repeat itself for the twelfth time, finally, a phone representative got back from a long, leisurely lunch and pushed one of the many blinking lights on her telephone. Like the sneaky customer service ace she was, before I could open my mouth to begin to explain my dilemma, she quickly assured me she wanted-to-do-everything-possible-to-make-you-a-satisfied-customer, how can I help you?

After her scripted greeting had passed, I filled her in

"Singapore! Is it cold there?" she asked excitedly.

"Nope, it's near the equator," I said.

"Oh! I've heard of that place. We studied Ecuador in school!" she bubbled obliviously.

I gave her a quick geography lesson on how Ecuador and the equator weren't quite the same, and Singapore was actually around the world from South America, but I felt this probably should have been taken care of earlier in her academic upbringing and certainly not at international telephone rates! The idea that Singapore was both the name of the city and the country would have blown her geographical gasket. I decided not to risk that tidbit.

I explained that though I was now in Singapore, I had first notified the bank of the theft while in Australia and had been promised that the card would reach me there. I had waited the aforementioned "three business days" to no avail, and in order not to forfeit my airplane ticket to Asia, I had decided to move on. I asked if a card could be sent to me in Singapore. She said that couldn't be done because the card was probably already in Australia although she wasn't sure if that was indeed the case. She also said that perhaps it had been sent to my former home address in Washington. I patiently explained that I had sold my condo and didn't live there anymore, so that wasn't going to work. To my further doubt of the efficacy of my homeland's educational system, she continued bravely on, "Well, if the card is in Australia, can't you just go over and get it?"

"Good idea," I replied. "Perhaps, I'll just walk over and get it right now. I'll be right back. Do you mind holding a sec? Or better yet, how about if I hail a cab to Australia? How about a bus? Maybe I'll just rent a bike and pedal right down there to Alice Springs across the Pacific Ocean and through hundreds of miles of uninhabitable desert. What do you recommend?" While the phone rep didn't know geography, she did know sarcasm when she heard it. She didn't take kindly to my rant, and I wasn't exactly ecstatic that my tax dollars had helped fund her inadequate education.

It took about another two-hundred-dollars' worth of telephone calls back to the U.S., but I finally got it worked out. I got a new card with a new number, and I hoped the thief in Australia enjoyed his new surround-sound stereo system. Bastard!

Singapore also has to be the cleanest major city in the world. Not a hair is out of place. It's a whole country of Eagle Scouts on their best behavior. You're more likely to see a monkey flying a helicopter than one word of graffiti spray-painted on an empty wall. The city is so spic-and-span it looks as if they have morning inspections by a drill sergeant to make sure that even their beds are properly made—with military corners. I had the urge to litter, just to be a rebel, but the powers that be in Singapore wouldn't have been happy about it. They take these matters quite seriously. There are huge fines for littering, spitting, and any kind of loud behavior. The fine for your first offense for littering is six hundred dollars U.S. Drivers always go below the speed limit and all traffic lights are strictly obeyed. It's the only city I visited in Asia where the nonstop honking of car horns wasn't the norm.

Any drug offenses in Singapore are treated with the death penalty, which is pretty much the ultimate "just say no" program. The strict government also uses public whippings with a cane for lawbreakers. Caning in Singapore is administered across your bare rump as I had read in a magazine article of the process: "The prisoner is stripped naked and shackled by strong leather straps to a trestle, and is held down in a bent-over position with the offender's buttocks protruding. The victim is then punished by a well-built warder wielding a flexible four-foot long length of rattan which has been soaked in water." I decided right then and there that I wasn't going to even so much as jaywalk while in Singapore. My plan was to avoid the public caning if at all possible. I hadn't been spanked in forty-plus years. I wanted to keep my streak intact.

Nonetheless, all these laws had made me curious about how the locals felt. I asked a cabdriver who was driving me to the Laguna National Golf Club from my hotel in the "Little India" neighborhood of Singapore about his native land's notorious restrictions. The driver was a young student who might as well have been working for the local chamber of commerce as he answered cheerily, "Singapore is great! We have many rules and regulations and we cherish them!" Wow, when's the last time you heard a cabdriver say something like that?

I asked him why he felt that all the rules were good; even, for example, the no-chewing-gum rule. With a sincere look, he said, "Of course, the government knows what's good for us. We like to obey." This chap had definitely drunk the Kool-Aid.

We pulled into the Laguna National Golf and Country Club, near the busy Singapore airport, and I quickly saw that golf there was definitely the sport of the rich. My cab was greeted by a doorman who not only opened my door but also welcomed me, personally, to Laguna National. My golf bag was immediately placed on a conveyer belt that quickly took it down into the bowels of the magnificent, gleaming white, ultramodern clubhouse. The place had the efficiency of a five-star hotel. Though the clubhouse was enormous, it exuded sleek, quiet elegance. The entire center area of the building held the club's reception area, with a lively after-golf restaurant and bar tucked in to boot. This area was covered by a roof, but had no walls. It was the effect of being both inside and outside at the same time, and the beauty and simplicity of the design was my first run-in with the Asian concept of feng shui.

Feng shui is the ancient skill of keeping a balance of forces in land or surroundings, or in this case, a golf clubhouse. It's all about the balance of opposite forces: yin and yang, fire and water, peanut butter and jelly, gin and tonic, Sonny and Cher.

I'm not usually one for fancy clubhouses, but Laguna National's grandness was humbly understated, and the open-air structure was designed for people to relax and have fun. It was lunchtime, and everywhere I looked, people were smiling and enjoying themselves. The light, amiable atmosphere was the polar opposite of the stuffy clubhouses that usually went along with exclusive clubs. Laguna National obviously catered to the moneyed, and they, at least, seemed to be enjoying it. The place was feng shui heaven.

I was at the Laguna National to meet with Mr. Peter Goh, the general manager of the club. At Joondalup Country Club in Perth, the general manager naturally had introduced me to Mr. Goh via e-mail, since Laguna National and Joondalup are owned by the same gentleman, by the name of Peter Kwee. Mr. Kwee bought Laguna National Club in 2001, and I have to give him credit for creating an awesome environment of first-rate golf and camaraderie.

At lunch with Mr. Goh, I was fortunate enough to meet the pleasant and unassuming Mr. Kwee. He had just finished playing a round on his course. An avid golfer, Mr. Kwee tries to play every day. Just a normal guy who happens to have a bunch of money, he would have been as content playing at West Seattle with me and my pals as he was playing his exclusive, world-class club.

As we dined on delicious sushi and talked golf, Mr. Kwee was curious about my golf journey so far. I filled him in on where I'd been—many courses he'd played and many places he'd been, as well. He agreed with my assessment that New Zealand was golf heaven as we chatted and dined. I could get used to this lifestyle in the blink of an eye! If I had an extra couple hundred million bucks lying around, I'd build a club like Laguna National—in a heartbeat.

Golf first presented itself in Singapore on June 17, 1891, when four gentlemen played the game on the grass infield of the oval horse racetrack of the Singapore Sporting Club. The first shot was struck by Sir John Tankerville Goldney, a British Supreme Court judge whose idea it was to form a golf club there in the land to which he had been posted. Singapore, at that time, was a British colony, and as we've already seen in points beyond, when the British arrived to govern, golf wasn't too far behind.

Having brought his clubs along on the voyage from England, Justice Goldney arrived in the late nineteenth century to discover a big problem: Singapore had no links. However, he did notice that the horse racetrack, owned by the Singapore Sporting Club, had a lovely grassed infield that looked to be an ideal spot to play golf. Golf courses on the infields of racetracks have been common throughout the history of the sport; what other use is there for a piece of land that horses run around? Royal Musselburgh, just east of Edinburgh in Scotland, is one of the earliest golf courses in the game and its racetrack infield setup dates to the early 1700s.

What I found most impressive about Justice Goldney and that initial round in Singapore was that he reportedly wore a bowler hat, knickerbockers, a long-sleeved red coat with gold buttons, starched collar, and white tie for the inaugural event. That's an impressive amount of clothing to be wearing in the Singapore heat of mid-June. He must have been sweating like one of the horses running the perimeter! There had better have been a ton of starch in that collar to keep it stiff in the steamy humidity. My money says it wilted after the first shot.

As I played the championship eighteen of the Laguna National courses, it was late January. I, however, played without the benefit of a red coat, white tie, or knickerbockers. As a matter of fact, if you ever see me wearing knickerbockers and a red coat with gold buttons while golfing (or not golfing for that matter) you have my permission to shoot me immediately. For me, it was shorts and a well-worn golf shirt that stayed dry for about one minute as the smothering heat encased me like a mummy while I stepped onto the first tee. I bet Judge Goldney had to burn those clothes after his initial round.

Laguna National was superb. The course is the home of the Singapore Masters tournament, which annually hosts some of golf's best professionals. Golfing greats like Ernie Els and Vijay Singh have won the event and almost every well-known golfer of the past fifty years has played in Singapore. Though not a golfing great, I proudly add my name to the list of golfers playing its elegant fairways and tricky greens.

The course was designed by Andy Dye, the nephew of the famed golf-course architect Pete Dye. It's never hard to tell when a course has been designed by the diabolical Dye clan because of the use of wooden railway sleepers that form the face of his deep, penal, Scottish-style bunkers. The sleepers also serve as the boundary walls on the edges of his treacherous water hazards. Dye's courses tend to be haunted houses of golf with mayhem and chances for disaster lurking throughout every which way you turn during the eighteen holes and Laguna National is no exception. The Dye family must stay up late gleefully planning ways to torture the poor innocent golfer.

Tropical vibrant flowers were richly in bloom and their sweet fragrance lingered in the air as I strolled along in the 100-degree temperature. After the Australian outback, my body was adapting to intense heat and I found the high temperatures not nearly as bothersome as I golfed my ball around the lush palm-lined fairways. That's not to say it isn't hot—you could steam vegetables fully-cooked within minutes under your golf hat—but all my time golfing under the intense sun of Australia had turned my skin into part reptile.

I discovered that after finishing your round of golf in Asia is when the real fun begins. Relaxation after a round of golf is taken seriously in Asia. Laguna National was my initiation into the creature comforts provided in the clubhouses of the region. After golfing, you strip and bathe in gloriously hot pools in soothing rooms designed for total comfort. Then you sweat in wonderfully hot saunas and steam rooms while attendants bring you ice-cold water and hot tea. This is followed by foot and back massages performed by beautiful women in colorful robes as their wise fingers unknot your spine, muscles, and bones, using secrets passed down for generations. Who the hell cares how bad your score was! After the local anesthesia of hot bath, sauna, and massage, you're so content you could have root canal surgery without Novocain. Man, this is the life! It didn't take long for me to forget my old views on golf for the common man. Screw that! I wanted another massage! I wanted more time in that hot pool! What in the hell was I thinking about public golf? When was the last time I got a foot massage at the West Seattle Golf Course? I have seen the light! I was looking forward to golf, and especially after-golf, in Asia.

Though the degree of luxury changed from club to club, the baths and massages were, almost always, part of the deal. Which element I looked more forward to—golf itself, or the after-golf—became a toss-up. Later, when I was asked about a certain course in Asia, I often couldn't recall the layout of the links, but could remember in vivid detail the color of tile in the hot pool and whether the masseuse had started on my feet or shoulders first. I became a slave to the golf comforts of Asia.

Through I did play Laguna National on my own, that was to be the last round I would play for the next three months without a caddie. Every golf course in Asia requires taking a caddie. This was something I definitely wasn't used to. I had been a caddie myself as a teenager at the Rochester Golf and Country Club back in Minnesota. That had been my first real look at golf, and it was love at first sight. Though, like calculus in high school, I had no real clue what was going on.

When I needed a summer job after my ninth grade year, a buddy of mine working as a caddie allowed me to tag along and check it out. Up until then, my summer jobs had always been as a newspaper carrier or a dishwasher in coffee shops; two jobs I'd absolutely hated. Never having even stepped foot on a golf course before, I immediately loved the green natural splendor of it all. Caddying outside in the warm air seemed a whole lot better than pearl diving in a greasy spoon.

My first job carrying a bag as a caddie was a disaster. I was absolutely dreadful! Unknowingly, I walked in the lines of the putts of the golfers—a cardinal sin! I didn't know how to tend the pin or the difference between a sand-wedge and a five-iron. I didn't know where I was supposed to stand, let alone any etiquette of the game, and must have looked like a complete idiot. I was a golfing philistine. My debut as a caddie was so poor the first golfer I caddied for refused to pay me.

My first caddie was in Batam, a one-hour ferry ride from Singapore. Batam is one of the many islands of Indonesia dotting the area. Many golfers can't afford the expensive clubs of Singapore and join clubs in Batam instead; it's just a quick boat ride away and much cheaper to join.

Peter Goh had arranged ahead for me to play the Southwinds Golf Club on Batam. Upon my arrival, a miniskirted young lady, from the looks of it in the marketing department, met me right away, smiling prettily. I believe her job included showing me around the club and regaling me with tales about golf in Batam, but her true passion was actually her own physical beauty. She seemed absolutely captivated by it. She whispered to me within seconds of meeting, "I should be modeling in Singapore instead of working here." Indeed, she appeared more than attractive at first glance. But as she sat with me while I had breakfast, she continued singing her own praises: "All the visiting golfers want to marry me. I could have any man I want." She became uglier by the second as she droned on and on.

Thankfully, I quickly headed off to a "golf specialist"—a woman named Alice whose job it is to play golf with visitors to the course. This lady, a thirty-nine-year-old former Sumatran track star, did her job with grace and ease. We didn't spend a single moment discussing her feminine attributes—which were impressive.

Unlike her marketing coworker, Alice had a beaming smile, gracious personality, and a silky-smooth golf swing. Peter Goh had set me up with the royal treatment! We were joined for the round by the third member in my golfing posse, and also my first caddie in Asia, a delightful young lady named Watti.

For the most part, caddying in Asia is done by women. Don't ask me why. Although they usually sported happy smiles, the female Asian caddies I met seemed to hate the sun, shielding themselves with layer upon layer of clothing, including long gloves to the elbow and wide-brimmed hats. Eskimos in the deepest winter months wear fewer clothes. The only exposed skin I could see was their bright, smiling faces peeking out from all the layers like a kitten from underneath a blanket.

The caddies tended to be unfailingly friendly. Though few actually played golf (not unlike that young version of me back in the summer of ninth grade during my first caddying job), they excelled at their jobs.

Throughout the region, caddying is a job in high demand. Golfers, rich enough to play at expensive clubs, tended to have money to tip. Yet, what is not a lot of money to a golfer can be a fortune to the caddie and her family. Peter advised me that tipping a caddie the equivalent of ten dollars was fantastic. I usually doubled that at least, and could see the pleasure in the caddies' faces as I handed them the cash. Having been a caddie, and a bad one at that, I felt a kinship with them and wanted them to go home smiling from their lucky day.

Watti, Alice, and I had a fine afternoon playing golf and talking about our lives. Watti, twenty-seven and married for just less than a year, was the breadwinner for her small family while her husband sought out elusive work. She felt lucky to have her position as a caddie, given the lucrative tips and wages she earned. Alice had been a sprinter on her country's national team. After her track years, she turned to golf and had become an excellent player. Alice had a textbook swing and she made par after par as I tried my best to match her golfing prowess. Her dream was to become a teaching pro in Singapore—where she could make more money. They giggled at everything I said, which is the direct way to my heart. On the par-three thirteenth hole, I made a fifty-footer for an unlikely birdie-two, and they both screamed with joy as my ball accidentally found the bottom of the cup. They were wonderful company.

On the boat ride back to Singapore, the threatening clouds finally broke and the rain came down in wet, black sheets of moisture, darkening the city as we pulled in to dock. I decided to move on, deeper into Asia. At the old Singapore railway station near the ferry terminal, I bought a train ticket north to Thailand through Malaysia.

The next morning, while the downpour continued, I arrived at the station early and eager to travel. The train, ridden by Malaysians and Thai people returning home from work in Singapore, their pockets full of Singapore cash earned working mostly as menial laborers, seemed a lively bazaar. Men and women dressed in more traditional clothing—rather than the trendy locals of Singapore's haute Orchard Street—jostled with bundles and parcels tied with twine. Muslim women, their heads shrouded in colorful scarves, reminded me that Malaysia would be the first Islamic country on my travel itinerary.

My plan was to take this train for six hours north to Kuala Lumpur and, after a five-hour layover, catch the overnight sleeper to Hat Yai in southern Thailand. I had bought provisions for the journey—this route didn't have a dining car and the train was a light-year away from the splendor of the Indian-Pacific. But, it was indeed a train, my ideal mode of transportation. I had a brand-new copy of the *International Herald Tribune* and books to read along with enough food and water to make it through the night, and plenty to look at out the window as we rolled through the rain-drenched Malaysian countryside. As I saw it, life was grand. We chugged out of the old Singapore train station exactly on time, and that was the last instant the train stayed on schedule.

It became a day of fits and starts. Veils of black rain had continued to fall from the dark, gloomy sky as the train whistle blew and the locomotive lurched forward as if startled from a nap. We quickly gathered speed, leaving downtown Singapore behind, and began our trek due north up the Malay Peninsula. Traveling seemed the perfect way to usher in the beginning of the 4,701st year of the Chinese calendar. It was the beginning of the Year of the Monkey, but I knew I'd still accidentally make the mistake of writing Year of the Sheep on my personal checks for the first month or so. That's an old David Letterman joke that I've always loved.

10

Blue Canyon
Country Club
Phuket, Thailand

8.15°N–98.5°W

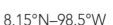

I settled back in my seat with my paper, the train finally at full speed. However, the train's joyride only lasted about twenty minutes and abruptly slowed to a crawl as we reached our first stop just across the border of Malaysia at Johor Baharu station. As we pulled in, the conductor informed us of a major delay—several hours at least—caused by mudslides in our path. A section of tracks between there and Kuala Lumpur had washed out in the overnight rains. I wasn't in a hurry to get anywhere, so I couldn't have cared less. My only goal was to play golf at the top of Norway before it snowed. And snow was the farthest thing from my mind in a train car near the scorching equator, where heat is as close as a tattoo.

After the long layover in Johor Baharu, we finally started up again, but after merely an hour, the train came to a dead halt out in the thick jungle of the Malaysian peninsula. The actual rain had stopped along the way, but the recent moisture had turned the blooming countryside into an intense steam bath. Dense, green jungle covered my window and the elephant-ear leaves seemed to be getting bigger by the second. Outside, it was hot and still and the closeness of the jungle pressed incessantly against my eyeballs, the wet leaves and steamy fog obscuring everything even inches away from the windowpane, making me claustrophobic. I wouldn't be happy until we started moving again.

We were stalled for an hour, but the engine finally woke up and started chugging again. It wasn't long before we came to the area of the mudslide. The train slowed to a snail's pace as a team of workers, caked in mud, busily shoveled the muck and tried to repack the ground beneath the track. From my window, the earth looked as soft as pudding. Such problems with the tracks had to be an ongoing concern during the long rainy season.

Inching ahead, the entire train suddenly tilted severely to the right as we crossed over the most precarious portion of the rebuilt track. I have to admit, I was more than a bit nervous during the train's "Leaning Tower of Pisa" impression. Laughing at my fright, I thought of my borderline irrational lifelong fear of flying. *All these years of worrying about dying in a fiery airplane crash after spiraling out of control at ten thousand feet to slam into the earth at eight hundred miles per hour, and you're going to die on a train that simply rolled over going one mile per hour.* Yet, once over the dodgy track, the train righted itself and quickly gathered speed. Off we went, northward bound. Once past the washed-out section of track, the locomotive brushed aside the overgrowth of jungle vegetation hopelessly determined to impede our otherwise steady progress.

After the ragged start to my journey, we reached Kuala Lumpur. The train station was surprisingly upscale. It teemed with passengers who had missed connections or been delayed by the washout, but luckily my connecting train hadn't left yet. I quickly boarded and found my compartment—the lower sleeping berth in the rear of the second-class car.

No sooner had I boarded than they announced our departure over the loudspeakers at the front of each car. I glanced across the narrow aisle and was greeted by five bright toothy smiles. A family from the Philippines was sharing the upper and lower berths across from me. Their three grinning tots stared, wide-eyed, at my golf bag. I could see them wondering at what could possibly be in my one large, abnormally lumpy piece of luggage.

Over the last few months, many people had asked if I was lugging around a dead body—my golf travel bag could have fit a small corpse with little problem. My normal reply was a wicked grin, responding, "Why, yes—I am! I always promised Grandpa I'd show him the world!"

No one ever got the joke except me, but that didn't stop me from repeating it over and over again for my own amusement. In the tightly packed sleeping car on the way from Kuala Lumpur to Hat Yai, Thailand, luggage was stowed in the aisle so passengers would have more room in their berths. Scanning up and down the car, I realized, once again, that there was only one passenger on board carrying golf clubs (or, a dead body!).

My sleeping berth, a large cubbyhole beneath another bunk, consisted of a bed and a reading light with a curtain that could be drawn for privacy. I sat on my bunk as the smiling Filipino children watched my every move like I was a real-life Disney cartoon. As I visited places where Westerners were rare, and golf clubs rarer still, being stared at became a part of my journey.

We arrived without further incident in Hat Yai, Thailand around noon the next day. On my map of the Malay Peninsula, the name *Hat Yai* had intrigued me. I imagined an exotic, sleepy destination just north of the Malaysian-Thai border. That image wasn't even close. There was little charm to the dusty crossroads town.

Peter Goh had recommended a golf course in southern Thailand with the lovely name of *Blue Canyon* in nearby Phuket on the Andaman Sea. I decided to see if I could get there by bus, since there was no train to Phuket from Hat Yai. I secured my bag at the train-station luggage check and caught a *tuk-tuk* (a three-wheel open-air taxi with a canopy over the passenger seat) to the bus station across town to inquire about my transportation options.

Good timing ruled the day: several buses were leaving for Phuket that very afternoon. I bought a ticket on the line that seemed to have the most up-to-date bus—since, judging by the buses lined up along the depot, there was a wide range of quality available. Most of them looked tired and uncared-for, with caked-on dirt and grime so thick they looked like they'd never been washed once in their long lives. Oil changes or brake checks seemed an unlikely occurrence. My trusty guidebook said that the road from there to Phuket was "mountainous" and "curvy"; after my previous experience with these two road conditions, I wanted a bus that at least had tires with some tread. I booked a seat on a "VIP" bus leaving in a few hours. The "VIP" part meant the bathroom onboard actually was in working order—which is what we VIPs require.

I had been looking forward to a simple trip to Phuket by bus, but that ride proved to be the most harrowing of all. The order and maintenance of Singapore was long gone as we moved deeper into Thailand. I quickly discovered that driving (or riding) in Asia is not for the squeamish. All drivers there tailgate, constantly honk their horns, pass on the shoulder or on blind curves, and speed, speed, speed. It's survival of the fastest in Thailand. As our bus was the biggest vehicle, the smaller cars scattered like mice when the cat comes out to play as our driver floored his way through the narrow mountain passes. Perhaps there are traffic laws on the books, but if so, they must be suggestions. The bus trip, a six-hour illegitimate roller-coaster ride, with no safety nets or *stop* button, made me pine for my cozy, smooth-riding train berth. Owning a car insurance company in Thailand would be a risky venture, indeed.

We finally reached the bus depot in Phuket at ten that night. I felt sure I'd gained a few gray hairs on the journey, but I was more or less none the worse for the terrifying ride. I just needed to lay my head on a soft pillow and get some rest. To my dismay, Phuket's taxis were missing in action—there wasn't a motorcycle or *tuk-tuk* to be found. The depot was closed, the cabs had gone home and the rest of the passengers had melted away into the inky night.

It was dark. I had no hotel arrangements. And my golf bag was certainly not looking like the ideal pillow right about then. Unsure of what to do, I sat down in the darkness on my bag and tried to form a plan. Out of the night, a young Thai fellow approached me, asking if I needed a ride.

Wary to be approached by a stranger in this unlit, lonely area, I weighed my options. He didn't seem menacing, and I was indeed in a bit of a dilemma. I replied that I was going to Patong Beach, which I knew had numerous hotels. We haggled a bit and he agreed to drive me there for five hundred baht, about twelve dollars. I had no clue if this was a good price or not, or how far Patong Beach was from the depot, but I wasn't exactly in a position of power from which to negotiate. So, I hopped in his two-door jalopy.

The jalopy, whose glory days as a motorized vehicle were long since past, was tiny and reeked of petrol. I thought I was going to pass out from the fumes as we chugged up the mountain pass into Patong. In between the waves of nausea, I thought my driver could be an operative of some kind, approaching innocent, stranded travelers and drugging them, so he could rob them and steal their precious tourist luggage. But we arrived without incident in front of a small hotel near the water and I tumbled out into the fresh air, clutching my golf bag.

The place looked respectable. I went in, checked out the room being offered, and thankfully booked it for the night. It was a touch disconcerting that a hired policeman escorted me to my room and then looked behind every closed door as well as behind the shower curtain to make sure that no one had hidden in the room before he allowed me to enter. Turns out my hunch in the cab hadn't been so far off—apparently there had been a major problem with thieves preying on tourists in the area. His thoroughness in checking the room spooked me completely. Man, the Year of the Monkey had been one wild and crazy year so far—and this was only the end of day one! Exhausted, I barricaded my door with my golf bag and fell into bed.

I slept the peaceful sleep of the innocent, the Golf Gods watching over my nightlong sleep, and no boogeyman even came close to disturbing my dreams.

I awoke the next morning refreshed and ready to explore Patong

Beach. It didn't take long to realize that Patong, at least while I was visiting, is one giant German tourist trap. Wall-to-wall Germans confronted me everywhere I wandered. I wondered if anyone had stayed home to run Deutschland, or if they were all there, with me, in Thailand.

Except for the herd of German tourists that had the nerve to be in Thailand the same time as me, I enjoyed Phuket. My days were booked solid. Between reading the newspaper over tea, having a mid-morning one-hour foot massage, lunch, an afternoon two-hour full-body Thai massage, dinner, and then another one-hour foot rub in the evening, I barely had time to fit in a round of golf every other day or so. I don't know where the time went. Busy, busy, busy!

Seriously, the massage possibilities in Thailand are endless; the Thai people are the Ben Hogans of the trade. Massage there is cheap (around five dollars per joyous hour). The skill has been passed on for generations. I couldn't get enough, especially after my appetite was whetted so skillfully in Singapore. Thai people seem to have naturally sunny dispositions and actually made me feel like rubbing my stinky golfer feet was more fun for them than cable television. A lifelong carrier of tension, I arrived in Thailand stiff as a surfboard. I would be leaving al dente. I love those people.

Relaxed as I've ever been, I decided to take Peter Goh's advice and try to play at the millionaire's Blue Canyon Country Club. I tentatively introduced myself to Roger Foo, the director of golf at the course, but quickly found out I had nothing to worry about. Roger, in his early thirties, is as friendly and welcoming as a person can be. He sports an impish, constant grin like a cat next to an empty canary cage. Best of all, he loves the game of golf. He graciously invited me to play the course and stay at the club for the night. I was delighted by his kind offer and it only took me a millionth of a second to accept his hospitality. For a wandering golfer like myself, if doesn't get much better than the elite, well-designed, high-living Blue Canyon. Indulge me while I tell you about the magnificence and charms of living the life of an Asian millionaire for a day, golfing at the wonderful Blue Canyon Country Club.

In case you haven't noticed by now, my childhood dream of becoming a millionaire by the age of forty hasn't come to pass. Next to being just under a million short, the fact that I'm forty-seven years old doesn't exactly work in my favor, either. Well, neither does selling off all my worldly possessions, but that's beside the point, and the point is: golf. That's not to say I can't live like a millionaire, and that's exactly what I did at the magnificent Blue Canyon Country Club and Resort.

I now have a pretty good clue how the other one percent lives (didn't it use to be how the other *half* lived?). They live very well in tropical, exotic Thailand—especially at the Blue Canyon Club, which boasts of having two world-class, extraordinary courses sitting on as fine a piece of natural golfing real estate as you'll find anywhere in the world. I have never been a country-club kind of dude, but things can change; and I love the calm, cheerful atmospheres of Asian golf clubs, most of which are private. Blue Canyon is expensive if nothing else, and, thoroughly charmed by its joyous ambiance, I found myself seriously contemplating a life of crime to be able to afford joining the delightful club.

Now, I know I'm not smart enough to be a white-collar criminal. I don't even have any white collars except on golf shirts. I decided I'd start knocking off the convenience stores that seemed to dot the corner of almost every block in the world. I figured two to three holdups per week should cover the ongoing cost of the club membership and its amenities with little problem.

But seriously, it's the Canyon Course, the elder of the two golf courses, which has the pedigree even the winner of the Westminster Dog Show would envy. It has been named "the Best Course in Thailand," "the Best Course in Asia," "the Best Championship Course in Asia," and "the Asia and Pacific Golf Resort of the Year," as well as holding numerous major world professional tournaments including the Johnnie Walker Classic—won by my fellow millionaire (not that I'm letting the whole experience go to my head or anything), Tiger Woods, in 1998.

The week before I played the course, two of my future clubmates—Ernie Els and Nick Faldo—had been at Blue Canyon, relaxing and preparing for the upcoming Johnnie Walker Classic to be held in Bangkok the following week. To think that I'm only one measly little million dollars away from saying, "Good morning, Ernie! That was one hell of a good shot you hit on eighteen yesterday, big fella." Or, "Hey, Nick! Fancy a game today? I'm just going to need my usual twenty shots a side." Oh, what fun we'd have!

Built on an old rubber plantation with natural ravines and valleys, Blue Canyon is a symphony of green fairways, fragrant flowering trees, and wondrous foliage that would force Monet to get the easel out of his golf bag and start painting. The Canyon Course has it all: large, fast, undulating greens, tricky water hazards, and naturally rolling fairways that turn each hole into a mini-SAT golf test.

Several holes are outstanding. My favorite was the par-four 390-yard thirteenth hole, a real gem, which horseshoes around a deep ravine that must be cleared on your drive. If successful, your second shot is 185 yards uphill to a severely bunkered green resting peacefully beside the grand, elegant clubhouse. Playing this hole when he won there in a playoff against Ernie Els in the Thailand Johnnie Walker Open in 1998, Tiger drove the green! Standing on the tee-box, it would never even occur to me that it was possible to drive the green. We're talking a carry of 340-plus yards straight across the unforgiving ravine to an uphill green that sits behind a grove of tall rubber trees standing watch on the edge of the cliff that must be cleared as well. No way! I couldn't think of a more difficult golf shot, or anyone (besides Tiger) with the ability—or imagination—to try such a heroic feat.

Showing he's at least a little human, after pulling off this incredible shot, Tiger three-putted. I, on the other hand, taking the coward's route, was on the green in three shots and one-putted. My delightful Thai caddie, Tig, was overjoyed for me as she said in her broken English, "Mr. David, Tiger on in one and three-putt. You on in three and one-putt. Same score!" I guess that's one way of looking at it, but I would have rather been the one that drove the green. Oh well, par is par, after all.

The next hole, the fourteenth, presents itself like a wolfish par-five wearing a lamb's par-three clothing. Playing the fourteenth is as scary as an IRS audit. While it looks nothing but beautiful, resting all peaceful-like in the middle of the lake, a veritable torture chamber of evil awaits your innocent little ball. The wind, the water, the tiny target, your nerves—you really don't have a chance. Best to just hit your shot quickly and know that it's going straight into the water, then proceed rapidly with a rueful smile to the drop area. This gorgeous hole is a double bogey on the way to Grandma's house.

Terrific golf holes abound. Course record-holder Freddy Couples calls the par-three seventeenth one of the best par-threes in golf. He's not alone; the 221-yard hole has been named in the top five hundred golf holes in the world. The finisher is excellent as well, with water flanking the eighteenth fairway to catch the errant drive. The second shot plays directly toward a peaceful waterfall cascading gently down from the hill atop, which the ever-watchful clubhouse rests. It's the perfect setting to finish playing a great course.

To be fully forthcoming, all the holes are remarkably memorable. I could gab on and on about this golf wonderland. How is it that I can never remember where I put my car keys, yet I can recall every blade of grass at Blue Canyon?

After playing, I sat on the clubhouse patio overlooking the course, simply mesmerized by all the colors as the sun started to slowly descend over beautiful Phuket. I dreamed of playing this course on a daily basis and then relaxing in that very spot, taking in the awesome view. What could be better? Purples, reds, greens, and blues—the full spectrum of the earth's finest colors—formed a serene palate, soothing my constantly restless mind. The spell was enhanced by an orange butterfly suddenly flittering directly past my gaze, as if to tell me that the glories of life are fleeting and time is racing by. I wanted to summon the cheerful waitress and ask, "Excuse me, would you please tell me where the nearest convenience store might be?"

But, before I could enact my plan to begin a life of crime to afford the membership and remembering that my true love will always be public golf courses (despite their glaring lack of hot pools and offers of massage in the clubhouse after a round), I came to my senses and caught a plane to Bangkok.

11

Santiburi Country Club Chiang Rai, Thailand

19.57°N–99.52°E

Not much in life prepares a first-time traveler for the onslaught of experience about to be gained by visiting pulsating, humming, busy Bangkok. Perhaps if you were to marinate your head in a vat of honey and then stick it directly into a swarming beehive, you might begin to emulate the sensory overload Bangkok has in store for you. With the terribly polluted Chao Phraya River sledging through the city, the smoggy, boisterous labyrinth of Bangkok proper is choked to its gills with people, cars, motorbikes, taxis, and street vendors.

As a visitor, presumably with ready cash to spend, it's a nonstop sales pitch the moment your feet hit the pavement in the morning. Any and everything is for sale. In Thailand, like many developing countries, bargaining rules the street markets; nothing has a set price and everything is negotiable. I am probably the worst haggler in history. If my bargaining acumen was handicapped, I'd be getting four hundred shots a side. You'll certainly never find me in a high-profile Donald Trump–style negotiation situation. But, somehow, I found myself enjoying the experience, in my own way. A typical Bangkok shopping session went something like this:

I inquire, "How much for the picture of Buddha?"

"One hundred baht," the vendor replies.

I confidently counter, "How about sixty baht?"

"Eighty baht," clips the Thai merchant, getting into the negotiations.

At this point I get nervous, start to panic, and blurt out, "I'll give you the hundred baht!"

The merchant then looks at me like I'm crazy, and says something in Thai to the effect of, "You American idiot! Didn't you just hear me say eighty baht?"

Me (panicking further), "Okay! I'll give you a hundred and twenty baht."

The Thai salesperson now looks completely stunned, and begins glancing around nervously like I'm insane. Seeing the confused look on the Thai merchant's face, I panic even more, exclaiming, "All right, two hundred baht! That's my final offer!"

Then, feeling so sorry for me and my complete lack of nerve and backbone, they insist I buy it for forty baht if I just promise to leave immediately, as I'm making the other customers uncomfortable. Works every time.

During my stay, the Johnnie Walker Thailand Open was being held at the Alpine Golf Course in Bangkok, so I decided to hire a cab and go see the golf in person. The Alpine Golf and Country Club is located well outside the sprawling city. My taxi driver, an older Thai man who spoke no English, nevertheless nodded that he knew where to go. We drove and drove and it became apparent after forty-five minutes that he had no clue where the golf course was. He kept driving, making sudden U-turns every five minutes, as we retraced the street we had just been down, followed by hairpin turns onto dead-end streets. He finally got on the highway, but quickly realized another mistake, did a U-turn right there, and was now driving against oncoming traffic back down the on-ramp. It was insanely traumatic.

Dodging the speeding vehicles that seemed about to crash into us at any moment, the cabbie pulled the taxi over to the side of the on-ramp, got out of the car, and started trying to flag down passing drivers for directions. Bangkok is the epitome of gridlock, so you can imagine, anytime a driver gets even a few car lengths' of open space in front, they floor it like a dragster taking off from the starting line. The freeway entrance ramp gave the oncoming drivers a rare chance to step on it, thus increasing the difficulty my driver had in getting a car to stop.

This went on for ten minutes with several close calls as the driver narrowly jumped back to avoid the speeding cars buzzing by him at breakneck speed. Finally, he managed to flag down another cab and got the directions to the course. We were still about ten miles away. All this time, the meter was running—what would have been a three hundred baht (nine dollars U.S.) ride ended up costing me fifty dollars. We finally reached our destination, to my surprise, relatively unscathed. The language barrier and the driver's surly grimace precluded any argument about how we hadn't exactly driven as the crow flies. With discussion out of the question, I meekly paid the meter fare and entered the Alpine Golf and Country Club.

The instant we arrived, my attention was diverted to that game I love: golf. The hair-raising, spendy trip turned out to be worth it, as I loved seeing professional golf in an Asian locale. The tournament, an annually sanctioned European Tour event, spends the first few months of the year globe-trotting in the warmer climates of Southeast Asia, Australia, and South Africa, waiting for most of Europe to thaw out before returning for the bulk of its yearly schedule.

Immediately upon entering the grounds, I could sense the laid-back atmosphere of the event—it was tournament golf Thai-style. Golf isn't high on the radar screen of the average Thai; once again, it's a sport for the wealthy, as the masses are wholly captivated by the elaborate rituals and violence of Thai boxing. The tournament wasn't as crowded as a similar event would be in the States, so there was little in the way of gallery ropes. You could wander wherever you wanted on the course. Thai people are way too polite to tell you not to stand somewhere, anyway. Being in proximity to those great golfers, whom I had long admired, was almost surreal. That was as up-close as a fan can get to the world-class golf games of Ernie Els, Nick Faldo, Thomas Björn, and Colin Montgomerie without getting a restraining order slapped on him.

Watching the graceful professionals that close-up caused me to become as depressed about my own game as I have ever been in my golfing life. I know I'm an amateur, but I've always dreamed of having a pro-caliber game. And for most of this trip, my game had been, I'm sorry to say, poor at best. Perhaps the constant excitement of seeing and experiencing new places hadn't been conducive to good play. There is always a price to be paid, and my erratic play was the levy for seeing and enjoying the world. I must admit, however, that if you're going to hit a ball out of bounds, it seems far preferable to do it in Thailand or New Zealand or Chile, rather than back in Seattle to the tune of the teasing taunts of your golfing pals.

The Bangkok tournament really opened my eyes to how good these pros are—like most sports, there is a wide chasm between the abilities of the professional and the amateur. To see, in person, the skill level of these top-flight professionals—the tremendous distances off the tee, short-games to die for, putts that have no choice but to go into the hole—and then realize how my game stacked up against theirs . . . it was enough to make me want to take up Thai boxing, if only to get the notion pounded out of my brain that I could play this game, golf, at a high level. I'm closer to becoming a nuclear scientist than a professional golfer, and I'm not even totally sure what a nuclear scientist does.

Despite my own personal depression, I thoroughly enjoyed watching the expertise of the professionals—especially how they looked so cool and calm as their shots soared through the tremendous heat. The intensity of the weather was second only to that of the Australian outback. Out on the course, even the shade of the palm fronds didn't deflect the roasting heat. It occurred to me how much multimillionaire golf pros like Faldo or Montgomerie must actually love golf to want to play in conditions that brutal. Of course, they weren't there for free, but they had reached the top of their sport and didn't need to play for the money. I respected them all the more for playing the exotic tournament stops where the travel and conditions were difficult. The European Tour strikes me as infinitely more intriguing compared to the PGA Tour with its America-only events. Seeing the world while playing golf and getting paid to boot—sounds perfect to me!

The heat and the spectacle didn't keep me from a moment of sheer terror that happened while I was following the somewhat testy Scottish golfing star, Colin Montgomerie. Monty has always intrigued me because his silky-smooth golfing genius is matched by an equally prickly public persona. Since the early 1990s, he has either been at or near the top of the golfers on the European Tour, and (as of this writing) bears the unfortunate and terrible label of being the best golfer to never have won one of the four major tournaments. The Golf Gods seem to love a tragic figure upon which to heap their considerable wrath, and Monty is one golfer who has received more than his fair share of their fury.

Monty wears his emotions on the sleeve of his well-logoed golf shirt, more than once going off on a fan that made a foolhardy misstep in his way. He's also known for possessing supernatural hearing, and can get distracted by a fan rewinding his watch four fairways over. At the tournament, I stood literally five paces away as he teed off on the par-four fourteenth hole. Where I was standing behind him, I could see that the hole doglegged slightly to the left. I was so close that I could feel the wind from his practice swings as he prepared to drive down the fairway, aiming to hit one of his notoriously straight tee-shots to the right-center of the lane. I could have practically reached out and patted him on the shoulder. He had lined up and was ready to launch his drive when a fierce red fire ant bit me on my left calf.

Fire ants may be tiny, but they aren't called *fire* ants for nothing. They have one heck of a set of choppers in their beady little heads, and my calf was no match for their sharp little incisors.

The sting shocked me and hurt so bad I almost let out a yelp.

Had it been anyone else but Monty I would have, but I knew he would have gone crazy on me. There was no way I was going to be the golf fan that turned Monty catatonic mid-swing and ruined the career of Scotland's greatest player. In my mind's eye, I could see ESPN showing the clip over and over as Monty attacked the hapless fan that harassed him in Thailand. To stifle the scream that began to explode from my lungs, I bit down on my tongue as hard as I could. Monty hit his drive wonderfully, exactly where he had aimed, and as he picked up his tee he looked back, directly at me, and smiled—he had been very pleasant and funny with the people following him. I tried to say, "Nice shot," except my freshly-bitten, rapidly-swelling tongue had become the size of one of those gigantic, 460cc, oversized driver head covers. The compliment came out of my mouth like, "*Nicphte sphoftt!*" Monty gave me the same look the Thai merchants did when I tried to barter. Taken aback, he hurried off down the fairway to his ball.

On my way back into town after the play was over, I shared a cab with a young Aussie doctor also returning to Sukhumvit Road. James, in his later twenties, was vacationing in Thailand for the sex, sex, and more sex. He enjoyed golf, travel, and vacationing in general, but the promise of all the abundant Thai sex was the real reason he was in Bangkok. He cheerfully filled me in on all the best-kept secrets in the sex trade, intimating the perfect places to go to receive even the most wild and outlandish "services" in town—all for the price of about a dozen golf balls—as if we were discussing the weather.

Not that James's debauchery lacked for outlets. Bangkok truly is the world's pinnacle of price-per-service passion. My hotel was located just off one of the busier areas of engagement, the Soi Cowboy. On Soi Cowboy, a sex-hungry fellow like James encounters block after bountiful block of bars selling anything and everything a sex fiend can dream up. As you walk down the street, hundreds of young women in sexy outfits vie for your attention. "Hello, welcome!" they call out, which in the high, soft voices of

Thai women comes out as one sweet, singsong greeting: "Hel-loooowellcooooome!"

At first glance, I had enjoyed the interest of the lovely ladies. The girls of Bangkok are indeed both beautiful and enticing. My first night there, I walked through the Soi Cowboy and passed a group of ten lingerie-wearing young ladies. Out on the sidewalk, in front of the lively bars and nightclubs, the girls looked more like a sorority group headed to a racy costume party than seasoned women of the night. As I walked past, they immediately encircled me, screaming and giggling, trying to get me to pick one of them for some prepaid hanky-panky. "Pick me, mister!" they laughed and cajoled, "Pick me!"

With the girls clamoring for my attention, I felt like a rock star. Still, not one to participate in paid entertainment such as this, I begged off as politely as I could. Nevertheless, I walked away thinking, "Hey, maybe they did want *me*! Sure, I'm forty-seven, but hey—I've still got it!" Just then, I heard the giggling and screaming start up again. I turned around only to see the ladies performing the same routine on an elderly man carrying a walker who looked old enough to be Father Time's great-grandfather. The girls were all over him like he was Jon Bon Jovi. Oh yeah, I still got it. Damn.

Golfwise, other than the Johnnie Walker tournament, Bangkok was a complete bust for me. The majority of the courses were well out of town and that initial cab ride—if you can call it a ride—to the Alpine Country Club had put me off.

All during the two weeks I stayed in Bangkok, my mind whirled at the greatness of the professional golfers I had witnessed at the Johnnie Walker tournament. This game, golf, is the game I love, and they played with an apparent ease and sophistication my lackluster drives and pathetic putts just couldn't manage. What did they all know that I didn't? What part of their being makes them so good at this crazy game—and me, so pathetic?

Witnessing the obvious physical gifts of Ernie Els and the single-minded quest for perfection of Nick Faldo up close and in person, the realization presented itself to my heat-addled, cab-crazed, over-massaged brain that perhaps both traits were sadly lacking in my own pursuit of the game. With no Herculean physical traits and the approximate attention span of a hummingbird on crack, I was just another golf hack.

This was not the first time these frustrating points had occurred to me. Throughout my golfing career, whenever I hit rock bottom—which happens more frequently than I would like to admit—you might think I'd throw my clubs in the nearest lake and head for another pursuit. But there's just no getting away from the sheer love of the game, the intoxicating, infuriating, often inexplicable but always irresistible game of golf.

My slump remedy, which I'd had ample opportunity to perfect over the years, has always been to hit ball after ball at a driving range until some heaven-sent spark sends my shots back on their intended course. That was exactly how, just a few days after I left Bangkok behind on my way to northern Thailand, I found myself hanging off the back of a speeding truck with my clubs slung over my shoulder and wondering just what in the hell I was doing.

I had just practiced for the first time in a long time at the Lanna Golf Club's driving range, a busy public course in the northern Thai city of Chiang Mai. To return to my hotel at Chiang Mai, I hopped a local taxi. Which, more accurately, was a small, old, exhaust-spewing Toyota truck with a hard-shell roof covering the truck bed. Inside the back, sitting on two facing wooden benches, were nineteen Thai people packed together like two-dozen eggs in a carton built for twelve. Along with two local men, I was clinging to the outside of the vehicle with my feet barely on the back bumper, holding on for dear life to the roof rack as the taxi hurtled back to town, all with my clubs bumping around on my back.

I felt like the ladder man hanging on to the back of a speeding fire truck, except my tools weren't pickaxes and hoses, they were my ten clubs and golf bag. The driver seemed determined to paint this picture even more vividly in my mind as he put the pedal to the metal like four alarms were ringing in his ears. He was going the speed that all Thai drivers seem to go when faced with a rare stretch

The Ushuaia Golf Course—the world's southernmost locale to play the ancient Scottish game.

The wild badlands of the "Valley of the Moon," which borders the La Paz Country Club.

Gonzalo Reynaldo Ballion, my English-learning caddie, in La Paz.

Your author on the tee at the Arica Golf Club.

The Arica Golf Club—the world's driest course—bordering the Atacama Desert in northern Chile.

The Australian Outback's Alice Springs Golf Club—said to be the world's hottest place to play golf.

A traveling golfer going on a walkabout in the Australian Outback.

Two golf spectators, Australian-style.

The dazzling beauty of the Remarkables and Lake Wakatipu seen from the Kelvin Heights Golf Club in New Zealand.

Russell Squires, a lobster fisherman from New Zealand's Steward Island, playing his tee-shot at the Ringaringa Heights Golf Club.

The author golfing on the "brilliant" scenic coast of New Zealand's South Island.

A potentially lethal lateral-hazard on the Elephant Hills Golf Course in Zimbabwe.

The cheerful caddies and ground crew at the Elephant Hills Golf Club near Victoria Falls.

Warthogs pruning the fairways at the Elephant Hills Golf Course.

Scottish golfing great Colin Montgomery at the Johnnie Walker Thailand Open in Bangkok moments before I was bitten by a fire ant.

Two smiling caddies at the Mission Hills Golf Club in Shenzhen, China.

Me, George Shay, Douglas White, and Patrick Lim (from left to right) at the Nick Faldo Course at Mission Hills in China.

On the road.

My faithful caddie and sidekick Farouk at the Mena House Golf Course near the Great Pyramid of Giza.

My Lawrence of Arabia impression at the Great Pyramids.

The wonderful golf oasis of the Soma Bay Golf Club near Hurghada, Egypt, and the Red Sea.

Lars Erstad, my golfing companion for my final round in Tromsø.

The dramatic setting of the Tromsø Golf Course in northern Norway.

My final hole after 60,000 miles.

of open road—about nine hundred miles per hour. The periodic speed bumps only seemed to encourage the driver to hit the gas. Maybe he liked the sport of tossing the twenty-five of us (there were three passengers up in the driver's cab as well) as high in the air as he could, as the truck bounded over the bumps like a gas-guzzling wildebeest stampeding down the road.

I haven't held on to anything that tightly since someone tried to take my blankie when I was three years old. I'm not sure if it was my golf bag slung over my shoulder, my golf shoes sliding around on the bumper, or the look of sheer terror on my face—or some combination of the three—that so delighted the beaming, giggling, captive audience in the back of the taxi. When the truck finally rumbled to a stop in front of the hotel after fifteen solid minutes of constant fright during which I had prayed to every god I could think of, I gingerly pried my fingers from the roof rack, jumped down off the bumper, and kissed the ground upon my safe arrival like the pope on the tarmac during an international papal visit.

Chiang Mai, with five local courses, was definitely more of a golfing town than Bangkok ever hoped to be. The city is a winter golfing haven for Koreans on vacation during the cold wintertime. At the Lanna Golf Club, roughly five miles from the town center, I had shared the range with a group of ten Korean teenage golf prodigies as I tried to get my game back in shape.

Their stern but passionate golf coach corrected them in fiery bursts of Korean. He had his players hitting the ball with almost no leg motion—flat-footed in fact—to create the speed of the hands at the point of contact with the ball necessary for long, accurate shots. I had never seen the simple drill before, but the kids all had beautiful power swings, so I had a feeling the coach knew what he was talking about. At rock bottom with my sorry, broken swing, I figured I had nothing to lose and everything to gain. Though I didn't understand a word he was saying, I mimicked the actions of his students as they practiced. After a few minutes, I got the hang of it—and was amazed at how far the ball was going with such minimal effort. By concentrating on keeping my legs completely still, I had allowed my arms and hands to return to harmony with my body as I swung the club.

Starting to feel more confident, I took out my driver, and started hitting the ball to the fence at the back of the range. I began thinking that perhaps it was time to move to Korea—maybe there was a whole country of golf teachers that good. You didn't even have to know the language to see instant results!

Happily feeling much better about my game, and down to my last range ball, I pretended the final drive was on the eighteenth hole at St. Andrews with par left to capture my first Open Championship. With the Scottish crowd worshipfully quiet and in awe of my command of their native game, I aimed straight at the clock on the Royal and Ancient Clubhouse in my mind's eye and sent my ball soaring toward the left side of the green and just short of the infamous "Valley of Sin" lurking in front of the short par-four finisher. My second shot would be a piece of cake as that great drive up the eighteenth had all but assured my victory. The Claret Jug would be mine!

"That was a beautiful power fade!" said a companionable nearby voice as I remained posed in my follow-through, relishing the sensation of a well-struck shot in the warm afternoon sunlight. I turned around, realizing that the giver of the compliment wasn't in my daydream, but was actually standing directly behind me wearing a big grin on his face.

The English-speaking gentleman was none other than nattily attired professional golfer and author Peter Andraes. Peter, an American, has led more lives than an alley full of cats. He played college golf at Stanford, inherited a family fortune at twenty-one, and lived the high life off the cash during his own version of the Roaring Twenties. Peter met a young Tiger Woods in the early 1990s while playing golf in Arizona and became a friend of Tiger and his family.

Peter became interested in Tiger's golfing makeup, which he felt combined the martial-arts teachings of Tiger's Green Beret father, Earl, and the inner serenity of his Thai Buddhist mother, Kultida.

Peter wondered whether the answers he was seeking in life and golf were in the Eastern cultures. Ready for a life change, Peter gave up the money, all his earthly possessions, and moved to Thailand in 1994 to study the ancient ways of the East. He studied the teachings of Buddha and practiced the disciplines of the Shaolin warrior monks who were the inventors of kung fu. The practice demands developing your physical strength and courage through intense exercise while learning to unleash the power of the mind. He became strict with his diet, gave up alcohol, and began a simple, but happier, life.

Peter's cosmic search for truth led him to Chiang Mai where he happily lives with his lovely Thai-Chinese wife, Apple. I had been working hard on my game for a couple of hours as I pounded balls and mimicked the sweet-swinging Koreans. Perspiration had drenched my clothing all the way through to my REI travel underwear. Cool, calm, and totally collected in his golfing attire of yellow Polo shirt and tan khaki pants with nary a wrinkle, Peter looked as if he had just walked out of an air-conditioned meeting at a bank. There are many sides to Peter, and that particular incarnation was his golf teaching persona.

Peter teaches golf and uses the Lanna Golf Club as base for his clients who have decided to commit to the strict regime required to follow his teaching. Part martial arts, part golf, and part Eastern philosophy, you better be ready to study hard with Peter because he never does anything partway. His process is a Zen golf boot camp. He teaches golf through the art of *qi-gong*, which works to uncork the powerful energy locked in our bodies through yoga, meditation, tai chi, and discipline. The idea is to get these forces working in our bodies in tune with the forces of nature: a beautiful, powerful golf swing becomes as simple as smelling a rose. As you can tell, he isn't your normal golf instructor. Hitting it off immediately, and both of us grateful for conversations in fluid English, we quickly became friends. I'd crossed paths with many interesting people on my trip, and they don't come much more intriguing than Peter Andraes.

As an American citizen living in Thailand, Peter has to leave and reenter Thailand every three months to keep his visa current. He had planned a weekend trip up to the Burmese border near the Golden Triangle to get his immigration papers renewed, and asked if I would like to keep him company, as Apple was going to Bangkok with friends for the weekend. I quickly agreed and was thrilled with the chance to see the Golden Triangle—the geographical convergence of Laos, Myanmar, and Thailand on the mighty Mekong River. There was a great golf course in Chiang Rai we could play as well. How could I resist?

We drove three hours north from Chiang Mai to Chiang Rai and reached the Golden Triangle. We crossed the border into Myanmar (formerly known as Burma until 1989). I could sense the desperation of the people living there immediately. Border towns tend to be rough, and it was plain to see that life there was no picnic. In-between the merchants hawking their fruits and vegetables, I spied several stores selling vicious-looking knives and weapons made from chains and spikes. I found this unsettling. The goods were all significantly cheaper than at a similar store just fifty yards away in Thailand, but the sinister storefronts and hopeless aspect of the inhabitants gave the place a lawless feel.

Young boys hocked counterfeit cigarettes and whispered that they had hash as well. A toothless money changer offered his exchange rates to me as we passed by; he was the first toothless banker I had ever seen. The hawkers were all desperate for a sale and their angst was palatable as they grabbed my arm and forced their goods in my face for inspection. As we walked through the streets, a strong tingle of dread crept up my spine: the feeling of crime and corruption and little hope, combined. Life was cheap. Though we only stayed there for a couple of hours, I was quite happy to cross back into Thailand. Myanmar's harsh military junta has long kept the country isolated from the rest of the world, and the Burmese people at the border had the wild-eyed look of animals locked up in a dilapidated zoo.

Peter had been searching for pure Burmese jade from dealers who obviously knew him from past transactions. The most valuable jade, a clear, forest-green, is worn around your neck or as the setting of a ring, or placed in prominent points in your home to generate positive energy and ward off evil spirits. I bought a few small pieces to fight off my recent evil golf play and to bring me luck and prosperity on the rest of my trip. A small jade monkey caught my eye and I bought it to remember the Year of the Monkey.

With my new bits of jade now standing watch over me, we drove back to Chiang Rai and to the wonderful Santiburi Country Club, a few miles outside of town. The course was built in 1992 and is the baby of Khun Santi, the tycoon owner of Thailand's largest brewery, Singha. The course was designed by that globe-trotting architect, Robert Trent Jones, Jr., who took a marvelous piece of land there in northern Thailand and used his genius to turn it into a special place to play golf. Northern Thailand is beautifully green and slow-paced. The sweet smell of the mountain springtime lingered in the air as if it had nowhere else to go. The sunny day was winding down and we arrived at the course with only time for nine holes on the backside. As my golf writing buddy Turk Pipkin says, "Sometimes just playing nine holes is perfect."

The setting there at Santiburi was glorious as the course wandered through the contours of a fertile valley with a canopy of magnificent shade trees alongside the vibrant flowering trees in the full bloom of early spring. The trees were so heavy with blossoms that the ground beneath the trees was covered with a blanket of brilliant ruby-red and vibrant white petals, tempting me to roll in them just as I had as a kid in the January snowdrifts in Minnesota, creating snow angels. With the verdant foothills and mountains of Chiang Rai in the distance, we golfed the day away as the giant sun slowly sank. I have never felt as peaceful on a golf course in all my years of playing the game. As I walked up the gradual incline of the eighteenth fairway to the final green, I was mesmerized by the setting sun, which seemed remarkably close—as if it was going to spend the night in nearby downtown Chiang Rai. It finally fell behind the mountains and gave the horizon a radiant buzz of golden energy. The grass and trees and flowers were bathed in an aura of soft sunlight. It was enchanting.

Walking alone with my thoughts as I took all this captivating beauty in, I realized Peter was nowhere near me. I looked back down the fairway and there was Peter a couple of hundred yards away with his clubs lying on the ground. He stood facing the wonderful sunset with his arms extended wide as if to take in every ounce of energy nature emits at its end-of-day glory. His eyes were closed; across his face, played an angelic smile. This was his form of prayer. I stood on the green looking back down the fairway at him while he remained as still as a statue for several minutes in his meditative pose. He later told me he had been "gathering *chi*," and the image of his extended arms in the beautiful surroundings of the Santiburi Country Club will be how I always remember Peter Andraes—another lucky person who has found his spot on the earth.

12

Dansavanh Nam Ngum
Golf Resort
Vientiane, Laos

17.58°N–102.36°E

Chicken sick!"

That wasn't exactly what I had expected to hear from the Laotian waitress after ordering scrambled eggs and toast in the coffee shop of my hotel in Vientiane. The traditional Asian breakfast of noodles and vegetables had been my staple over the past few weeks, but since the menu had offered scrambled eggs, a more traditional American breakfast had sounded good to me as a change of pace. But . . . *chicken sick?* It took me a moment to realize that the waitress was talking about the "chicken flu" currently sweeping Southeast Asia, not a specific free-range hen that had just come down with an earache or a case of the shingles. "Chicken sick" also meant there wasn't an egg to be had there in Laos or anywhere else in Southeast Asia while the fear of an epidemic of avian influenza was spreading like wildfire from coop to coop and country to country. I sighed. It was noodles for breakfast once again.

"Chicken sick" did make me wonder: if a chicken was actually sick, would chicken soup make it feel better? But I decided to keep that little tidbit to myself. I also wondered if a chicken tasted chicken, would they think it tasted like chicken? I decided to keep that tucked under my money belt as well. When you travel as much as I had been, you have quite a bit of time to think of these things. If a chicken is too scared to cross the road, does the chicken's friend call it a chicken? I'll stop.

The opportunity to travel and play golf in Laos had just popped up, as it hadn't been on my initial itinerary. While in Bangkok, I had gotten a visa for Vietnam, and was planning to go there next and play golf at Kings' Island—the only course in the former North Vietnam. Peter Andraes had told me that Kings' Island is said to have been built on top of an ancient snake pit and that intriguing thought, combined with golfing in a Communist land, had made it a must-see. Golf and communism don't often share a cart (so to speak) and I was curious to see how the two got along. However, the chance to play in another Communist country, before Vietnam, had presented itself first.

My final round of golf in Thailand was at Royal Chiang Mai— a scenic, gently rolling course an hour from the city out in the middle of peaceful Thai farmland. I had joined up with two other golfing singles playing that day—Mike, a chief warrant officer on a golf vacation leave from the U.S. Army in South Korea; and K. K. Cheong, a Malay businessman who runs the only golf resort in the neighboring country of Laos. K.K. has the size of a powerful pulling guard in the NFL, but rather than participate in the sorts of rough, physical sports where his size would have been used to his advantage, K.K.'s loves are scuba diving and golf. Full of good cheer, with a slight British lilt to his English, he's a gentle soul in a strong body. You don't meet people nicer than K.K.—as he'd insisted we call him, friendly and unassuming from the start.

It was a fun day as our motley threesome played our strokes, chatting and enjoying the sun-drenched northern Thai countryside. Royal Chiang Mai is a comfortable, easygoing resort set all alone out in the countryside. Just off the main highway headed north toward Myanmar, you turn off and meander down a dirt road through rice paddies and a tiny village, home to a couple of old wooden shacks, and then find the course sitting on a gradual rise in the otherwise mostly flat landscape.

Royal Chiang Mai has what Peter Andraes calls "the rhythm of three," which is a shaded gazebo every three holes with cold refreshments and respite from the tropical heat. This setup is actually typical of many Thai golf courses. Normally (as in back in temperate Seattle), stopping and sitting and having refreshments every three holes would drive me bonkers. Usually, I don't even liking stopping after nine holes at the turn for a sip of water. I prefer to get on with it. Golf is too important an endeavor to be mixed up with ordinary mundane tasks like eating and drinking.

However, Thailand had massaged my "full steam ahead" ways out of me. My muscles and spine now possessed the consistency of creamed spinach. I found myself relaxed, even enjoying the periodic breaks as K.K., Mike, and I sat under the canopies, cooled down, and told our stories. I had never enjoyed a six-hour round of golf before until Thailand. It was the perfect way to spend a day.

Mike had been a military man for twenty-seven years and had visited Royal Chiang Mai on many leaves from his duty in South Korea over the years. I asked him if there was any chance he might be called to go to Iraq for the current conflict. He hoped not, but said he'd go if he had to—with "no questions asked." He was a true soldier who followed orders. Personally, if told to go to Iraq, I'd be asking a ton of questions, with the first one being: "Why don't you post me in Thailand instead and let me guard Royal Chiang Mai?"

K.K. was just happy to be playing golf anywhere. K.K. and I are kindred spirits in our futile quest for trying to tame the elusive game, which consumes an unhealthy amount of our waking hours. He's as goofy for this maddening sport as I am. K.K. and I talked about the pros we follow (we both are Tiger fans) and the latest and greatest in golf equipment, a subject on which he is an absolute master and one I know next to nothing about. K.K. was going on about the new hi-tech Cleveland irons that do everything but put themselves back in your golf bag after hitting your ball straight and true no matter how awful and unathletic your swing. All this technical mumbo jumbo was lost on me. He was talking to a guy with a set of twenty-five-year-old blade irons who was thinking of going to the hickories of ancient Scottish golf if he didn't start playing better. But golf talk is golf talk, and I enjoyed talking golf with K.K. It can be therapeutic when an addict meets an addict going round the bend.

After our round, over drinks on the clubhouse patio that looks out over the course and the serene surrounding vista, slick-talking businessman to the core, K.K. invited me to come and play in Laos, then go to Vietnam from there. He knew just what to say: "All you have to do is fly to Vientiane and we'll pick you up at the airport and take you out to the resort. You can play golf and relax. Flights leave daily to Vietnam from Laos, and you can leave whenever you like." Like a direct order from Don Corleone, it was an offer I couldn't refuse.

Never in my wildest dreams did I think that some of the best days of travel I would have in my around-the-world golf extravaganza would be in Laos. That's right, Laos! The Lao People's Democratic Republic (its formal name) is one of the last Communist countries on earth. I haven't had much dealing with Commies in my life, but these Commies are cool. The Lao people are so sweet, laid-back, and groovy, I was ready to get my own personal hammer and sickle, buy a Lenin T-shirt, and just hang out.

There is an innate sweetness to the Lao people, due, in part, to their isolation. They are the only landlocked country in Southeast Asia. Long and skinny like a mini-version of Chile, Laos is sandwiched between Thailand to the west and Vietnam on the east, with China at the top, and Cambodia completing the hemming-in to the south. The awakening roar of the economic super-heavyweight China has sent tremors of prosperity thundering throughout the region. The economies of Thailand and Vietnam are speeding down the highway while Laos and Cambodia are stuck in the corner of the garage like a couple of old worn-out, discarded persimmon drivers.

There was a dawdling, rural charm to Laos. Without a port city, greed has to travel overland to get there, so that ugly trait hasn't yet firmly taken root. No one is storming the gates to enter the country and spend wads of cash—neither tourists nor investors, although both trickle in. Simply put, other than the wood in the forests of the northern hill country, there just isn't much of value for other countries to pillage. Laos is largely left alone. As a result, Laotians have yet to become jaded by the chase for money at all costs and seem to love being helpful for the joy of serving. It's wonderfully refreshing.

Massage-wise, Laos was fantastic as well. Their expertise in this ancient skill was every bit as good as Thailand, and it was even cheaper! I had a one-hour sauna followed by a two-hour massage for the equivalent of two dollars. It was too good to be true. How would I ever adjust to a life of no massage back home?

Laos has two golf courses, with the major one being K.K.'s course—the Dansavanh Nam Ngum Golf Resort, a co-venture with the Laos department of defense. If you want to do business in Laos, it helps to get the military on your team. The resort is a Lao version of Las Vegas with a golf course, hotel, and casino. In that bastion of socialism, capitalism is running rampant there at Nam Ngum, complete with slot machines, roulette, and baccarat to take all your dollars, baht, kin, dong, or whatever your currency of choice. There is a retro Rat Pack Las-Vegas-of-the-Fifties feel to the endeavor. It's just a matter of time before a Communist version of Wayne Newton works the hotel lounge.

The golf course and resort are tucked away in a peaceful, secluded valley forty-five kilometers from Vientiane. After the constant whirl and noise of Bangkok, it was wonderful to hear nothing but the wind and birds of the Laotian countryside. Though a work in progress, the golf course has the potential to be great. No big-time golf-course design firm had a hand in this layout, just a few guys with a bulldozer and some jungle to clear. The course follows the natural cut of the land, and the holes seem to have been patiently waiting to be discovered under the dense tropical foliage.

Framing the gentle rolling fairways is the thriving green jungle, freckled with brilliant orange, purple, and white wildflowers. Graceful herons fly over silent, still ponds that once served as rice paddies and now flank the excellently mounded putting surfaces. You have to plot your way carefully around this challenging course because Mother Nature has given you all the hazards you can handle with the flourishing forest or the abundant ponds swallowing up your errant shot as quickly as a monkey eats a mango. It's one solid golf hole after another. As you play, you're lulled into a serene meditation of Lao golfing bliss out in the peaceful countryside.

I played with my two new friends: K.K. and Richard Ang—the director of golf at the resort, both from Malaysia. All of us were living the good life in Laos. For several days we had nothing but fun—playing golf, eating leisurely dinners in the hotel, laughing, telling golf stories, and enjoying the smooth, easy flow of Laos.

Richard is a golf-loving, funny, easy-to-laugh kind of guy. Also a fine golfer, he is sixty years old going on twenty-one. Richard gave me the best piece of advice I received in my travels. Before I let you in on his pearl of wisdom, let me set the scene.

Life in this part of the world makes you live one day at a time, because whenever you get into the car to drive anywhere, it could be your last day on earth. Driving (or being a passenger) in Laos is an all-too-familiar free-for-all and is as frantic as everything else there is peaceful. There is no road rage in Southeast Asia; for road rage to exist, there would have to be traffic rules, regulations, and thus, expectations for drivers to drive in a certain way. The only rule there is to drive as fast as you can, wherever there's room and try not to hit the other cars, trucks, bicycles, motorbikes, rickshaws, chickens, goats, cows, water buffalo, and people using the same dusty two-lane road. There might be a striped line down the center of the road, but they must think it's just a decoration, because no one pays it any mind.

Richard's sage advice came when he caught the unmistakable look of terror on my face as we were driving through the countryside back to Vientiane so I could catch my plane to Hanoi. Our van was dodging the oncoming onslaught of trucks, cars, and motorbikes that whizzed by on our left and right—it was mayhem. Several times en route the traffic was four abreast on a road that barely had room for two. This wasn't even taking into account the dozens of beasts of burden pulling carts, herds of goats, intermingled plaid-uniformed schoolkids going home on bicycles, and pedestrians laden with goods bought at market—all sharing the narrow road—as well. As I stared open-mouthed out the front windshield at the chaos bearing down on us, the odds for catastrophe had seemed highly probable. I tightened my seat belt as tight as it would go with nervous, sweating hands. Just as I was about to foolishly ask if the rickety van had passenger airbags, Richard gently patted my shoulder and gave me his astute, wise recommendation: "Close your eyes. It's better when you don't look." We made it, after all.

13

Kings' Island Golf Club
Hanoi, Vietnam

21.05°N–105.55°E

From Vientiane, I flew to Hanoi. Hanoi, the capital of the Socialist Republic of Vietnam, had an international reputation of not welcoming travelers. The exact opposite was my finding, in fact. The Vietnamese now seek visitors from the world over with open, friendly arms. The grumpiness of the past could have something to do with the fact that the Vietnamese have been almost continually at war with outsiders or each other since 40 AD. That's more than enough conflict and a good reason to be wary. After thirty years of no one trying to take away their lovely spot on the earth, they have lightened up a bit. But it's well worth noting that in the past fifty years, the Vietnamese have been in five wars without a loss on their home turf. These are resilient people.

The Hotel Du Nord had looked comfortable on its Web page and the price was well within my meager budget. Plus, the locale was good—a quiet (for Hanoi) side street just a few blocks from the main arteries. The gentleman who ran the hotel, Mr. Hieu, had been kind and helpful in his e-mails, and said he would pick me up at the airport. He was worried I'd have trouble finding his hotel on my own and he was probably right. I was grateful to have transportation from the airport taken care of as well.

My flight leaving Laos had been delayed for six hours (no reason was given), and this was information I couldn't get to Mr. Hieu
because we passengers were held at the boarding gate like cattle in
a pen as we waited to leave. Not wanting to miss my arrival in
Hanoi, Mr. Hieu stayed at the airport eight hours awaiting my arrival. His courtesy was typical of the Vietnamese I came in contact
with there—they seemed to relish contact with outsiders. It was
still a whole new world to the North Vietnamese. Mr. Hieu told me
in one message that he was excited to test his newly learned English out on me, as well as show me his country. The Vietnamese
have tremendous national pride.

Finally, I reached Hanoi. As Mr. Hieu was loading my golf bag
into his car, he got into a major altercation outside the airport terminal with a stern military guard who was upset about where Mr.
Hieu's car had been parked while he was waiting for my flight.
They argued back and forth for several minutes in rapid Vietnamese, almost coming to blows. Mr. Hieu had to produce some papers before the guard relented and let us pass. When I asked him
what the ruckus was all about, Mr. Hieu laughed and said, "I don't
think he realizes the war was long ago."

As we entered Hanoi, I realized I wasn't fully prepared for how
lovely Vietnam's capital would be. Hanoi was hidden from the eyes
of the Western world until the mid-1980s, but the curtain has
dropped, and travelers are the beneficiaries of the unveiling. There
is a surprising elegance and old-world charm to Hanoi, with its
city lakes, shaded wide boulevards, and leafy public parks. A
French colony going back to the 1880s, the Gallic architecture has
prevailed and many of Hanoi's buildings would look right at home
in Paris or New Orleans's French Quarter. The streets are wide and
grand and absolutely crammed with Vietnamese on motorbikes.

Like the view of La Paz clinging to the side of the Andes, my first
sighting of the sheer volume of people riding motorbikes in Hanoi
won't soon be forgotten. You stand on the side of the road flabber-
gasted at the thousands and thousands of motorbikes screaming
down the boulevards. When I say thousands, I mean thousands and

thousands! I tried to quickly count the number of scooters stopped at a traffic light directly in front of me. I was at 142 and counting, but wasn't even close to the total as the light turned green; they revved up and continued en masse on down the street.

No one in Hanoi was idle. The streets are teeming with people trying to make a buck. Black-market money changers on street corners ask for your dollars, old ladies sell oranges and mangos and garlic, small kids try to sell you bus tours. Crowded back streets are full of peasant women in black silk pajamas balancing yokes of vegetables on their small shoulders. Markets seep from the sidewalks into the streets; I walked past barrels of fresh eels and ducked under bunches of plucked dead fowl drying in the air. I passed a man selling chunks of raw meat off a side of beef on the sidewalk. He had a movable tree stump on which to hack away and a small cleaver. You identify which part of the carcass you want and he hacks if off and wraps it in newspapers for you—blood and all. It was so ghastly unhygienic I had to turn away. I vowed to eat nothing but vegetables until that grisly image left my brain.

Seeing their entrepreneurship, I would have to say the Vietnamese are more capitalistic than even Americans. The Vietnamese as passive Communists? Boy, did those politicians who started the Vietnam War get that one wrong. Get real. Talk about not knowing your foe.

Well, my foe is the game of golf and it was off to Kings' Island Golf Club—the first course constructed in the former North Vietnam. Mr. Hieu arranged a taxi for me. My driver spoke no English, but Mr. Hieu had given him firm instructions on where to go and to stay there and drive me back when I was done. Feeling guilty that the driver had to just wait in the car all day just for me, I told Mr. Hieu that the driver could come back at an arranged time. Mr. Hieu set me straight with a snappy, "He'll be happy to wait for you. It's his job."

Though golf in Vietnam dates as far back as 1922, the game started on a grander scale in the early 1990s. On August 7, 1993, at the brand-spanking-new Kings' Island Golf Club twenty-two miles west of Hanoi, Vice Prime Minister Nguyen Khanh became the first member of the politburo to actually strike a golf ball. No details are known if he hit it right down the middle of the fairway with a slight draw, or if he whiffed several times first before making contact, or if he hit it into one of the many water hazards that surround the fairways at Kings' Island, but what is known is that this shot initiated the start of the golf boom in Vietnam. The official Communist Party newspaper *Nhan Dan* cheerfully announced in an article upon the opening of the club, "Golf is a good sport for health and the spirit." The newspaper failed to mention that three-putting on the eighteenth hole to lose twenty dollars to your gleeful golfing buddies destroys not only your health but also damages your spirit for life. They'll learn.

The twenty-mile ride from Hanoi to the Kings' Island Golf Course was a scenic treat. The countryside was fertile and well-tended with flat rice paddies spreading off into the distance. The back roads were full of activity. We passed horse-drawn carts full of produce, herds of cows and water buffalo, scores of bikes, cars, and trucks all heading toward Hanoi. I saw a small motor scooter precariously weaving down the road with a family of five all clinging to the two-wheeler like the Flying Wallendas on the high wire. The family all looked content as they puttered along, but it seemed remarkably unsafe. The smallest child, who couldn't have been more than three years old, was riding balanced on the handlebars with a big grin on her cute face.

The twenty-mile drive took forty-five minutes as we passed through a few small villages and then took a secluded back road down to the shore of the Dong Mo Reservoir—a beautiful U-shaped lake with the humpbacked Bavi Mountains watching grandly in the distance. The course is accessible only by boat and I was thrilled by the ten-minute ride over the lake to my first course in a formerly forbidden golfing land. I felt like Colonel Kilgore in *Apocalypse Now*, but rather than a beach to surf in Vietnam, I was after golf. In addition to confirming my long-held view that taking a long back road to a golf course usually delivers an interesting golf course, having to take a boat to go play is even better. Kings' Island loomed ahead with the clubhouse peeking out above the low-lying fog of the morning. I liked the place instantly.

There was a curious touch of mystery to the Kings' Island Golf Course as we pulled up to the dock in front of the clubhouse. This intrigue quickly turns to something significantly lighter when you meet the director of golf at the club. Never did I expect to find a hilarious Boston native who once worked as a stand-up comedian in the Catskills to be the first golf professional in Vietnam. When thinking of what type of golf professional I'd find there, I had pictured a more serious type—perhaps British, with little sense of humor and finishing out an unsuccessful career in golf's backwoods of Southeast Asia. I couldn't have been more wrong. Robert Bicknell is an adventurous chap who wanted the thrill to live abroad, but is as American as Twinkies. He moved to Asia twenty-five years ago and he has been an integral part of the growth of golf in Thailand and now Vietnam from the early 1980s to the present. Mr. Bicknell is a different breed of cat.

After a quarter century in Southeast Asia, you'd think his Boston accent would have dissipated over the years, but his East Coast drawl is as thick as a cop working a beat in front of Fenway Park. He loves the Red Sox and American food and is up on the political world of Washington like he's a K Street lobbyist. He's proof that you can take the kid out of Boston, but you can't take Boston out of the kid. I asked him what he missed most about not living in America. "I'd kill someone in a New York minute for a real pizza," he answered with a sly grin. I wondered if language was a problem with his staff as he is the only nonnative at Kings' Island and Robert is a talker to say the least. "No, I get my point across—they listen to me," he said in his Northeastern Joe Quimbyesque brogue and chuckled. "I am proud to say that I'm functionally illiterate in four languages."

With an ability to hit a golf ball an unbelievably long way, as I was to witness firsthand as we played golf that afternoon, coupled with a rat-a-tat delivery of nonstop hysterical stories and jokes, Robert is the wisecracking Bugs Bunny of Asian golf pros.

He enjoyed being out playing golf—it was a rare event for him. Between running the day-to-day business and managing several hundred employees, giving lessons, and hosting weekly tournaments, there isn't a lot of time for him to play the sport at which he excels. Robert was having fun blasting the ball down the wide, forgiving fairways with his violent but well-timed swing. I have never seen anyone hit the ball as far as he could and he was roughly the same size as me (and though I'm no ninety-pound weakling, I'm not exactly brawny, either). After another tremendous wallop of over 300 yards, Robert said with a grin, "It's better to play golf outside. My wife gets mad at me when I practice full golf shots in the house."

As we walked along the lake bordering the green of the 330-yard par-four fifteenth hole that Robert had reached in one mighty swing, I commented to him about the amazing amount of motorbikes in Vietnam. Just on the road from Hanoi that morning, I told him, I had seen people hauling any and everything on the back of their motorbikes: giant mirrors, grandmothers, sometimes grandmothers and grandfathers at the same time, furniture, toilets, mattresses, coops of chickens, dogs. I had even seen one motorcycle toting a dozen wicker baskets stacked eight feet high on top of each other like a circus act as it zipped by me. Those motorbikes had me mesmerized.

I then told Robert about the family of five I had just seen riding all on one tiny motorbike. "That's nothing," he said excitedly. "One time I was stopped at a traffic light in Hanoi, and I looked over and alongside me, there was a guy with a water buffalo riding on the back of his motorcycle. The water buffalo was five times bigger than the driver and was just sitting there with his hooves on the back pedals and its front legs resting on the shoulders of the driver. Just as the light changed, the water buffalo looked over at me and shrugged with an incredulous expression on its face that said, 'Can you believe this idiot has me on the back of this thing?'"

14

Spring City Golf and Lake Resort Kunming, China

25.04°N–102.41°E

Marco Polo, that infamous Italian world traveler of the thirteenth century, and namesake of the obnoxious swimming-pool game that kids seem to delight in playing for a minimum of ten hours straight, first ventured into China from his home in Italy in 1271. Over seven centuries later, I headed into that formerly forbidden land as well; though not on horseback as Polo had, but in a comfortable air-conditioned minivan that ferries golfers daily for the ninety-minute trip from Hong Kong to the Mission Hills Golf Club just outside Shenzhen. It had to be easier motoring into China's countryside while resting my behind on a cushioned seat rather than on a sweaty, tired steed galloping across the Asian steppe as Polo had done; but, then again, he wasn't lugging golf clubs. I had him there.

China! The ancient land of wisdom and ingenuity! The home turf of Confucius! The birthplace of paper, gunpowder, the compass, umbrellas, the wheelbarrow, whiskey, and chess! Astronomical observatories, printing, decimal mathematics, and the seismograph all were first discovered and put into practice there. The Chinese even played a form of golf as early as 300 BC—*ch'ui wan*—which translated, means "beating a ball."

You know a game is great when everyone wants to claim it as their own. China joins Italy, England, France, Holland, Egypt, and Belgium who all maintain that a form of the game of golf was first played on their turf. As far as the game's true originators go, I'm going to stick with those lonely shepherds on the windy links land of the eastern coast of Scotland. Here's my reasoning. Is the world's first golf course, the Old Course of St. Andrews, in France? Holland? Egypt? Italy? Belgium? China? Perhaps these countries had some ancient idler hitting some form of a ball with something resembling a club, but they didn't build a golf course back then, did they? Scotland did. Your honor, I rest my case.

Now unchained economically, China isn't doing anything on a small scale—even in the world of golf. China currently has around two hundred courses and that number will be growing as fast as the numbers of hamburgers sold at China's seven hundred McDonald's—especially when every backwater Chinese villager gets a chance to have their cholesterol rise with daily doses of Happy Meals. Southwest China's Mission Hills Golf Club is the largest golf complex in the world. The Chinese have figured out that they can't buy tradition in golf—those pesky Scots have a six-hundred-year head start—but with their cheap labor and land, they damn well can be the biggest. Mission Hills, with ten golf courses side-by-side and 180 holes of championship-caliber golf, is the new big golfing bully on the block. By the way, did you like the way I quickly figured out that ten golf courses equal 180 holes? Who says we Americans aren't keeping up in math?

Each of the ten courses at Mission Hills bears the name of a famous golfer. Jack Nicklaus, Nick Faldo, Vijay Singh, David Duval, Jumbo Ozaki, Ernie Els, Annika Sörenstam, Jose-Maria Olazabal, Greg Norman, and even teaching guru David Leadbetter, all have signature golf courses there. Many golfers double as true golf-course designers in their spare time. Nicklaus, Norman, and

Olazabal all had a hand in designing their respective course at Mission Hills. However, one of the executives there told me that as far as he knew, the Japanese superstar, Jumbo Ozaki, has never once been to his signature course. Oh, to be a world-class elite golfer! Checks arrive in the mail for millions and millions of yen and you don't even have to show up. How good is that?

The leaders-that-be in China know that businesspeople like their golf (as do we non-businesspeople), and there's no doubt the enormous scope of Mission Hills was built, in part, to attract more investment to the area. It is, indeed, one attractive carrot they're dangling. If corporate bigwigs are seeking a spot to build a new factory in Asia, why not next to ten designer golf courses! If I was a corporate board member, which is about as far-fetched as me being a professional golfer, I know how I would vote. Raze the Des Moines plant (no offense, Iowans)! We're moving to Shenzhen!

Like China as a whole, it's impossible not to discuss the numbers when describing the scope of Mission Hills. With over one hundred million people living within a two-hour traveling radius, Mission Hills averages fifteen hundred rounds played per weekend day, and anywhere from five hundred to one thousand per weekday. And you think your local muni is swamped! Think about that—one-third of the population of the entire U.S. lives within a two-hour travel radius of Mission Hills! Only a small percentage of Chinese need to become golfers to make Mission Hills wildly successful. Like everything else there, golf is going to explode as it gains popularity as China increases its burgeoning middle class. Yet again, it's a numbers game: China is going to have more and more of the world's best golfers—the odds are in their favor with their gigantic population base. Plus, the game suits their disciplined, goal-orientated nature. These factors make China the sleeping golf giant of the world, and they are waking up quickly. I predict that in the next fifty years the Chinese will dominate golf on all the major professional tours. Kindly remember you heard it here first.

Everything at Mission Hills is the biggest or the most in the world of golf. In addition to the most golf holes in the world, they were building the world's biggest clubhouse during my visit. If you're going to have the most courses, you might as well have the biggest clubhouse! During a tour of the property, I looked down onto the gigantic structure under construction. It looked more apt in size to hold an indoor NFL football game than sell golf balls and cheeseburgers at the turn. I've seen smaller Wal-Marts. Mission Hills is also the world's largest buyer of golf carts, and just in case you want to play real golf and actually walk, there are over twenty-five-hundred caddies to tote your bag. That's right—twenty-five-hundred caddies! These folks aren't kidding around: in China, bigger means better, and they'll go as far as they have to, to be the best.

Mission Hills isn't planning on stopping their expansion any time soon. I envision a day when every professional golfer in the world will have their own signature course at Mission Hills. You'll be able to play golf across the entire country right up to the border of Afghanistan and never once leave the perfectly groomed fairways of Mission Hills. I asked the vice president of Mission Hills, David Lim, what they would do if another golf company somewhere off in the world built ten or eleven courses to match them or move ahead. He replied confidently, "Oh, we'd just build a few more." There you go.

Roger Foo, the director of golf at Blue Canyon in Phuket, had called his friend, Francis Poon, who is the rooms division manager of the five-star hotel there at Mission Hills, and told him to take good care of me. Francis was charming and welcoming and couldn't have done a better job of filling his friend's request. Rather than seeing me as a tired, slightly rumpled, globe-trotting golf-seeker, he welcomed me like a long-lost relative and showed me straight to my room personally. The suite was huge and luxurious, with a king-sized bed and wide-screen television with worldwide cable. There was a free DSL line for rapid-fire Internet access and a large bathtub to soak in. My balcony looked out over the Nicklaus course. Chuckling, I thought to myself: *So this is China! Who knew?* Whatever I had expected of the golf world in China had already been far exceeded.

As nice as the rooms were, the golf courses were even better. Nothing less than top-notch, the bent grass and zoysia fairways were as well groomed as the pristine Augusta National. With 180 holes to choose from, the golf seems to go on forever—you need a trail of bread crumbs and an atlas to find your way back to the hotel. In a golf cart, Francis gave me a tour of the new Greg Norman course, which is designed to be the most difficult course ever built in Asia. From what I saw, it looked as brutally intimidating as any you'll find in the world. The Great White Shark has designed something that only he and his peers will have a chance to play well. It looked harder than advanced trigonometry. The bunkers are as deep as water wells and the forced carries from the tees to the landing areas in the fairways require steroidal strength to reach. Apparently, the course is being designed for the next strain of superhumans.

Francis arranged for me to play the more benign, but still challenging, Nick Faldo course. The Faldo layout was perfect golfing terrain as the fairways wind through banked mounds clearly showing the correct route to the green. Among my golfing mates were Douglas White, a tall, funny American who has the daunting job of overseeing the golf-course maintenance of all ten courses— that's quite a bit of mowing and watering. Douglas sought adventure in his chosen profession by going abroad, and loves living out in the world. Joining us was George Shay, the affable director of golf, with a beautiful golf swing to match his even temperament and good humor. George had recently joined the club after a stint at a golf club in Shanghai. Our fourth was Patrick Lim, a funny, wisecracking Chinese golf-course photographer who lives in Kunming in south-central China.

Douglas and George were excellent golfers. They both hit the ball like true golf professionals, eliciting that crystal-clear whack!— just like the sound of a rifle shot—piercing the tranquil Chinese air as they made solid contact with that poor stationary golf ball waiting on the tee. Both were impressive to watch. My golf, on the other hand, barely warranted a passing glance. Though I started off okay with four straight pars, I double bogeyed the par-five fifth, which destroyed my fragile confidence. My game, as always, was a flimsy house of cards. I limped home with a fury of bogeys. Thankfully, I don't have to make a living with my spotty golf game.

Meanwhile, Patrick Lim, the photographer, was a fascinating chap. His job consists of traveling around the world and photographing the great courses on our planet. Boy, do I wish that "golf course photography" would have had a booth at the "career day" at my high school. Where do I sign up? I can't think of a better occupation. Patrick said that he mostly works with Robert Trent Jones, Jr.—the builder of wonderful courses all over the globe.

Patrick Lim's home is in the Kunming province, which is a couple of hours due east from Mission Hills via air. He asked me if I was planning to play at the Spring City, his home course. Spring City has two courses, both of which are rated as the top two in China. I was thinking that if they were better than the ten at Mission Hills, they must be quite special indeed. I had heard of Spring City often during my travels in the past weeks in Southeast Asia, as it is known for being not only scenically beautiful, but also world-class, golfwise. At first, I told Patrick that Spring City wasn't in my plans. I was headed for India and said I wanted to get there as soon as possible.

"You can't come to this part of the world and miss seeing Spring City," he replied emphatically. "Let me call them for you." Before I could get a word in edgewise, he whipped out his cell phone and called Spring City right on the spot. He chatted for a few minutes explaining my quest, hung up, and said, "It's all set up. They're expecting you tomorrow. I'll call the travel office at the hotel and get you a plane reservation from Shenzhen to Kunming." I guess I was going deeper into China: Spring City was on the itinerary. India would have to wait a bit more. Besides, I wondered again, how hot could India possibly get, really?

The crazy chain of events that eventually led me to Spring City was really quite an amazing example of serendipity. It had all started when I had played at Joondalup in Perth and the general manager of the club, Mark Duder, had recommended I contact Peter Goh when I got to Singapore. The gracious Mr. Goh had called ahead for me to his protégé Roger Foo at the Blue Canyon Club in Phuket. Roger had called Francis Poon at Mission Hills, and Patrick Lim had called Spring City and that was where I went. Sitting back at my desk in my old condo on the shores of Lake Washington in Seattle, I never could have imagined anything remotely like this. Those finicky Golf Gods can be fantastic travel agents when they get right down to it.

The next day, I said a heartfelt thanks to Francis who presented me with a Mission Hills golf umbrella as a going-away gift. It was a nice gesture; I was touched. His last words to me were, "Speak well of China."

I taxied out to the Shenzhen airport, which was a true modern affair with industrial gray carpet and glass walls and a broad, pointy-domed roof overhead. It was so gleaming and new it looked as if had just opened that morning—you could smell the fresh paint. While waiting for my Kunming flight, I had my first encounter with the exasperating Chinese habit of cheating-in-line. In China, line-jumping is as normal a thing to do as eating with chopsticks. It's very demoralizing.

The first incident occurred while I was lined up at the airline counter about five passengers back from the front while waiting to show my passport and get a boarding pass. All of a sudden, a small Chinese gentleman squeezed in and stood right in front of me as if I wasn't there. Just as I was about to dip into my bag of expletives, another Chinese gentleman did exactly the same thing. There were at least ten people in line behind me. I looked back to see if perhaps the same thing was happening to them. It seems it was just me, the obvious visitor, who they chose to jump in front of. Was I invisible there in China?

I decided to let it pass, but I did edge up to the second cheater so the only way another person could slip in front of me was if they were the width of a number-two pencil. Having never cared for line-jumpers, which I equate with cattle rustlers of the Old

West and cheaters in golf in the new one, these two interlopers had pissed me off mightily. Though I was fuming, I decided to play it cool. The line was slow-moving, so by the time I received my boarding pass the whole incident had left my thoughts. The woman at the airline counter said I was required to go pay the tourist airport tax at a booth across the terminal before I could to go to the boarding gate for my flight to Kunming. Travelers in China are constantly made to pay extra.

As I walked across the terminal to go pay the extortion fee, I saw there was a line of two other travelers at the booth; I became number three. The other two paid the tax, got their receipt, and as I was taking the final two steps to the counter, another Chinese man suddenly darted in ahead of me. Enough was enough! I grabbed the interloper's shoulder and said, "Hey man, I'm next!"

To be fully forthcoming, I should note here that this line-jumper was much smaller than me and that was the sole reason I grabbed him. Normally, I'm about as physically imposing as Truman Capote. The gentleman rather forcefully removed my hand from his shoulder, and showing a command of good old American English, loudly exclaimed, "It's my country! You wait!"

I hadn't had much of any kind of altercation or confrontation for months, but this little weasel had me riled up, so my reply was a witty retort of, "Oh, yeah! Screw you, pipsqueak!"

This outburst of mine had surprised me because not only had I never used *Screw you* and *pipsqueak* in the same sentence before, but I don't think I had ever in my life uttered *pipsqueak* aloud even once. Apparently, *pipsqueak* had been patiently hiding in my brain like a recessed gene and waiting for just the right moment to enter my spoken vocabulary. This was the moment it had been waiting for. After I had blurted out, "Screw you, pipsqueak!" the utterance just hung in the air like a kung-fu movie actor caught in a freeze-frame in the midst of performing a karate kick.

My response set the little bugger off—he went crazy as he screamed at me with spittle flying and his eyes filling with rage. "Screw me? Screw me? Pipsqueak? I kill you! I kill you!"

Having someone tell me that they were going to kill me was a first, and I started to look around for help as I didn't want to die at the Shenzhen airport. I certainly didn't want "death by pipsqueak utterance" on my autopsy.

Another disclaimer should be introduced as well: I have never been in a fight in my life. Though I have long been a wiseacre, I have as strong a flight response as a startled deer in the forest. At the first sign of trouble, I usually run away as fast as my little legs will go. Being a complete coward in this respect has served me well. I have made it to the age of forty-seven with no black eyes or bruised knuckles; but as the pipsqueak's eyes were starting to bulge out of his raging, beet-red face, I thought my reign of non-violence was about to be broken.

The crazy little dude continued to scream at the top of his tiny Chinese lungs that he was going to kill me. My only plan of action was to just keep smiling at him like a moron, which was only making him angrier. "Screw-me-pipsqueak!" had become one solid word spouting out of his frothing mouth. "I kill you! I kill you!" he panted. I started to believe him.

Just as I was about to take a foolhardy made-up kung-fu stance in hopes of scaring my assailant, a tall, young Chinese student came to my aid. He went right up to the ranting rodent and spoke to him harshly in Chinese as he poked the small man in the chest with his index finger. He was much braver than me, and the pipsqueak cowered. Whatever the young guy said had done the trick. My killer-to-be calmed down, paid his tax, and moved on. I thanked the young guy for his help with my heart break-dancing inside my chest from all the adrenaline. I had been seconds away from running like Bambi after spying a grizzly in the forest.

He said in perfect English, "No problem. You have to remember you're in China. Be patient."

Lesson learned. Shut up, let people cheat in line, and be careful when you say *pipsqueak*.

It was a couple of hours by air to Kunming. Kunming is the

capital of the Yunnan province, which borders Myanmar, Laos, and Vietnam to the south. Kunming has the wonderful reputation of having temperate, springlike weather year-round. The Wumeng Mountains to the north stop any cold weather headed south toward Kunming and heat rises from the Bay of Bengal to the south. The two influences create a constant spring hovering over the clear, blue skies of Kunming. What a pleasant dilemma to have!

The timing of my visit to Kunming was perfect: I was in the "City of Eternal Spring" right smack in the middle of actual spring. The dogwoods and azaleas were in full flower and their sweet aroma filled the air, and, at least, wrestled to a draw the thick, brown smog that is now the norm of any Chinese city of size. The temperature was ideal for short sleeves. It seemed to be a perfect climate for a great golf course.

Well, I was wrong. It was the perfect climate for two great golf courses! *Holy smokes, Batman,* I found one of the best thirty-six-hole golf complexes in the world! And it's in China of all places!

The Spring City Golf Club is flat-out as good as it gets. If you're a golfer, do what you have to do to get there. Mortgage your house, sell your car, cash in your IRA, take your kids out of those expensive private schools and put them back in the cost-effective public system—just do whatever needs to be done to travel to Kunming and play both courses at Spring City. You'll thank me for years to come.

The aptly named Spring City Golf and Lake Resort sits grandly up on a broad hillside a few miles inland, off the highway in a tranquil world of its own. The complex is billed as the "golf paradise of Asia"—the moniker fits as snug as a brand-new golf glove.

You enter a world of tasteful villas and town houses set around the resort's comfortable hotel and elegant clubhouse, which both gaze out over the oblong azure-blue Yang Zhong Hai Lake. Flowers and cherry blossoms abound as birds flit through the sugary-sweet air. Emerald-green fairways framed by overgrowths of golden fescue and fragrant pine trees transverse the gently sloping hill down to the lake's edge. Across the vista, rounded green mountains peek through the misty late-afternoon fog, giving the whole area a hint of mystery. The scene is beguiling. It's as beautiful and soothing a setting for golf as any you'll find in the world. I couldn't wait to play.

Spring City is, indeed, a self-contained world. You never have to leave Spring City once there. Except for the menial workers who are locals, all the other employees—who mostly come from Singapore, Malaysia, and Thailand—are housed there on the grounds. Everyone eats in the clubhouse restaurant, working and socializing together. The employees seem to have as good a time as the pampered guests. Though golf is a game of the wealthy in China, there isn't a discernible snob factor yet, as people seem to be enjoying, rather than flaunting, their good fortune.

Upon arrival, I was met by Mr. Lau Tong Chye, the gentleman whom Patrick Lim called from Mission Hills on my behalf. Mr. Lau, along with the head honcho, Mr. Arthur Yeo, runs the joint. They are both living the high life there at Spring City out in the serene countryside. Mr. Lau immediately suggested I do the same. It seemed an assignment well within my meager abilities. I enjoyed a large, comfortable room with a television showing the Golf Channel beamed in from the U.S. "Relax," Mr. Lau told me. "Play both courses, and stay as long as you like." Like Francis Poon at Mission Hills, he couldn't have been kinder or more welcoming. I was digging Chinese golf.

To enter the world of Spring City is to have your blood pressure free-fall to next to nothing. If you can't relax there—what with the incredibly easy pace and natural spring color show surrounding you—your only hope is heavy medication. The flowers alone are worth the visit. The dogwoods only bloom for three weeks a year, and my visit was right in the middle of those three weeks. I had lucked out once again.

I settled into blissful days of playing the Jack Nicklaus "Mountain Course" and the Robert Trent Jones, Jr., "Lake Course," which sits closest to the lake. The two courses are extraordinary, and both have been named at one point in time as the top course in

China. Currently, the Trent Jones eighteen is ranked number one, and Jack's is number two. There are going to be a ton of courses built in China in the coming years as their economy roars, but I can't imagine any exceeding these two. Like New Zealand, this was golf heaven! If the two courses there weren't so far removed from the rest of the golfing world and the bluebloods who dole out the annual ratings, they would surely be ranked among the best courses of the world. Spring City is one special golfing locale.

First, I played the Nicklaus course, a real gem, which weaves around the higher ground. It was one terrific hole after another as I golfed and strolled along the perfectly coiffed fairways snaking between the wonderfully blooming trees with pink and white petals fluttering in the breeze. The thickets of azaleas aligning the fairways teemed with songbirds chirping to their hearts' delight. The setting was as lovely and challenging a place to play the game as you'll find anywhere on the planet. Perhaps encouraged by my surroundings, I played well. On the diabolically slanted par-five ninth green, I had a birdie putt to shoot a three-over-par thirty-nine. I asked my caddy how the putt would break.

Though barely five feet tall, she barked out with the authority of a drill sergeant, "Downhill, very fast, keep it inside left!" This wasn't Steve Williams reading a putt for Tiger, this was my delightful twenty-one-year-old Chinese caddie, Lynette Li, telling me exactly how to putt my twenty-footer.

Over the past three months of playing golf in Singapore, Indonesia, Thailand, Laos, Vietnam, and China, I had a series of female caddies who were, for the most part, so excellent at their job they put any male caddie I have ever had to shame. The caddies, required at every course I visited, speak "Caddie English"—the only English they know, which is all golf related. They wouldn't have a clue what I said if I inquired in English if they had brothers and sisters, or what village they came from, or tried to ask any questions on the myriad of topics I was curious about regarding their life in China. Not a word would get through our cultural divide. But on a tee-box Lynette would hand me a driver, and declare in perfect

English, "Four-par, three hundred and seventy-nine yards, OB right, water left, two hundred and forty yards to carry the bunker, Mr. David. Hit it straight at the marker!"

The most interesting caddie I had so far was in Chiang Mai's Lanna Golf Club in Thailand. Her name was Kai, she was twenty-three years old, and though it was over 100 degrees and I was sweating like Don Rickles in front of a tough crowd, she had on the normal Asian caddie attire: turtleneck sweater, T-shirt, golf shirt and caddie bib, two pair of pants, and long gloves that went all the way past her elbows. She was a walking yard sale. To top off her caddie outfit, Kai sported a wide-brimmed pink bonnet along with a towel wrapped around her neck so only the top of her nose and eyes were visible. Most women in this part of the world have an aversion to the sun that makes Dracula look like he's a lifeguard on *Baywatch*. Every female caddie I had in Asia wore as many layers as Kai.

What I loved about Kai, in addition to her just handing me a club of her own choosing without any input from me on every shot I was to play, was how the reactions and caddie duties she would perform depended on how well I played. She was tough. Pars or better were met with a full-wattage grin and cleaned clubs. Bogies earned a poker face, and I had to put my putter back in the bag myself. Double bogeys received a look like she just ate some gravel; I performed all of her caddie duties while she angrily walked to the next tee *sans* golf bag. She was ninety pounds of attitude (even with all those clothes), and I have never tried to par golf holes as hard as I did that day. I just wanted to see the grin of my Thai taskmaster!

Lynette Li was anything but tough or demanding. She was as sweet as Kunming's spring air. She would have gladly jumped up and down with joy had I made that putt for a thirty-nine on the front. Her read was dead-on, but I pushed the putt to the right and settled for a four-over-par forty for the first nine. I had to say that I wasn't discouraged in the least; it's hard to get upset at joyous Spring City.

I ended up staying for a week, and one of the aspects I enjoyed the most during this time was witnessing the weekly golf war between Mr. Lau and Mr. Arthur. Even old rivalries like the forty-plus years of head-to-head battles between Arnold Palmer and Jack Nicklaus have nothing on those two competitors. Though friendly, it isn't hard to tell from their respective body language which warrior is in the lead. The current leader walks proudly down the fairway with his chest thrust out as if he were wearing a suit of armor. The other slumps along quietly while planning the next shot with the hope of taking back the lead and deflating his opponent's momentary glee. They don't quite cheer out loud when the other hits a poor shot, but the corners of their mouth can't seem to stop, at least, the hint of a grin from forming. It was great fun to watch the bantering duo's dual up-close.

We played the wonderful Robert Trent Jones, Jr. Lake Course on just another perfect day in southern China as the warm, welcoming sun combined with a fresh breeze that blew through the gaps in the mountains and formed gentle ripples on the picturesque lake below. The Lake Course was one of the most dramatic and beautiful I have ever played. Mr. Jones didn't have nearly the same amount of land that Nicklaus had on the top of the broad mountain for his course, which was built first. Mr. Jones constructed his design on the sloping hillside that cascades down to the water's edge—which comes into play on several dramatic holes at the bottom of the property. Jones squeezed every possible inch of golfing land out of the hillside terrain and the results are spread wonderfully before your eyes as the holes crisscross the incline with groves of pines surrounding the fairways and greens. The Lake Course has it all: difficulty, sweet-smelling pine forests, grand views of the countryside, greens set on beguiling mountainside ledges, ravines, vibrant flowers, and the gorgeous lake itself. Jones borrowed from every bit of nature available to perfect effect. The result is a golfing masterpiece!

Despite all this, it wasn't all golf for me at Spring City. I hung out in the clubhouse chatting with the locals, and had wonderful meals nightly with my new friends. After dining, we listened to a band featuring two beautiful sisters from the Philippines who sang as wonderfully as they looked. After these nightly festivities, I would take a wonderful moonlit walk back to my room to write and watch the Golf Channel broadcast from back in America. Did I ever have to leave?

I did everything there was to do there. The company that owns Spring City is Singapore-based and the club is patterned after the comfortable Singapore golf clubs such as Laguna National with all its creature comforts. At Spring City, I spent hours in hot baths and steam rooms sipping tea and soaking after playing golf. After bathing, a beautiful young Chinese masseuse named Gigi gave me two-hour foot massages as I sat in a comfy recliner that looked out over the beautiful lake. My tension didn't stand a chance! Gigi was as beautiful as the view.

Every day, I would tell Mr. Lau that I was going to move on, as I had to travel to Bangkok to obtain my visa for India and get moving. Every day he would reply, "Why don't you stay another day?"

I'd think of the awesome golf and the hot baths in the locker room and Gigi and I'd say, "Okay, one more day it is." If I ever go back to Spring City, I'm not sure I'll ever leave.

I became great friends with Mr. Arthur, who as far as I could ascertain, seems to be having about as fun a life as someone can have. Spring City is his baby. He loves world travel and golf and good food and his weekly match against Mr. Lau. He's a tall guy with sleepy eyes and a constant, mischievous smile like he's about to shake your hand with a joy buzzer. His goal was to create one of the best places in the world to enjoy the game of golf. He has succeeded grandly.

Mr. Arthur is quite funny as well, as he loves to tell a risqué joke or two. He's quick to chuckle and loves stories. I filled him in on my adventures to that point as I went off on my love of Thailand and New Zealand. He loved hearing about my trouble in the Andes. "You wouldn't catch me up there, Spring City is as high up as I need to go!" he said with a big laugh.

I was intrigued about the building of Spring City as Mr. Arthur had worked directly with both Nicklaus and Jones on the initial designs of the two courses. Mr. Arthur isn't shy, and he said he put in his strong opinions on where he thought some of the holes could be located on the extraordinary piece of land. Great designers can have large egos, and I asked him if Nicklaus or Jones actually took his advice. He grinned and said, "Of course, silly boy! I was the one writing the check."

15

Qutab Golf Course
Delhi, India

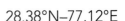

28.38°N–77.12°E

On a sidewalk somewhere in the world, two people walking from opposite directions approach each other. As they draw near, both pedestrians look up, determine which portion of the sidewalk the other is using, and make precautionary moves to avoid walking directly into the other person. Sounds simple enough, doesn't it? This elementary procedure is a fundamental component of moving via one's own volition and has evolved through ascent of humans over millions of years as Homo sapiens learned to not bump into other members of their species while walking erect, thus avoiding the crash and inevitable tumble. Just trying to find fire was hard enough without knocking heads with that troglodyte from two caves over. Yet, whatever strand of DNA is in charge of that basic function of foot travel simply does not exist in India! Just as surely as a parakeet in flight will smash its little beak by flying directly at its own reflection in the mirror, a person in India will walk directly into you as you proceed by foot anywhere in that country. You could be separated by a four-lane highway, yet somehow find yourself in a head-on collision with that kindly-looking fellow coming up the way. That very event happened to me roughly forty million times during my first three days in New Delhi.

Furthermore, I maintain, you could place two people from India on opposite ends of a football field with no one else around, and then ask them to walk to the other goal line. There is a 100 percent chance that they will smack directly into each other on the fifty-yard line. I believe you could take this experiment even further. Place one Indian on the North Pole and the other on the South Pole. Spin them around twenty times and tell them to start walking. I'll bet everything I have in my meager Roth IRA that they bump heads somewhere near the equator.

With over a billion people, India has the world's second-largest population, and by the time you can say "Deepak Chopra" one hundred times in a row without messing up, they will overtake the current number one, China. I'm not sure what type of birth control is used there, but whatever method it is, it isn't working. This awful population problem stems from the old, yet tragically flawed, concept that every family has to have a male offspring so he can take care of the elders. One son is good, two or three are even better. Families in India keep having kids until they have enough sons to be the *nan*-winners of the entire clan, and since 50 percent of the time they might have a girl (and in India girls don't count), families keep breeding like rabbits on Viagra. China solved this endemic problem by adopting the "one-child rule." India seems to have a "one-child-per-year rule" as the families there are super-sized.

Result: there are hordes and hordes of people everywhere! Not only that, the concept of personal space doesn't exist in India. There isn't even enough room for an imaginary friend. Never did I suspect I would look back at Saigon or Bangkok as beacons of civic order, but compared to Delhi they are both as spic and span as Disneyland.

In India, livestock live right in the city with everybody else. Pigs, goats, monkeys, water buffalos, and the ever-present, and very sacred, cows are all jostling for elbow (and hoof) room with all the humans. Cows rule the roost there. They are the only living beings that no one really bothers because they are considered holy creatures in India. Reincarnation has its perks.

I also quickly learned how the concept of *baksheesh* works. From

the moment you enter India, almost every person you meet is trying to perform a *rupeeotomy* on you and your purse strings. As a
tourist, you are the golden goose, the holiest of holies, the pot at
the end of the rainbow, the walking ATM card with a Western passport and ugly shorts and sunburned legs. You are Bill Gates, Jed
Clampett, and Daddy Warbucks all rolled up into one. Baksheesh
is basically an unofficial traveler's tax in India, and everyone wants
their fair share—100 percent. They don't even have the good manners to at least give you two-hour foot massages first. Baksheesh is
the way it is, and you have to get used to it if you plan to stay in India for any length of time. Everyone has their hand out, not only
professionals such as taxi drivers, waiters, and bellmen, who, of
course, earn their living from tips. Every person you meet on the
street has their paws in your pocket. "Something for my trouble,
pleeeeese?" It's more of a statement than a question.

Baksheesh gets old quick. People demand a tip just to get out of
your way. It boils down to simple arithmetic: there are way too
many Indian people, there are not enough rupees, and you (the
tourist) have dollars or euros or pounds that can be converted into
many rupees. And no matter how much you tip, I guarantee you, it
won't be enough. Any gratuity offered will be met with a negative
shake of the head and a frown suggesting your generosity was just
an average down payment. You better keep digging. You could tip
someone there one million dollars, and the rueful reply would be,
"This will suffice for me . . . but, what about something for my
family?"

I also finally found out exactly how hot India can be. Brutally
hot! India's heat is in a whole other category of temperature; it is
so close to your skin, it might as well be a layer of your epidermis.
It's one thing to be in 110 degrees of heat in the middle of the
Australian outback with no one else around for miles, but to be in
the middle of fifteen million people with hundreds of thousands of
cars and animals around as well—that's a whole different story.
Delhi's heat had me reeling, and it's actually in the cooler northern part of the country!

After that initial dose of being physically overwhelmed by India, I needed to find trees and green grass and nature, if for nothing else, the extra oxygen. I was pleased and relieved to see that the Asian Golf Tour's annual India Open golf tournament was being held during my stay in Delhi.

I taxied by *tuk-tuk* in the free-for-all traffic from my hotel in Old Delhi to the New Delhi Golf Club, which was as British-feeling as a course could be outside the UK. By the way, any day you survive without becoming a traffic fatality is a good day in India. As a by-hell-or-high-water traveler, you learn to lower your standards on what constitutes a good day. I had incorrectly assumed I had seen the worst the world offers in congestion and chaos and mayhem on the roads, but compared to Delhi, Bangkok, Vientiane, and Saigon are a bunch of pikers.

The Delhi Golf Club is rated as the number-one golf course in India and is an oasis of greenery in the midst of that urban demolition derby. There aren't any cows strolling around there—just Indian fat cats. The club is a gated enclave of stately trees with a grand Tudor clubhouse that screams wealth. It could have just as easily been in a leafy suburb of London. If you were airlifted into the grounds, you would never know that just outside the gates, looms the pandemonium of Delhi.

It was a practice day for the three-hundred-thousand-dollar tournament, which is enough of a payday to attract golfers from all over the globe, trying to ply their chosen trade of golfing for money. The Asian Tour is a breeding ground for the bigger professional golf tours. Golfers like Greg Norman and Tom Lehman honed their considerable skills on this tour, and Tiger Woods has played in Asian Tour events in his mother's homeland of Thailand.

I decided to go out and simply walk the course to enjoy the grass and trees and watch the players get used to the layout before that coming Thursday's opening round. To protect myself from the blazing sun, I lathered up with sunscreen, put on my hat, and made sure I had plenty of water—you'd have thought I was trekking across the Sahara instead of eighteen holes in the middle of Delhi.

Little did I know I was about to meet a most unusual professional golfer.

I had started chatting and walking down the fairways with some friendly Australian golfers who had wondered what the hell I was doing in Delhi. There were no other spectators but me. I explained my golf trip around the world, and it turned out we had a mutual friend back in Australia in Paul Daley, an excellent golf writer from Melbourne, so they invited me inside the ropes as they played the course. It's always fun to see golfers of this caliber up-close, especially in such an unusual golfing location as India. They all seemed as shell-shocked about India as I was as we laughed about the chaos and heat. Misery loves company.

The Aussie foursome all looked the way most professional golfers look: neat and clean and well-groomed with effortless, unhurried, beautiful swings that hit the ball a mile. Then I espied their antithesis—Bryan Saltus.

Bryan was out playing the course by himself, and I had never seen a professional golfer that looked quite like him. He was more hippie than golfer. His pants were extra baggy, and his loose-fitting golf shirt was barely tucked in. He looked more dressed for yard work. Bryan, a small thin guy with longish bushy hair, was wearing his golf hat backwards with sunglasses resting on top of his head. He had a string of puka shells around his neck and looked like a guy who probably made surfboards for a living or perhaps checked your lift ticket at a ski resort.

I thought he was maybe a caddie who was just out fooling around on the course while the golfer whose bag he was carrying that week was having lunch. I saw him swing the club from a distance, and it certainly didn't look like the grooved swing of someone who made a living playing tournament golf. Noticing my gaping, surprised stare, one of the Aussies told me then that he was a professional golfer. *No way*, I thought.

I had to meet this guy, so I went over and introduced myself. After a welcoming smile and a pleasant, "Nice to meet you too, bro," the first words I heard out of his mouth were, "I used to be on the Grateful Dead tour, now I'm on the professional golf tour." There's a sentence you don't ordinarily hear a professional touring golfer say, but this was no ordinary golfer. Bryan Saltus is a thirty-three-year-old Grateful Dead–loving Deadhead who was in New Delhi from his home in California to compete in the Indian Open.

I was fascinated. I asked if he minded if I walked with him while he practiced. He replied right away, "That's cool with me. The next few holes are awesome!" I liked him immediately. I learned that Bryan plays on both the Canadian and Asian tours, and is the winner of fifteen events on the very competitive California mini-tours. "I kill them in California, bro!" he declared in a nonboastful way with a big grin.

His biggest win was the San Francisco Open in 2001, for which he received twenty thousand dollars, and publicly dedicated the win to the late Grateful Dead leader and guitarist extraordinaire, Jerry Garcia. Most professional golfers grew up idolizing Jack Nicklaus or Arnold Palmer or Ben Hogan, not the founding member of a band whose audience considers LSD one of the major food groups.

Bryan had no air of a being professional athlete—he was just a regular dude playing a game he loves. If he wasn't playing for money and trying to make a mark on the world's professional tours, he'd be playing for fun back in California. Bryan's game is self-taught: his setup and swing are anything but orthodox. Like a true Deadhead, he's got a style all his own. He stands by the ball as if he's casually watering the lawn with a garden hose. He couldn't have looked more leisurely or unready to strike a golf ball with force and velocity. He takes the club back about halfway to what is considered a full normal swing. As he swings forward the ball explodes off his clubface like a rocket. It was extraordinary how well he repeatedly struck the golf ball. Shot after shot flew into the hot air of Delhi like a bullet, straight as a string tied to the flag waiting at the hole. He was playing five balls during this practice round and each shot was as gorgeous as the last. That Deadhead can play golf!

Bryan travels the world playing the game he loves. He is on a gallant pursuit on a stingy budget. After India, he was flying back to California for a week, and then it was back across the Pacific to play the China Open in Beijing. I told him how beautiful I found the Chinese women while I had traveled there as I fondly thought of my beautiful masseuse, Gigi, at Spring City. He gushed, "Cool! Bro, you couldn't believe the girls we met last night at a party for all the players. They were all models. There was free booze. It was awesome!" He seemed to have his priorities straight.

Bryan Saltus is my new golfing hero. No traveling swing gurus or sports psychologists or sports agents for that man; just a guy seeing the world and trying to make a living playing golf. I envy him. I asked him if he felt he could win the tournament. "Who knows, man? I could start making putts and shoot sixty. I've done it before. It's all up to the Golf Gods." Anyone who knows the power of the Golf Gods is my kind of golfer!

Seeing Bryan hit his low, straight-boring rockets to the greens made me want to play too. I decided to go back to my hotel and get my sticks and find a place to play. The caddie master there at the Delhi Golf Club suggested I try a course called Qutab. He said it was a course that he and his buddies played regularly. Off I went.

Though I'm not sure exactly how it happened, I had acquired my own personal *tuk-tuk* driver who, no matter where I went, was always waiting to drive me somewhere else with his beaming smile and three-wheel taxi. I decided to hire him for my complete stay. What the hell, I needed to get around, and I wasn't about to rent a car anyway. I'd rather eat glass than attempt to drive in the mayhem of India.

Shatish Sharma, my driver, wore a crisp uniform of white long plants and a white buttoned-down shirt like an ice-cream man or a tennis star in the 1930s. It was remarkable how clean and pressed his clothes were in the grime and heat—it didn't seem possible. His full head of black hair was coiffed as elaborately as Carlos Menem's lacquered do and his David Niven moustache was painstakingly groomed. Shatish is the father of three and, like most Indian males, provides for them as well as for his own mother and father and brothers and sisters and cousins and probably a couple of cows as well. As the firstborn son, he's in charge. I asked him if he had any hobbies like cricket or yoga. He laughed at my question. "Providing for my family is all the yoga I have time for."

We went and got my clubs back at my hotel and then headed off in search of the Qutab Golf Club. I was itching to play my first round of golf in India.

The history of golf in India is a surprisingly old one, as India was the first country outside of Great Britain to build a golf course. The first was the Bangalore Golf Club in 1820, which was also the birth year of St. Andrews's Old Tom Morris—the first star of the game. To put that date in perspective, in 1820, the governing body of golf—the Royal and Ancient Golf Club of St. Andrews—was still fourteen years away from being formed. The old feathery, the golf ball whose core was a top hat full of bird feathers, was being played as it was still another twenty-seven years before the rubberized gutta-percha would revolutionize the game in the late 1840s with its longer flight and more durable cover. It was thirty-one years before England's Willie Park would become the first person to try and make a living strictly from golf as he put out the shingle—"Golf Professional." The U.S. was still sixty-seven years away from its first golf course—the St. Andrews Golf Club in Yonkers, New York. All that time, golf was being played in India.

The Royal Calcutta Golf Club was established in 1829 and is the second oldest golf club outside the British Isles. The Calcutta Golf Club added to their pedigree when King George V and Queen Mary conferred the title of "Royal" to the golf club during a visit to Calcutta in 1911.

Although the Qutab Golf Course of Delhi may never obtain "Royal" status like its neighbor, how it came to be is just as noble a cause, in my opinion. Qutab is the first public golf course built in India. Funded by the Delhi Development Authority, the first nine holes opened in January 2000 and were followed by nine more in May 2002. The course is a cheap place for locals to learn and play the game. While the three-dollar greens fee is expensive to the normal Indian citizen—this is a country where three hundred and fifty million people live on less than one dollar per day—at least it's a start.

As Shatish and I motored into the parking lot of the course, a dozen caddies started running after us in pursuit. There were no other cars in the lot, so the competition was fierce for the paying job of toting my clubs. It seemed whoever grabbed my bag first was the winner. Only one of them would be earning rupees that afternoon.

The course was low-key and welcoming to anybody who wanted to tee it up. The white clapboard clubhouse was old and obviously had been there long before the course came to be. There was a prominent sign on the outside of the clubhouse that was the best warning sign I had ever seen on a golf course. The sign stated, simply: PLAYERS ARE REQUESTED NOT TO SEND THEIR CADDIES FOR BRINGING TEA FROM THE OUTSIDE. It would have never occurred to me to send my caddie out for a spot of tea, but at the Qutab Golf Course the problem seemed dire. Good thing they had a sign, or I might have been tempted for some of that "outside tea" myself!

My caddie was unusual, in that he was a he. So far, all my caddies across Asia had been women and, as I've mentioned before, wonderful. Rinku, my twenty-seven-year-old caddie, had some tough acts to follow. Rinku said he'd been playing golf at Qutab for the three years it had been open. He said his handicap was twelve, but I let him hit a few shots later, as I played, and I would say the actual number was probably double that. We golfers like to exaggerate a wee bit. Rinku was a total sports nut. He plays cricket on the weekends and golf there at Qutab on Wednesdays, when the course is open for the caddies to play for free. He told me, "Sports are my life. I don't smoke or drink. I just play cricket and golf." Rinku was easygoing and rather shy. It was nice that he spoke English well, as did most Indians who were schooled in the no-nonsense British-style school system.

The Qutab Golf Course was rather plain and nondescript, not nearly as flourishing as the wealthy Delhi Golf Club. In fact, *flourishing* was a word that would probably never cross your tongue when describing the layout. It was really just a bit of bland parkland—a field actually—on which they had installed nine simple putting surfaces, constructed a few tee-boxes, and called it a golf course. But I nevertheless loved playing the first public course in what was, for me, a new golfing land. Rinku and I pretty much had the place to ourselves. The only other people on the course were the grounds crew—all Indian women in colorful red and gold saris doing all the weeding and mowing by hand. I didn't see one piece of motorized equipment anywhere. They worked silently in groups of two on the sun-browned turf as they plucked the intruding weeds. For a public course, with little revenue, and in India of all places, it was immaculate—these smiling ladies did their job well. The clippings were gathered up into wicker baskets and then carried off the course on top of their heads. I had never seen a sight like that before on a golf course and it added color and an exotic flair to a banal piece of land.

Yet, the strangest vision on the golf course was the dozens and dozens of brown eagles that had full run of the place. You would have to go to the wilds of Alaska to see that many eagles in one location in the Northern Hemisphere. The eagles were huge and chocolate brown, with giant fierce-looking talons. The winged assassins were stoically perched in the trees, eerie and silent, as they scoped the course for prey. On one hole, a dog was sound asleep in a bunker by the green. I looked up into a nearby tree and twelve eagles were staring down at the sleepy mutt with dinner on their minds. I was tempted to wake up the dog to get him out of there before he became an entrée for the fierce-looking predators, but he was snoring soundly in the intense afternoon heat. The dog looked healthy, which can't be the easiest feat in India unless you're a cow, so I figured he knew the territory and the hazards lurking.

After a week in Delhi, I decided to get out and about and travel to Jaipur and Agra, the two other cities, along with Delhi, that form the well-beaten tourist track that is called the Indian version of the Golden Triangle. The circumference of the triangle is around five hundred total miles, with Jaipur and its many Mughal palaces as the western apex and Agra the eastern point with the ultimate tourist attraction—the Taj Mahal. There was golf to be played in Jaipur and I understood there was a nine-hole course in Agra near the Taj Mahal. It seemed a good excuse to see the countryside and play the game I love in a country that I couldn't quite seem to get a grip on.

Shatish drove me to a local travel agency he shills for. All *tuk-tuk* drivers make extra cash by taking their passengers to shops and agencies. Shatish had tried this a few times with me, but I quickly put a stop to it by telling him that I'd tip him more as long as he drove me exactly where I wanted to go. You have to be firm with the *tuk-tuk* drivers or they'll take you to shop after shop. It's all part of the baksheesh system of fleecing tourists.

Shatish had said the cheapest and best way to get around was to hire a driver who would spend five days driving me around the Golden Triangle. I wasn't eager to get on a bus as I seldom saw one that wasn't packed to at least twice its original capacity. The agency would book the hotels, which was fine by me, as India had rendered me clueless on where to stay. The whole deal, including driver, was less than fifty dollars a day. I would tip the driver at the end whatever I felt was right. I went for it.

The next morning my new driver, Bhuppi, picked me up at my hotel for the five-day sightseeing adventure. Bhuppi was another first son supporting a big family. He was thirty years old and married with three kids. As part of his livelihood depended on my tip, he tried to impress me with his English—which seemed to be one cliché after another. I wrote them down as he said them: *Old is gold. If they don't lie, they don't walk. One lie leads to many lies. No hurry, no worry. Don't worry, chicken curry.* Though we had only been driving for a short while, the thought of hearing this babble for the next five days straight seemed daunting. Bhuppi loved to talk nonsense, nonstop.

A couple of other worries dominated my thoughts once we got out on the open roads: the autos are chockablock except now everyone is driving as fast as they can too. Cars literally tailgate one another within a few feet of each other at high speed on the two-lane byway. We're talking NASCAR close! Every mile or so we passed the twisted remains on the roadside of violent traffic crashes that surely had no survivors as the metal and frames were in obscene configurations like a clash of warring robots.

We were in a small compact car owned by the travel agency, which was the other worry on my mind. Our oil light was shining as brightly red as a Christmas bulb. The car's hand brake was tied down with an old white T-shirt to keep it from springing up. The side-view mirrors were missing, and there was a jagged crack down the middle of the windshield separating the two glass halves into east and west. Worst of all, there were no seat belts! All of this and the violent traffic to boot—we were living on the edge.

I asked Bhuppi if he had his own car and learned that he didn't. Bhuppi's dream in life was to someday have his own car. "Then life will be easy! No worry, chicken curry!" he said. It was roughly the thousandth time for "No worry, chicken curry!" and we had only been driving for an hour. It was going to be a long five days.

It is 170 miles from Delhi to Jaipur. After two hours of driving, the car finally gave up trying to go forward. The oil light had indeed signaled something was desperately wrong. We pulled off onto the side of the road as steam bellowed from the engine in the already stiflingly hot air. Bhuppi called back to the travel agency on his cell phone and said another driver and car would be coming to rescue us in about four hours.

There was a tented, dirt-floored, roadside restaurant a quarter of a mile up the road, and that's where we waited. There were two cooks on duty, both of whom were barefoot and worked by a hot griddle as they pounded dough ball after dough ball into flat pudgy pancakes for a customer rush that never came the whole time I was there. There was no running water, just a dozen bottles of Pepsi and six Mountain Dews. Flies were everywhere as they lit on the cooks' arms and me and a sleeping dog that was lying next to my chair with scores of the winged pests on his back. The flies were so common no one bothered to shoo them but me. What good was it taking malaria pills if you're not going to put them to work? And my malaria medication was in for a workout.

The heat was intense. The sun was unrelenting in the parched countryside—there wasn't a shade tree as far as the eye could see. I was glad for the cover of the tent—a wimp like me wouldn't have lasted in that desolate, thirsty land for long. There was nothing appealing like a mountain or even a sandhill on the horizon to take my mind off the situation of being stranded for several hours in the middle of nowhere. A few times I tried to count the amazing number of flies that continually lit on the back of the snoring dog, but that trick only worked to alleviate my boredom once or twice. Bhuppi piped up and said, "No worry, chicken curry," about every five minutes or so. I wasn't exactly in Hell, but I was certainly on its outskirts.

I had started to get hungry and decided to try the food. No worry, right? The rolled cooked dough was called *parantha* and was eaten with something that tasted like mango chutney and white, lumpy curds. The cooks were watching closely to make sure I was enjoying the food and I have to say it was indeed quite tasty. I ordered two more *parantha* and the proprietors were so overjoyed you would have thought they had just won the lottery.

Twenty or so *paranthas* later, the new car and driver arrived and I said good-bye to chatty Bhuppi and said hello to my new driver, the quiet and reserved Ramesh. It was a good trade.

We arrived in Jaipur a few hours later. Known as the Pink City because of the red limestone buildings that signify the place as a Mughal center, it was a welcome retreat from the dingy chaos of Delhi. It's not that Jaipur wasn't crowded—it was packed like every other Indian city—but it was more manageable, since you only had to fight the onslaught of cows, people, and vehicles most intensely in the old walled section of the ancient city.

After a good night's sleep, I had Ramesh drive me to the Rambagh Golf Club, which is the only place to play golf in Jaipur. The eighteen-hole course has nine greens with grass and nine "browns" that are dirt "greens." The flat course was in dire condition in that dry area of northern India, and if there hadn't been flags on the putting surfaces, you would have never known it was a place to play golf. You would have assumed it was a derelict field down the street from the moon.

I again had the course to myself, along with my caddie Mukesh. Mukesh looked to be a hard-living forty or so, but I had the feeling he knew the game of golf well. Mukesh looked like a golfer. He wore one of those gold copper bracelets that golfers wear to heal their ailments through the magic of magnets or zinc or whatever the hell it is. He sported a grimy yellow alligator golf shirt and white golf shoes that had paid their dues from what looked to be twenty years of use. Mukesh gave me the impression he felt he was doing me a favor by being my caddie—the whole round seemed to be about him. I was actually hitting the ball well as I tried to emulate the rocket shots of Bryan Saltus, but the grass on the greens hadn't been mowed for several weeks and they were as rough and uneven as the greens had been at Ringaringa on Stewart Island. I had trouble hitting the putts hard enough on the ramshackle surfaces—I just wasn't used to having to hit a putt with that violent of a swing to get it to the hole. My lag putts would come up eight feet short time after time and Mukesh would snarl at me with repugnance, "Don't leave it short! That's awful!" Like baksheesh, Mukesh got old quick.

On par-five fifth hole, Mukesh ordered me to hit my drive to the left half of the fairway for a better chance to reach the green in two. I tried to follow his advice, and although I hit the ball long and well, it landed just in the right rough alongside the hard-pan fairway. Again, my ineptitude met with admonishment from Mukesh as he slammed my driver back into my bag. He spit out, "I said the left side!" as he stormed off in disgust to find my ball, mumbling about my lack of golfing expertise under his breath. Oh, how I pined for the good-natured female caddies of Thailand, Vietnam, and China. Walking down the fairway, I attempted to put the ill-tempered Mukesh out of my mind and focus on the exotic surroundings of the hills around Jaipur.

The dramatic Moti Doongri Palace was visible from the course. The palace is a hilltop fort built like a Scottish castle and sits grandly on the high ground dominating the entire area. The palace reminded me of the wondrous Edinburgh Castle in the busy downtown of that splendid Scotland city. I tried in vain to focus on that dramatic landmark rather than on my abusive caddie, on whom I had started to wish a case of severe leprosy.

The fairways of the golf course in Jaipur share their turf with the Rambagh Polo Grounds and horses were being led on their morning walk around the perimeter of the grounds while I played. Perhaps they let the horses graze on the greens, which would explain why they were so ill kept. With the heat and lack of grass and smog, I couldn't imagine a worse place to be a horse.

The road from Jaipur to Agra is the longest portion of this particular Golden Triangle and so it was one full day of nonstop terror for me as Ramesh and I made the drive the following day. After my round of golf with the foul Mukesh, I was glad to put that course and its evil caddie in our rearview mirror, which, of course, our car didn't actually have. Why would anyone need something silly like a safety mirror to drive in India?

That day of travel proved to be one of the most horrifying of my life. Driving in India has to be one of the most frightening endeavors in the world! The drive to Agra was eight nonstop hours of cars, trucks, and buses barreling straight ahead at us before swerving over at the last second, avoiding collisions by a whisker. We're talking hundreds of near-misses in which there would be no need for an ambulance and the only way your corpse could be identified would be with dental charts—if you haven't ground your teeth off from the tension before it happens. Every driver in India feels that every other driver should get out of *his own* way— they take road rage to a Herculean level. Horns are honked nonstop and every driver's goal is to pass every other car on the right or the left or right over them if you're going too slowly—they don't mind banging bumpers.

The whole experience was so frightening and terror-inducing, I just started laughing manically every time I escaped almost-certain death, which was every other minute or so. It was the only way I could handle my anxiety.

We finally arrived in Agra, miraculously intact, in the early evening. All I wanted to do was go to my hotel, eat dinner, and sleep. It was a good plan except for the eating part. I ordered room service at my hotel and after an hour became violently ill. I knew instantly I was in big trouble. This was food poisoning at its evil worst. I'll spare you the details, but it lasted a week, and I was surprised I didn't lose any organs. It wasn't pretty. I had to stay in bed the next day as I was so dizzy and weak I could barely raise a finger without extreme discomfort. However, I was determined to see the Taj Mahal, as golf in Agra was entirely out of the question—I wasn't even strong enough to put a tee into the ground let alone make a complete golf swing. Just bending over was enough to induce my guts to empty once again. I could only stand up for about a minute at a time, but I desperately wanted to see the grand mausoleum for which Agra is world-famous. Perhaps in a feverish delirium, I became driven. How could a person go to India, much less the host city, and not see its most celebrated attraction? Around four in the afternoon, I rallied as best I could, and had Ramesh drive me to the Taj Mahal.

It was glorious! All thoughts of mere bodily sickness were wiped from my aspect as I gazed upon one of the marvels of the world. The Taj Mahal lives up to its billing. Built almost entirely from white marble, the Taj Mahal seems to float on the horizon like the grandest of mirages. You don't even want to blink for fear that it might, indeed, be just a product of your imagination and could disappear like footprints in the sand with the swish of a gentle wave. It's best viewed from a distance, where the center domes and corner spires can be seen as a whole. It's the definition of flawlessness. Even as sick as I was, I couldn't take my eyes off of it. It seemed as good a place as any to die, as I was certain was going to happen at any moment; my fever was racing with my intestines to see which could produce more havoc in my system.

I sat on a bench and wiped the flood of sweat swamping over my brow and gazed at the Taj Mahal in complete awe in the hot afternoon. It does make one wonder how a people can build something that remains so technically perfect after three hundred and fifty years, and yet can't build a sewage system in the twenty-first century, but that's for another conversation. While at times it was touch-and-go, I didn't throw up on one of the Eight Wonders of the World, but only just.

16

Royal Nepal Golf Course
Kathmandu, Nepal

27.45°N–85.20°E

"Don't worry, they're small bombs."

That was meant to be reassuring, as I had just asked my taxi driver about the reported explosions the Maoist guerrillas had been setting off in Kathmandu in the ongoing Nepalese civil war. Reassurance was exactly what I sought while being driven to my hotel in the Thamel section—but I wasn't getting any promises. During my incoming flight from Delhi, I had read in the newspaper that the New Zealand government had followed the United States in issuing a warning against traveling there because of the bloody conflict. The dreamy kingdom was anything but peaceful.

One hundred and fifty soldiers had been killed in a battle in western Nepal the week prior as well as another seventy-five in the past couple of days. In addition to those skirmishes, there were also violent riots in Kathmandu between the government, which had suspended democracy, and the Nepali people, lead by university students who weren't at all happy about that governmental move. This particular conflict had begun in June of 2001, when the crazed prince-in-waiting, who, after getting tired of just hanging around the palace, shot and killed his mom and dad who happened to be the king and queen of the country. He also shot nine others, including his big brother, the heir apparent. The murdered king's brother became the new king and suspended democracy as a show of force against agitators who had, of course, immediately smelled a rat. Many felt the newly crowned brother was the brains behind the shooting spree. Those events had all come to a head and there was violence and unrest seeping into the sweet spring.

My taxi driver had stated the obvious right off the bat: "Things aren't good here right now." That was plain to see. There were armed military personnel and police in riot gear at all the major street intersections during the thirty-minute drive into the center of town. They looked ready for conflict with their gray military helmets, battle fatigues, and riot shields. Rifles were slung over their shoulders and menacing-looking black batons were ready at their sides.

Tension swirled in the air. It was almost like the atmosphere of a big prizefight in Las Vegas as there seemed little doubt as to whether both sides were going to come out swinging or not. Personally, I hadn't cared about the possible violence because I was, at least, out of India. The thought of small bombs and riots actually sounded like a step in the right direction compared to how I had been feeling the past few days. Uprisings or not, I was relieved to be in Nepal. My stomach had still been doing the rumba with my intestines, and I was still quite ill from my room-service meal in Agra.

For my first few days, I stayed in bed and battled against the evil microbe that had taken control of my body. The hotel manager was kind and kept bringing me tea and bottled water and oranges. He seemed used to treating this affliction with guests just arriving from India—I wasn't the first.

My aims for Nepal were simple: improve my health, play golf at the Royal Nepal Golf Course, and figure out my next travel destination. Either I would give India another shot, or head off to South Africa and start the long, final climb up the globe to Norway. Hopefully, my goals would be met without bringing me near one of those "small bombs" that made the headlines of the news-paper each morning.

Despite the unsettling specter of political unrest, I found Kath-mandu both appealing and interesting. The city is ground zero for a tug-of-war of the centuries as the customs of the past try to hang on while the modern world bullies in via the Internet and television and SUVs. Ancient incense-clouded Buddhist shrines, swarming with monkeys, and windy backstreet bazaars, unchanged for hun-dreds of years, now struggle with diesel fumes and KFCs for space. Rickshaws compete for passengers with motorbikes and yellow sedan taxis. Old family-run fruit and vegetable stands now abut brand-new glass-fronted shops with the latest in technical gad-getry. Nepal has its feet in several different eras and is being pulled like taffy as the old and new ways are so diametrically opposed. Forced to handicap the race, I'd say the lure and ease of the modern world is too tempting and is well ahead as they come down the final stretch. Nonetheless, there is still a whiff of the exotic to the city.

It all made for good viewing to a voyeur like me. Even with the threat of violence, there was a groovy vibe that was both engaging and calming. Everyone there just seems to calmly do their own thing in the incense-scented air, unconscious and probably uncar-ing of how the world outside perceives them. There were dusty backstreet bookstores in Thamel's thriving shopping area to browse in; I found a newsstand that got the daily *International Herald Tribune* flown in and each day the merchant would gush the moment I en-tered his shop, "I saved you a copy! I know you love this paper!" Things were looking up! Slowly, but surely, I was getting back in business and decided to go try and play golf before the political sit-uation or my health got worse.

Nepal first got the golf bug in 1917 when their self-declared Prime Minister Rana returned to the mountain kingdom from a trip to Scotland with a set of golf clubs and a hankering to play the ancient game. A hastily constructed golf club was built on the land on which the Kathmandu airport runway now exists. It was believed that a full complement of eighteen holes were in play those days with the "browns" constructed of a dirty mixture of oil, sand, and tar for the putting surfaces. Over the years, as the airport needed more space, golf gave way to economic necessity and the holes were paved over to land planes ferrying in those tourism dollars. The course was moved, but not too far away.

Originally named the Gauchar Golf Club, it now bears the lofty name of the "Royal Nepal Golf Course" and takes up residence on a hilly slope across the street from Kathmandu's airport on the outskirts of town. The club was given its "royal" status in 1965 by his Majesty King Mahendra Bir Bikram Shah Dev (try saying that name three times fast!) and has to be the shaggiest "Royal" course in the world. Royal Melbourne it ain't.

My taxi pulled into the parking lot in front of the small clubhouse and I immediately had somehow procured a whole team of personal caddies that would all accompany me on my round. I didn't seem to have much say in the matter. One caddie was to carry my bag, while two others would sprint down the fairway before I would hit to be ready to find my ball as it flew over the blind landing areas that are common to Royal Nepal. On the first tee, I pulled out my driver and whacked it hard and straight down the middle of the opening par-four and my caddies took off like greyhounds chasing a rabbit. Their enthusiasm made me laugh and I realized it was my first chuckle in many days. Oh, it was good to be healthy and playing golf again!

After two holes, I was joined by one of my caddie's brothers, who had been playing golf by himself behind us. Krisna was the top dog of local caddies at twenty-two years old, and though he was small like most Nepali people, he was an excellent golfer as he got every inch of ability out of his diminutive frame. Krisna's swing and setup were perfect—someone had taught him well. I enjoyed the fact that he was a skilled golfer, and he knew that he was good—he was calm and confident, almost cocky, but polite, nonetheless. When I asked him if he was a good golfer before I saw him actually hit a shot, he had replied simply, "Yes, I am." And he was.

Krisna and I played a match over the tricky hilly course for four hundred Nepalese rupees—about five dollars. I played well, but he ended up beating me in match play as he was three holes up with but two to play. I was closed out. We shook hands and I complimented him on his excellent play; and he replied, simply, "Thank you, sir." It surprised me to find a golfer that good in Nepal. He would easily beat me nine times out of ten. Well, probably ten out of ten, but hey, it's my book.

Meanwhile, the political climate was getting worse by the day. As I walked through the city the nervous tension of potential hostility was palpable, like a bulging skin of water in an over-full glass. My fifth day there the glass shattered. A student demonstration had gotten violent and several students had been injured by the well-armed police riot squad. Their bloody faces were all over the morning newspaper and the conflict ratcheted up all around me. A nationwide strike was immediately called against the government. Huge fires of burning tires were set in the streets. Lampposts and sidewalk rails were torn down and placed in the street to stop traffic as well. Businesses were closed down and windows were boarded up. Thousands of people went to the streets and marched with armbands and flags as they chanted fiery slogans against the king. Armed guards were everywhere and noticeably more nervous than when I had arrived a few days earlier. The time bomb was ticking. I could hear it through my open hotel window in the streets below.

I was fascinated by the whole event, in direct opposition to my cowardly nature—I found I liked to be near the confrontations, as they were starting to increase in frequency. What in the hell was wrong with me? Mind you, I wasn't in the middle of the action, but rather, off to the side where I could clearly see as the protesters and the police got nose to nose. I was ringside. Neither side was going to budge. Something had to give.

Near one major confrontation, I was on a crowed side street when, in response to a series of thrown rocks, the police fired tear gas into the crowd not more than twenty yards from me. All of a sudden everyone panicked and started running down the narrow lane where I was standing. Immediately, the tear gas was burning in my eyes and I was coughing from the smoke. There was a metallic taste on my tongue. I quickly ducked into a doorway just off the street to avoid the onslaught of panicked people trying to get away from the foul gas. Luckily, the small alcove helped me avoid the stampede.

Wising up, I knew it was time to get out of there. Things were not going to get better any time soon. A little more food poisoning in India wasn't looking quite so bad all of a sudden.

I found a travel agency just a few blocks from the tear gas incident that was open for foreigners only. I booked a flight for the next day back to Delhi. Because I reacted immediately, I got the last seat of what would be the last flight leaving for a few weeks due to the strike. My last obstacle, and the only danger facing me then was how to get to the airport. There was no way I could walk that far with my golf bag. The manager of my hotel kindly said that he would provide me with a ride because there was a good chance a vehicle wouldn't be harmed with a Western tourist onboard. I hoped he was right.

The next morning the entire city was eerily quiet as no cars were on the normally packed streets. The barricades of burning rubber and steel had been doubled. Blood was in the air. My driver was very nervous that his windshield would be stoned as we crawled past the roadblocks. We were the only car on the streets. The protesters menacingly peered into the car to see who was breaking the strike. I tried to look as touristy as I could in my golf cap and uneasy grin—it certainly didn't require acting for me to appear nervous. We were let through. I'd be lying if I said I wasn't scared, but they weren't after some idiot golfer with a goofy look on his face. It was the king whose head they wanted on a stick.

17

Bangalore Golf Club
Bangalore, India

12.58°N–77.35°E

During the flight back to Delhi, I decided I would see about getting a train to Bangalore in the south of India. Bangalore is the hotbed of the technology boom in India and was rumored to be a pleasant city with a couple of golf courses. That seemed to be a good enough reason to go.

The British-built Indian train system was supposed to be good and the thought of seeing the Indian countryside from a comfortable sleeping car sounded better yet. It was two days by train to Bangalore; I could read and nap and watch the landscape pass by. That thought put a spring into my step.

I was told at the train station there was an open sleeping berth in first class that might be available that evening for a little baksheesh. Not wanting to stay an extra minute in Delhi, I wasn't in much of a bargaining position. I did have the ticket clerk promise me that I would have my own cabin on the train and wouldn't be sharing with anyone else.

"No worry! You have your own cabin with sheets and blankets. All your meals are served in your room. It's like a five-star hotel. I dream of taking this trip!" he assured me. The thought of my own cabin was too good to be true. Having experienced near-five-star-worthy train trips on my journey several times so far, I paid the bribe.

Train stations in India are worlds unto themselves. This central station was once grand with its high cool ceilings and arched entry-ways, but now it was overrun by travelers and porters carrying luggage on their turbaned heads. Scores of beggars and entire families had set up camp inside—they had nowhere else to go. Thousands of people live on the platforms or near the tracks in the worst of hovels, if they're lucky. Most have no roof at all and live within a few feet of the tracks. You walk past hundreds of crippled people with no arms or legs, or suffering from leprosy. Entire families, from mother to babies, suffer with physical defects and plead for alms. It's heartbreaking to see. I felt guilty striding to my first-class berth where I would live in splendid isolation for the next two days.

Splendid isolation didn't come to pass. I arrived at my berth to find that not only didn't I have a cabin to myself, I would be sharing quarters with three members of the Singh family from Delhi—and a chicken. *Brutal*.

I double-checked the posted roster of berth assignments on the platform, but there it was in black ink: Singh 3, Wood 1. It wasn't the final score I was looking for. I found the conductor and protested, but the train was full and nothing could be done, even as I offered baksheesh.

The Singh family was well-entrenched in the cabin with Mama and Papa Singh taking the bottom sleepers and their thirty-year-old chicken-wielding son up on the other top bunk. Their clothes and bags of food were spread out all over the berth—it looked as if they were moving in forever. Totally defeated, I climbed up onto my little narrow ledge of a home for the next two days as the chicken chirped across the way. Splendid isolation was as far away as Tromsö.

The Singh family was actually quite friendly and welcoming. Once I was over the initial shock, I decided to make the best of things and at least learn more about family life in India. It quickly became apparent that families are the same the world over. Papa

Singh was a radiologist who had grown tired of the medical field and was now in the trucking business with his brother. He said cheerfully, "We're doing quite well." The Singh family did look like money wasn't a concern. Mama Singh lived to eat and continually was putting candy or cookies into her mouth. She constantly complained about her weight, which was considerable, but it didn't stop her continuous munching. Mama Singh just sat in her seat as unmovable as Mount Rushmore. I don't think I've ever seen a person move as little as she did: the only calories she burned were from chewing. Yashwant was their oldest son, and it was plain to see that he was a major disappointment to his parents.

Yashwant had been schooled to be a lawyer, but had given up the world of business to study yoga and was in training to become a guru. Yashwant had long black hair tied into a ponytail and a beard that reached down to his chest. He looked like a yogi-in-training, which was what he was, I guess. His parents wanted him shaved and in a three-piece suit. He was the disciple of a holy man whose book he continually read every moment when he wasn't arguing with his parents. Like parents the world over, they wanted their son in a secure profession with a steady income, not a life in which worldly possessions were considered evil. Yashwant still lived at home under the financial umbrella of his dad's worldly possessions, so he hadn't fully given up creature comforts. Yashwant's beliefs had their limits.

Coming from a family of means meant Yashwant didn't have to take care of his parents financially, as would the vast majority of first sons in India. He was off the hook and able to be an agreeable bum, much to the consternation of his parents. Whenever he would go to use the loo down the hall, the parents would both immediately start telling me how lazy their son was. "He sleeps until noon every day!" Mama Singh wailed in between popping candy drops into her mouth. Papa Singh added, "His chicken has more ambition!" Yashwant's chicken was a recent addition to the Singh clan, having just been recently hatched. I never learned if the chick's parents minded that he was hanging out with a deadbeat-yogi-wannabe.

To kill time I would walk through the train and spy on my train mates—each car, seat, and sleeper was packed with humans and bundles of food and clothes. Luckily, I found a small two-seat berth with a curtain for privacy a few cars back that wasn't being used. I claimed it for my own to get away from the Singh family squabbles and the chirping chicken. I would go there, pull the curtain shut, and read and look out the window. This was what I had wanted to do on that leg of my journey, not be the fourth wheel of the devilsome Singhs.

I enjoyed the solitude, but Yashwant came looking for and found me. He slipped into the seat across from me and asked, "Want to join me for a smoke of hashish?" *Why not*, I thought, *perhaps it'll make me feel better*. I said, "I'd love to," which put a big grin on Yashwant's face. He quickly added, "Don't tell my parents."

We sat on the dirty floor of the couplings between cars at the rear of the train (well away from his parents) and passed the cigarette he had rolled. There were no doors to the outside—the sides were completely open, so we sat there as the hot wind of the late afternoon flowed through the car. We watched rural India pass by in our stoned stupor. The enormous, mesmerizing sun was lowering on the horizon as the last rays of the day gave the stark landscape a glint of gold. It was beautiful. I leaned back against the jostling train car and took a deep breath and for the first time in India, I felt peaceful. Mind-altering drugs are mandatory for serenity in India.

We arrived in Bangalore in the early morning, which, in my opinion, is always a better way to be introduced to a new locale—before the destination wakes. The streets were mostly vacant and it was plain to see how Bangalore is called the "garden city." The landscape had changed overnight. Southern India is tropically lush and the wide streets were canopied by leafy oaks. Spring was in full bloom, with deep-purple jacarandas and orange gulmohurs adding to the greenery. The trees were magnificently vibrant, especially the glowing gulmohurs. Gulmohurs are ornamental flowering trees that stay in flower longer than other similar species. They are brilliant in their dazzling color as their limbs are covered with the brightest orange flowers imaginable. It was the single most beautiful tree I had ever seen and startled me into an ogling stupor every time I came across one.

Bangalore has grand government buildings and beautiful greenspace parks. The sad thing is that the parks are fenced in and locked up tight like nature under glass. If the parks were open to the public, thousands of Bangalore's six million inhabitants would be living in them. You just stand outside the bars and look in at the trees and plants and pedestrian walking paths like you're checking out the lions in a zoo.

The economy of Bangalore is booming—it's also known as Indian's Silicon Valley. There are now hundreds of technology companies there and chances are when you dial an 800 number for technical assistance in the U.S., the call is answered by a polite, eager young adult in Bangalore.

After sitting on a train for two days I wanted to walk, and as long as I was walking I thought I might as well whack a golf ball as well. The two go so nicely together. I checked in at my hotel and did a cow search of the premises and found none—it was a good omen. By the way, I have nothing against cows; I just don't want their smelly hides standing where a sous-chef should be. I got my clubs and headed for the Bangalore Golf Club.

Golf was first played in Bangalore in 1820, although the Bangalore Golf Club was properly established as a sporting club in 1876. There is a feel to the place as if the British never left. The clubhouse is quiet, with wood-paneled rooms and ceiling fans providing an easy, cool draft. Photographs on the walls show the club over the years and trophy cases display the cups the proud club has won against other Indian golf clubs. The club has the distinction of hosting the oldest interclub tournament in India, dating back to 1878. More than any club I'd visited in awhile, it was a place where golf was the only focus. As always, I was eager to play.

The caddie master assigned me to Burnard, who would tote my

bag. Glad to have a job on a slow day, Burnard grabbed my clubs and quickly strode to the first tee. I was about to follow Burnard, but the caddie master stopped me and said in a low voice, "Don't keep your wallet and money in your golf bag. Some of the caddies here have sticky fingers."

Grateful for the warning, I replied, "Thanks for the information. By the way, what would be a great tip for a caddie?" He answered, "three hundred rupees would be exceptional."

The course was another nine-holer with two sets of tee-boxes to make eighteen holes. It was well-gardened and plants and trees were abundant—it was as classy a layout as the elegant clubhouse. The course was challenging, with tucked greens well-flanked by bunkers and slight doglegged fairways making you think you knew where you needed to hit your shots, but challenging you to come up with par. It was really one of the finer nine-hole courses I'd ever played, and was, by far, the best course I'd been on since Spring City. I was happy to have given India a second chance.

Burnard was thirty-one and single with no kids. That alone made him a novelty. I asked him why he didn't have a wife. "They're too expensive!" he blurted out. Burnard had worked as caddie there for twenty years. His father had been a caddie at the club and he had followed in the family trade.

I was, yet again, playing terribly as I wasn't doing much of anything right on the course. All parts of my game—chipping, putting, driving—were violently off. My errant drives were knocking the orange flowers off the beautiful gulmohur trees.

Burnard was getting a little pissy after I kept hitting poor shot after poor shot. He had to go and find my poorly struck ball, and the worse I played the more sour his attitude became. What is it with these critical male caddies in India? He started giving me unsolicited pointers on how to be better, which was exactly what I didn't want to hear. For the second time in India, I didn't like my caddie and I wished he would just go away so I could hit some balls, work on my game and just enjoy the scenery. I needed a bit of practice, not Burnard's condescending sneer.

On the next to last hole, he gave me a driver and said that the tee was fifty yards back and he'd wait for me behind a hedge out of view. Sounded good to me; caddies often try to shorten their walk. Plus, I was glad to have any moments away from his scowl.

As I walked back to the tee alone, I thought about the warning of theft I'd gotten from the caddie master. Of course, I had forgotten to follow his advice and my cash was in my golf bag in a black pouch that stores tees and ball markers. Not being able to see Burnard had me worried. I hit another distracted drive and started quickly walking to the hedge where Burnard, my golf bag, and my money were out of view. I reached him and said I needed to get something out of my bag—I wanted to see if all my money was still there.

I opened the pouch and could immediately tell he had been snooping. The money was all messed up, which wasn't in tune with my neatnik style of crisply folded bills. I have never been a member of the "crumpled money club." Burnard wore a sheepish look on his face. I didn't accuse him of anything, but was fairly sure he had grabbed a few bills. When we finished the round, I tersely tipped him the amount the caddie master had said—three hundred rupees. I just wanted him out of my sight.

Incredibly, he was dumbfounded at the tip. "Three hundred rupees! But you're an American!" he complained.

I replied, "I may be an American, but I'm not stupid!" I was about to accuse him of stealing, but thought better of it, as I'm sure he needed the job and a stink raised with a guest complaint wouldn't be good for his livelihood. Plus, I had been forewarned, so I was partly to blame. So that only he could hear it, I told him to scram or I'd tell the caddie master he was a thief. He got the message and scampered away quickly.

After a few days in Bangalore, walking the city, going to the movies, and enjoying the absence of livestock on the sidewalks, I flew to Mumbai (formerly Bombay) for my final stop in India. When purchasing the ticket in Bangalore for Mumbai, I also purchased another airplane ticket from Mumbai to Johannesburg, leaving in a week—it was the earliest I could get a direct flight to South Africa. I wanted to see Mumbai, but I was more than ready to cross India off my itinerary: *been there, done that, lost part of intestines.*

Upon my arrival in Mumbai, it didn't take long to see that India's premier port city has all the problems of India's other major cities, only more so. Mumbai is the quagmire of India in a nutshell. Similar in size to the limited space of Manhattan, Mumbai's twelve million citizens live on land built on a series of islands and surrounded by the Indian Ocean. Because of the natural water boundaries, Mumbai doesn't suffer from urban sprawl; Mumbai is an implosion. With nowhere else to go, life has moved to the only open bits of land—the streets. It has more of everything: more wealth, more poverty, more beggars, more people living on the streets, and more people trying to fleece you and your money. As a tourist you are never left alone, and when I say *never*, I'm not kidding. In fifteen minutes of walking you'll be hit on hundreds of times. If you were new to the game, you might find it charming. But I had been through the wringer and knew the score.

To walk down most any block in Mumbai is to pass the truly huddled masses: cooking, washing, sleeping, selling goods, and simply trying to survive in this hot, muggy, urban jungle. I often felt like I was invading people's privacy just by walking down the sidewalk; in essence, I was, because the street is the only home to thousands and thousands of people there. Combine this with the Indian inability to avoid walking into each other, throw in a few million cars, trucks, cows (of course), and taxis all honking their horns at the same time, and like a two-year-old with an open can of Hershey's chocolate syrup, you've got chaos on your hands.

It's bedlam! I tried to change my ticket to Johannesburg and escape earlier, but it seems everyone else was just as eager to flee as I was and had beat me to the punch. My ticket couldn't be changed without me having to eat nine hundred dollars, but I would be lying if I said I didn't seriously consider it. I pondered calling the airline: *I know I can't get to Johannesburg until next week. How about something to Afghanistan? I hear there is golf in Kabul.*

I ended up playing golf a couple of times in Mumbai at a ragtag course called the Wellington Golf Club. The course was dreadful; its only charm stemmed from the fact that it was in India, and you know my opinions on the charms of that land. The course wasn't memorable in any way that I can recall other than that both of my caddies on separate days were barefoot and walked over rocks and sharp twigs like it was shag carpet. The only other aspect of the course I will recount here is that the course had multiple workers tending the grounds on nearly every hole, and yet the grounds looked disheveled and ill-cared-for. Rather than cleaning the place up, they seemed to making more of a mess. It was puzzling.

To be accurate, I should say that I *tried* to play golf at Wellington: in the fantastic heat, I was sweating so much I couldn't swing the club without it flying loose from my sweaty mitts. I was wearing a golf glove, but it quickly became useless, immediately as wet as if I had held it under a running tap. Every shot was a race to see which would go farther, the flying club or the ball. It was supposedly just the start of the hot months in India, but I couldn't fathom it getting any hotter than it was. We're talking the kind of heat that even lizards say, "I am not going out in that!"

India was, in the end, more of an endurance test then anything else. Even leaving was difficult, as my flight left Mumbai at three in morning. I took my last harrowing car ride in India as my taxi raced through Mumbai's streets, still thronging at midnight. The cab had no working headlights, of course, which certainly wasn't the best situation as driving there is like dodgeball with automobiles. India had hardened me up. I just took the no-headlights situation on a dark road with thousands of other cars speeding around us in stride. Nothing could shock me in India—or, seemingly, anywhere—anymore.

Against all odds, the stealth taxi made it to the airport accident-free, and I slipped at last out of India under the cover of darkness.

18

Durban Country Club
Durban, South Africa

29.53°S–30.53°E

A monkey, sitting in a tree, is eating a just-cooked grilled cheese and tomato sandwich on toasted whole wheat. This statement is:

A. The first thought in Dr. Timothy Leary's head after he dropped LSD for the first time.

B. The setup of the last joke comedian Buddy Hackett ever told in a Las Vegas showroom.

C. An actual incident witnessed by yours truly.

The correct answer is C. I had just finished playing the front nine at the ebullient Wild Coast Golf Club, located just south of Port Edward in the province of KwaZulu-Natal on South Africa's gorgeous eastern coast. Wild Coast, a dramatic Robert Trent Jones, Jr.–designed golf course, resides on a bluff overlooking natural sand dunes tumbling down to the warm, intensely blue Indian Ocean. *Wild Coast* is the perfect name for the layout with its untamed, wheat-colored grasses paralleling the rippling bumps and hollows of the fairways. The holes meander up and around the craggy ocean-side slopes, and then crisscross a deep gorge of the Umtamvuna River. Wild Coast is one fantastic site on which to play the old game.

Playing decently, I had shot a thirty-eight (hallelujah!) on the front-nine, and was celebrating with that delicious toasted sandwich to fuel my hopeful to-be-continued assault on the back-nine. The landscape there was so breathtaking, and I was so enthralled by my good play, I had anxiously looked forward to seeing what the final nine holes would bring. Visions of a score in middle-seventies danced in my head.

In the two seconds it took me to put my sandwich down and put my wallet back into my golf bag, the aforementioned monkey swung down from his perch, nabbed my lunch, and was now back up on his limb removing the aluminum foil that had kept it warm. Before I could say, "Hey, you furry simian bugger!" the monkey crumpled the foil into a ball and casually tossed it down onto my astonished head. To add further insult to injury, the monkey then gave me a cheese-stained grin that suggested having opposable thumbs wasn't all it's cracked up to be. That theft by monkey became an omen for my bad play on the back-nine as I lost five golf balls to the wilds of Wild Coast. I quit keeping score to assuage my pride.

As much as I disliked India, I loved South Africa. Well, not quite the same love I reserve for my family, highlight films of Pistol Pete Maravich, tap-in birdie putts, sushi, the Old Course, and the arrival of the new Victoria's Secret catalogue, but nonetheless, an immediate and fairly considerable fondness. I left India at three in the morning in the sweltering early summer heat (even at that hour!), and with the time-zone change, I arrived eight hours later at seven in the morning in the balmy, sun-drenched autumn of South Africa.

It seemed like wondrous time travel, almost too good to be true. I had left the very definition of chaos, and arrived in what appeared to be pristine civic order. People were driving on the correct side of the road, traffic laws were obeyed, and cars actually stopped for pedestrians. Cows were grazing in fenced-in pastures rather than sashaying down the middle of the boulevards. I had already been there for thirty minutes and no one had bumped into me or asked me to buy some useless piece of crap for "only ten rupees!" My first financial transaction—a newspaper bought at the Johannesburg airport—had resulted in correct change being given to me, no questions asked. Things were looking up.

Though things are on the upswing in South Africa, I want to be careful not to paint too rosy a picture. The initial joy of my first glance at South Africa reflected my happiness to be out of India. The seamy underbelly of South Africa becomes apparent upon closer inspection.

The effects of apartheid are glaring. The shantytowns, with scores of impoverished inhabitants jammed together outside Johannesburg and Cape Town, were among the worst living conditions I had seen on the trip, worse even than India and rural China. The shantytowns struck me as more dire because the inhabitants seemed forced to live there, as the spoils of good, South African real estate were long since picked clean. The residents are boxed in. It was mile after mile of poverty of the worst order. Whole families were living in pens unfit for animals as the shantytowns were comprised of the barest of homes. Actually, *homes* seemed far too fancy a word for the cardboard shacks and lean-tos, no running water or sewage and dirt floor beneath the feet. In an industrially modern country blessed with the economic riches of diamonds, a plethora of valuable minerals, and soil as fertile as Iowa, half the people still have no access to clean water. This is after ten years of *improvements*, which gives you a clue how bad things were during the heyday of apartheid.

The unemployment rate still hovers near 50 percent and crime is prevalent—mostly due to hunger. Desperate people do desperate things. Most every South African you chat with has chilling tales of grisly robberies at knifepoint or being robbed as they were forced to look at the business end of a gun. Carjacking is as common as jaywalking. Homes and places of business are all heavily gated and watched by rifle-toting guards. You have to enter through manned gates in Johannesburg just to buy a carton of milk in a convenience store. AIDS is a wildfire burning out of control as people are dying so fast from that deadly disease that cemeteries are recycling burial plots and putting several caskets into one burial hole. All of this hardship was crystallized for me in a conversation with my caddie, John, while playing golf on the excellent layout of the Durban Country Club.

Durban, the capital of KwaZulu-Natal, sprawls along the shore of the Indian Ocean. The thriving city is South Africa's busiest port and boasts of having summery weather all year round. The weather had been, indeed, perfect for golf, with the sky sparklingly clear and a light, salty breeze blowing in off the nearby sea. I was playing golf at the Durban Country Club with the club's genial general manager, John Terry-Lloyd, and his happy-go-lucky brother, Michael, who now lives in San Diego. Michael was back in the town of his birth for the marriage of John's daughter. They are both affable chaps—I was grateful they included me in their golfing party as I was getting a touch lonely again after so many months away from home and so many days of losing myself in the crowd in Southeast Asia and the Indian subcontinent. Their brotherly joy of being in each other's company after a long absence was a kinship I missed from my family and friends back home. Like a double bogey at the end of an otherwise sound round of golf, loneliness rears its ugly head when you least expect it.

In addition to the much-appreciated company, playing the Durban Country Club was a sheer golfing privilege. South Africa is blessed with dozens and dozens of fine golf courses, and Durban is right up at the top of the list. No other golf club has hosted the prestigious South African Open (the second oldest "Open" championship in golf) more than Durban—a record fourteen times. Bobby Locke, Bob Charles, Gary Player, and Ernie Els have all won South African Opens played at Durban. Great players tend to win on great courses. To my eye, the Durban Country Club is as fine a course as any in the world. The course has been named as the second best in the Southern Hemisphere, behind Royal Melbourne. It's a joy to play!

Just a few hundred yards or so inland from the Indian Ocean, the course is a narrow strip of links-land with huge, grassed-over dunes and thriving tropical flora giving way to one excellent golf hole after another. Many of the putting greens are similar to the mounded tabletop surfaces of the fabled Dornoch Golf Club in the north of Scotland. The epitome of this design, at Durban, is the domed par-three twelfth green: its steeply raised putting surface is as treacherous a place to land a golf ball as you'll find anywhere. The green slopes sharply down on all sides, mocking you to try and land your golf ball onto a target seemingly no bigger than the hood of a car parked 175 yards away. The hole is known as the "Prince of Wales" hole because the hacking prince, during a royal visit to Durban in 1924, needed seventeen strokes to negotiate the mounded green as he ping-ponged his ball back and forth across the steep banks. Being born into a royal family might give you a birthright, but it doesn't automatically give you a sound short game.

Though every hole is, at least, good, one alone puts the course into the stratosphere of the world's elite courses—the 500-yard par-five third. The stout par-five has been called the greatest third hole in the game of golf. Playing from a high tee to a narrow fairway with dense, bush-covered dunes flanking the contours, a sinister-looking bunker on the left-hand side of the fairway demands that you hit your ball nowhere near it—if you are to have a chance at par on the hole. The fairway pitches every which way, but levelly, and your ball bounces around like a pinball headed to the gutter. Concentration and perfectly executed shots are required at every turn as you negotiate the grassy slopes and sharp-faced bunkers, continually lurking on all sides and all too happy to swallow up your ball. Your work is only half done when you reach the skewed, tricky green, which seems determined to reveal the flaws in your jittery putting stroke as your ball scampers away from the hole if you borrow too much break. Dreams of a par quickly turn to bogey, or, usually, worse. It's as demanding as a golf hole can be, revealing your deficiencies as efficiently as a doctor with a medical chart. The Durban Country Club isn't for beginners—you need to lace your golf shoes up tight and have a pretty good clue as to what you're doing with that little white ball and those long, sticklike things in your backpack before attempting to play there.

Let me get back to my caddie. John was a cheerful, thirty-four-year-old, black South African who caddies there at the club and is happy just to have a job. He had worked in a warehouse as a loader over the years, but was laid off. He landed the caddying job and said he would rather be working outside in the sunshine anyway. John said he was the only one of his buddies who could find work. "We all want to work and earn money, but there aren't many jobs for people like us." He seemed far more capable than a job as a caddie required. Like many black South African people I met, John had an appealing air of playfulness and was quick to laugh and find humor. His life seemed anything but easy—I doubt I would have had his good cheer had we switched lives. As we chatted about life in Durban in the benign sunlight, I said something his reply to which absolutely floored me.

"I'm heading for the ripe old age of forty-eight," I said, after asking John his age and mentioning to him that my own birthday was coming up in June. This birthday had been on my mind as I wondered which country I would celebrate it in. "Doesn't that sound old?" I asked John, laughing incredulously.

John's stark reply was, "Most people like me don't live that long. None of my friends or family have ever lived that long." He said this plainly—I knew he spoke the truth. That harsh realism was heartbreaking. His statement stayed with me as I thought about all that South Africans have been through. Despite all this, it is still hard not to feel the current of hope that was flowing through the crisp autumn air. People there, like John, are trying to move forward. Trampled down for too long, the people of South

Africa have some catching up to do. John said it best: "At least, now, we have hope."

Golfwise, South Africa is blessed not only with great courses, but great golfers as well. South Africa's golf history is full of golfing legends: Bobby Locke (known as the greatest putter of all time), the physically gifted Ernie Els who's nipping at Tiger's heels, and the amazing Gary Player. Player is one of only five golfers ever to have won the "Grand Slam of Golf" by capturing each of the game of golf's four major titles. Even more impressive to me, Player is also regarded as the "most traveled athlete in history," with over eleven million miles flown as he globe-trots from country to country and tournament to tournament.

South Africa was one fantastic course after another and no matter where I played, someone always told me that a certain hole on whatever course I happened to be on was in "Gary Player's top eighteen holes of South Africa." Now, there are only supposed to be eighteen holes recommended by Mr. Player in his lofty group, but I personally played at least thirty holes said to be in the chosen eighteen! It made me laugh every time someone would start telling me, "I'll bet you didn't know that this very par four you're currently playing is in Gary Player's 'top eighteen holes in South Africa!'" Mr. Player does get out and about.

After my disappointing train journey with the squabbling Singh family in India, I was still aching to take a train ride with my own sleeping compartment. After a week in Jo'berg, I booked a train to Cape Town. I could finally relax and see the countryside from my comfortable seat—the perfect way to wander. The daily Trans-Karoo links Johannesburg with Cape Town. The rail journey is an overnighter covering the eight hundred miles between the country's two major cities. The railway bisects the heart of South Africa into east and west halves, going right down the spine.

I had paid extra as a single traveler to secure my own berth on the Trans-Karoo. The train wasn't as fancy as the infamous, upscale Blue Train, which runs the same route but for several hundred dollars more. My train was older but clean, with a dining car and a shower at the end of the first-class car. My own berth was spacious, and the seat folded out into a comfortable, roomy bed. There was a washbasin and a writing desk—perfect for my meager needs.

We pulled out of the station and slowly motored out of the city. It was mile after mile of urban blight: barbed wire–enclosed junk-yards, dilapidated buildings that looked completely ransacked, and run-down homes with barred windows. South Africa has to be the razor-wire capital of the world—there must be hundreds of thousands of miles of it guarding every property line and subdivision in the country. The train gathered steam as the car gently swayed, the sound of our engine echoing back off the nearby buildings.

I stuck my head out my open window like a golden retriever on the passenger seat of a moving car. As we roared under a trestle, we passed two teenaged boys who were down on their haunches along the tracks working intently on a task—it was definitely a posture of someone up to no good. I looked down on them from the vantage of my window and realized they were both loading bullets into handguns. It was an unsettling scene, to say the least. I quickly pulled my head back inside in case they were seeking a quick target for practice. I thought on all the vicious crimes I had read about in the Jo'berg newspapers—usually page after page of ghastly murders. A crime-beat reporter doesn't lack for material around those parts.

Nearing the final outskirts of Jo'berg, we passed bored mo-torists stopped at rail crossings as we thundered past. For some un-healthy reason, I always enjoyed seeing the frustrated faces of the impatient drivers as they waited for us to go by. We train travelers are a superior sort. We have the right of way! We're on a train! Stop for us or else! Had I been in charge of the train whistle, I'd be blowing it constantly at the stalled cars just to rub it in.

My window was open once again as the thought of child gun-men receded and the speeding train moved on past the outskirts of town. I let the warm autumn breeze flood my cabin as I savored the joy of travel by train. I had my books and food and notes to write. Oh, I love it so.

Heading due south, the landscape became barren quickly. The Karoo is a stark, semiarid land hogging the middle of west-central South Africa. The land is relatively flat and deserted and reminded me of a less-hostile version of the Australian outback. After jostling with humans all over India and the scary, secretive tension of Jo'burg—the wide-open spaces of the Karoo were liberating. My peace ended abruptly, however, when the train stopped in Kimberley and a drunken South African couple boarded our car.

It was in the early evening, but I could tell these two had been drinking all day. They reeked of booze and alcohol-soaked perspiration. They were literally stinking drunk and couldn't walk without stumbling. The woman was wearing unflatteringly tight black spandex pants and a glittery blue tube top that kept falling down instead of performing the chore it was designed for. She was the kind of woman you would rather not see revealed.

Upon seeing me in the doorway, she blurted loudly at me, "Where's my seat?"

Taken aback, I replied, "Perhaps you should ask the conductor."

"You show me!" she demanded. I sheepishly looked at her ticket and showed her that her cabin was right next to mine. Oh no!

"Help my boyfriend with our luggage. We'll pay you," she snapped.

Obeying orders isn't high on my list of virtues.

She slurred as she again blurted out, "Help my boyfriend with our luggage!"

"You keep your money, sweetheart," I said as I went in search of the human being that actually found that shrew appealing. Anything seemed better than continuing that conversation.

I thought that I hadn't met someone I disliked that quickly in quite awhile, but then again, I hadn't had the pleasure of meeting her boyfriend yet. He was drunker than she was, which hadn't seemed possible. The front of his tattered, dark-blue T-shirt was wet from . . . slobber, I guess, and he reeked from a hazardous cocktail of too many odors to decipher. There was also a wet blotch down the front of his jeans; I realized, to my slow-blooming horror, that he had pissed his pants as well. His bodily functions seemed to have all gone off on their own accord. He was an olfactory nightmare. As he swayed unsteadily, I wondered if he had more brain cells or teeth—neither of which seemed to enjoy a full complement.

His first words to me were, "Don't just stand there, man! Give me a hand."

I toyed with the idea of letting him try and load all his gear by himself, but the train was only a few minutes from leaving. Deciding to take the high road, I began helping him. Their pile of possessions looked like they were having a yard sale on the station platform. There were eight tattered suitcases held together with twine and several large, black garbage bags full of clothes and shoes and God knows what else. The cord of an electric hair dryer trailed on the ground from one bag full of empty wire hangers. They even had a large, framed velvet picture of a German shepherd that looked as if it had just eaten a couple of children with gusto. The picture was big enough for a living room wall. Why would anyone want a fuzzy picture of a vicious-looking dog?

I couldn't figure out why they had so much stuff. Were they moving by train? I reluctantly started helping the guy load their belongings onboard, but the drunk soon quit and sat down to watch me at work hauling his possessions. That wasn't going to fly with me: I already detested the fact that these two had ruined the peace and quiet of my previously idyllic train ride. I quit and went back to my cabin. *Screw them,* I thought. *Drunken pipsqueaks!* I went back to the low road. Thankfully I never saw them again.

We arrived in Cape Town at two in the next afternoon to more sunshine and sweet breezes. Cape Town is a city that charms immediately. Table Mountain, the imposing city backdrop, defines and dominates Cape Town: its dramatic vertical 1000-meter thrust upward to a wide, flat summit is like a giant anvil made by nature. It looked as if an entire mountain had been to the barber and gotten a crew cut. With it vast size, Table Mountain dominates the surroundings, dwarfing everything under its silent gaze. From the base of that immense anvil, pastel-colored buildings gradually flow downhill all the way to the rebuilt waterfront, bursting with restaurants, malls, and museums to entertain the locals and tourists. Perhaps it's from the steady breeze blowing in from the sea, maybe it's the warm sunshine, but even in the fall, there is an air of freshness to the city—Cape Town is downright alluring. Robben Island, where Nelson Mandela spent much of his incarceration as a political prisoner, lies just offshore. It seems especially harsh to have been locked up in a dreary cell so near to so much natural beauty.

Happily, I settled into pleasant Cape Town life for a week. I rented a modest apartment well within my budget in the nearby beach community of Fish Hoek. The four-room apartment had a full kitchen and a comfy sofa in the living room with a nice television complete with a VCR. Joyfully, I cooked my own meals for the first time in a long time, rented movies from an outlet around the corner, and pretended to be a normal South African for a bit.

The golf around the area was first-rate, to top it off. I first played at a local municipal course called the Metropolitan Golf Club near Cape Town's waterfront. My golf mate was a welcoming local lawyer, John Commins, who would become a good friend of mine and later have me as a guest at his fine home course, called Mowbray. Like me, he had just come out to play a quick afternoon round under the magnificent gaze of Table Mountain. The slowly setting sun was still providing a glow of warmth; the weather was perfect for a casual round of short-sleeve golf before night fell.

After exchanging pleasantries, John and I had both driven straight and well down the first fairway for a couple of good starts. We were both putting the head covers back on our drivers and shouldering our golf bags to begin our pleasant afternoon walk when the starter asked us to wait a moment so another single could join us.

Our third was a brash young Afrikaner named J.P. He was twenty-five and built like an NFL linebacker. His hair was cut militarily short, and upon first glance he looked a bit intense as his eyes had an immediate, piercing quality. With his bulging muscles stretching his Polo shirt to the brink, he blasted his drive down the first fairway with an incredibly fast swing. It was a vicious clash of balata and metal, with the metal the overwhelming victor. It was the fastest, most violent, golf swing I had ever seen in my life. Though fast, his swing was impeccably well-timed and the ball became a tiny pill off in the horizon as it looked like it would soar all the way to Table Mountain. As he watched his ball sky-rocket off into the distance, he turned to John and me and his first words to us, two complete strangers, were, "I hit the ball farther than Tiger Woods!"

Nice to meet you too, I thought.

J.P. didn't lack for confidence, continually talking and boasting about his golfing prowess and how far he could hit a golf ball. I'll admit: it was truly amazing how far he could pound that golf ball! He was also exceedingly rude. When John hit his first putt well short of the hole on the first green, J.P. said mockingly, "Where's your tampon, old man?"

Shocked at his crudeness and braggadocio, I decided then and there to beat the guy in that round of golf. Sure, he could hit the ball a long way with his steroidal strength, but he wasn't quite as adept around the greens where real finesse was required. It was all about distance to this simian interloper. His overly cocky attitude made me feel competitive and fired up—I wanted to kick his ass, well, golfwise. With my mission foremost in my mind, I started matching his scores on the next few holes, and then slowly began pulling ahead. On our tee-shots, he was outdriving me by fifty yards or more, but I continually outplayed him near the greens as my chips and putts became crisp and well-executed. My focus was laser-sharp in my intent to prevail against this buffed-up braggart. You would have thought I was in the lead in the final round of the U.S. Open—I was that intent on my goal to beat this goon.

I outplayed him hole after hole. It killed him as I repeatedly kept the honor on the tee-box. I could feel his impatience as I took my time teeing up my ball, and then taking repeated practice swings just to make him stew a bit more. Frustrated, he tried to hit before me off the fifteenth tee, but I stopped him as I said, stepping up, "I believe I'm up first, J.P., my par beats your untidy bogey, I'm afraid." *Game, set, and match.* He didn't care for my little dig, but John and I had a big laugh about my cheekiness over a drink later in the clubhouse.

After my victory, it was golf, golf, and more golf for me in the warm sunshine of South Africa as I played daily. I played with John at the excellent Mowbray Golf Club in a weekly tournament, enjoying its chummy camaraderie in the high-ceilinged clubhouse after the round. I played a wonderful course called Clovelly near my rented pad in Fish Hoek, which would become one of my favorite courses I played on the trip. Clovelly sits in a narrow valley near the bay of Fish Hoek and possesses wonderful, rolling, sandy turf that was ideal for golf. The property featured gnarled, twisted pines, growing almost horizontally from the years of harsh wind off the cape, which added a hint of Scotland to the grounds. The natural course was well designed, with constant surprises on where the greens were nestled into the sandy hills. It was a joy to play. The welcoming atmosphere in and around the clubhouse was nicer still—this was a club I would love to join if I ever lived in the area. When I learned that Clovelly was the thirty-ninth ranked course in South Africa, I though to myself that if there are thirty-eight golf courses in South Africa better than this glorious little gem, you're really in a land of great golf!

The general manager at Clovelly, a welcoming, charming gentleman named Jeremy Lindquist, took a liking to my goofy adventure and called other golf-course general mangers in the region and set up games for me. He suggested I travel along the Garden Route—the spectacular southern coast area—to the town of George and play the George Golf Club as well as the prestigious Fancourt Links where the inaugural 2003 Presidents Cup was held as Tiger Woods and Ernie Els played a gritty back-and-forth match against each other that will live throughout the ages.

I wisely followed his sage advice. I played golf up and down the

Garden Route to my heart's content. South Africa has more than enough outstanding golf courses to keep an addict like me happy for decades.

One final goal remained for South Africa. After all that golf, I wanted to see the end of the African continent and the Cape of Good Hope. The Cape was an hour's drive south from Fish Hoek. The drive was scenic, transversing the side of the hilly terrain leading down to the very tip of Africa. The seascapes kept getting grander and grander the farther south I went. I knew I was headed somewhere special on the globe. It was like the gradual building of a Beethoven symphony toward a crescendo—there had to be a dramatic clash of cymbals at end of the road.

As I drove into the national park of the Cape, a family of baboons was holding court on the roadside to the delight of park visitors. One bold baboon had climbed onto the roof of one of the cars and the family inside didn't know whether to be thrilled or frightened as the baboon just sat on top and scratched his head. I drove down through the dunes to the end of the road, and walked the final mile out to the land's end and found myself alone at the Cape of Good Hope.

Standing high on a bluff looking out over the turbulent point where the warm Indian Ocean and the cool Atlantic meet and become one, I stood as far south as a person can possibly go on the dark continent of Africa. My heels were in Africa and my toes inched over the cliff's edge into no-man's-land. With the jagged shoreline echoing from the relentless pounding of the surf below, the Cape of Good Hope was stunning. You had to figure a continent containing the Nile, Victoria Falls, the Sahara Desert, the Zambezi River, and the Congo wouldn't have a bookend that wasn't amazing all by itself.

I looked out over the magnificent cape that Vasco da Gama rounded in 1497. His voyage had opened the first known sea route from Europe to Asia. Out on the edge of Africa, the next point of land straight south was Antarctica. I felt so lucky to be standing there as the blue sea foamed against the jagged cliffs below. There is hopefulness about the great vistas of the world as these citadels of nature's wonder take us outside our daily worries and concerns and fears to something grander—something better. Perhaps, there is a good reason, after all, why we're all down here on this water-logged planet spinning around our local star in this neck of the universe. Taking all the grandeur into my lungs in a great, deep breath, I smiled to myself, turned around, and started heading north to Tromsö and the world's northernmost golf course.

19

Elephant Hills Golf Course Victoria Falls, Zimbabwe

17.82°S–31.05°E

"Pleasure!"

Whenever I replied, "Thank you!" for whatever nicety a Zimbabwean seemed to be continually doing for me—with a shy, but genuine smile—they always said, "Pleasure!" Their whole face lights up as this melodious word flows like beautiful music out of their mouths and into the hard and desperate spaces the average person there lives in. When speaking English, Zimbabweans pronounce each vowel fully, and when combined with their high, singsong voices, heartfelt words like *pleasure* come out as sweetly as a Yo-Yo Ma solo.

Zimbabwe is a country coming apart at the seams economically, and yet, even faced by the cruelest hardships, those folks were among the kindest, nicest, and most ready to laugh and find humor in what others say as any people I have ever met. They are bright, educated (the country has a 91 percent literacy rate), funny, and there is absolutely no work for them in that country in all its self-destructive turmoil.

During my visit, Zimbabwe was going through yet another myriad of troubles. The economy had almost completely collapsed. One U.S. dollar on the black market could fetch as much as nine thousand Zimbabwe dollars. You would need a duffel bag just to carry the cash needed to buy a loaf of bread—if you could even find one. In a ramshackle grocery store in Victoria Falls with bare dusty shelves holding only a few scattered canned goods, I saw Zimbabwean currency on plain white typing paper—it looked to have been printed that very morning. The back of the currency was completely blank. It didn't make for confident transactions.

Basically, the Zim dollar was as worthless as an eight-track tape. Zimbabwe's trading partners won't accept it for payment. Because of this situation, deadbeat Zimbabwe can't import much-needed goods like fertilizer to grow crops or fuel for tractors. Parts for broken-down equipment are another matter entirely, as most machinery sits idle and rusting in the fields. In a country that needs a scant fifty thousand tractors to tend the land and feed its people, it is reported that as few as five hundred actually function. Most governments won't deal with Zimbabwe without full payment up-front. Besides no fuel for machinery, there is almost no petrol available for the ordinary citizens—who couldn't afford to own a car anyway. Unemployment is as high as 80 percent, and the people are hungry—for both a chance to work as well as having food to eat. It's a heartbreaking situation.

I had been repeatedly warned not to go to beautiful but distressed Zimbabwe. Most of the fifty or so South Africans I had asked about visiting there had said the people were lovely, but it was too dangerous. But, then again, I had been told that very thing about visiting their country as well as Nepal and Bolivia. Once I was in these troubled lands, I never felt as if I shouldn't have visited—well, I didn't regret visiting, anyway; and was always glad to have made the effort despite the warnings. The U.S. State Department had a two-page traveler alert on its Web site about the perils that await its citizens abroad the minute they land at any airport within Zimbabwe's borders. The warning strictly said not to visit any farms in Zimbabwe, which are considered ground zero for violence as black Africans reclaim white-owned land through force. My goal was to see the country's natural wonders and play a bit of golf. It seemed well worth the risk.

At the threadbare Victoria Falls airport, I was met by a representative from the hotel I had booked—the Elephant Hills Intercontinental. I had been unable to call into Zimbabwe from South Africa to make my own reservations, as the national telephone system, like everything else, only works sporadically. Through a travel agency in Cape Town, I had booked a weekend at Elephant Hills so I could see the Zambezi River, Victoria Falls, and, of course, play golf. I had also booked a four-night safari in the Hwanga National Park—a game reserve said to have the "big five": lions, elephants, leopards, rhinos, and water buffalo.

Sam, my jovial driver from the airport, had two buddies of his in tow for the day—Shamiso and Edmore. We loaded my golf bag into the huge trunk of their old red Chevrolet sedan and drove through the warm, sweet air of eastern Zimbabwe. All the car windows were completely open and the breeze blowing in from over the bushland washed away any apprehensions I had had about traveling there. It was a feeling of being well away from the world at large. Nobody I knew had a clue where I was. I found that thought liberating and thrilling. It was just me off in the world with my golf clubs. Best of all, I was in Africa!

I was immediately struck by how polite these young men were: they kept calling me "sir" and graciously laughed at my travel tales. I liked these guys right off the bat as they included me in their easy camaraderie and banter.

We discussed the current political climate and their thoughts of Robert Mugabe as we drove down the empty, tree-lined highway into the small village of Victoria Falls. Shamiso sighed wearily and said, "Mr. David, we all wish he would just leave."

Mugabe has become the pariah of Africa as well as the rest of the world as the resettlement of the long-owned "white farms" into black hands has brought violence and chaos and, worse still, no crops. The farms were often taken over by people who had no clue how to farm and the government couldn't supply them with the necessary tools or the know-how. In 1988, half of the white-owned farms were decreed to be turned over to black hands with no compensation and little notice. The resulting violence and chaos has led to severe food shortages within Zimbabwe.

All of these factors had me more than apprehensive about visiting, as I knew the tension in Zimbabwe could be far greater than even Johannesburg or Kathmandu. However, there was no way I was going to be in Africa and not see Victoria Falls or the Zambezi River. More importantly, the renowned Gary Player–designed course at Elephant Hills was only a couple of miles from Victoria Falls. I badly wanted to play golf there—it was what my trip was all about: unusual golf in unusual locales. Plus, I wanted to see more of Africa. The continent gets into your bloodstream quickly as you marvel at the splendor of the land and beauty of the people. As a fellow travel-lover in Cape Town told me happily, "When you're in Zimbabwe, you're in the real Africa!"

On another plus side (I must note), due to its colonial past, the white population introduced the sports of Great Britain to Zimbabwe as they had done throughout the British Empire.

Once introduced, golf grew like wildfire on Zimbabwe's fertile, scenic land and along with New Zealand, the two countries have the most courses per capita in the world. The country itself has produced world-class athletes in rugby, cricket, soccer, and golf. Golfing superstar and three-time major winner Nick Price learned the game on Zimbabwe's courses. Unfortunately, unlike tourists—who now avoid the country like the plague—the average Zimbabwean doesn't have the money to play the game. A full belly is more important than chasing a little white ball.

As we rode down the back dirt road leading into the compound of Elephant Hills, I asked my three escorts if they played golf and they all said no; but they did play a weekly pickup soccer game in a field alongside the first fairway of the golf course. As we neared the property I could see that the Elephant Hills Intercontinental, situated on a small hill about a half-mile from the Zambezi River, was by far the grandest structure around. From that higher vantage point, the sprouting water gusts of Victoria Falls could be seen billowing into the powder-blue African sky like smoke signals. The falls are a mile or so away from the hotel, but I could still hear the faint roar of the water. The steamy clouds spiraling up from the distance created an atmosphere of anticipation: Victoria Falls was going to be something special to witness. I could hardly wait.

The Elephant Hills Intercontinental Hotel would be luxurious in any country on earth. We drove past the guarded gate and into the peaceful, shady grounds. Large, thick-trunked baobab trees grandly filled the quiet courtyard as we parked at the hotel's entrance. Though immaculately clean and cared for, the upscale hotel was as empty as a ghost town. I had never seen a major hotel with this little activity. The hotel contains three restaurants, five bars, a casino, two squash courts, a volleyball court, a bowling green, a sauna, two outdoor swimming pools, two floodlit tennis courts, and eighteen holes of golf. There are 276 elegantly appointed suites with two telephones per room, satellite television, room service, and complimentary robes and slippers. It was lavish and comfortable and excessively elegant and had exactly one guest. Me.

There were hotel employees everywhere: front desk clerks, waiters, bellmen, bartenders, cooks, caddies, courtesy van drivers, and maintenance crew members. Everyone seemed to have tasks to do, but I think it was more wishful thinking as I was literally the only source of revenue for miles. These employees were the lucky locals—the ones with jobs, but I wondered how anyone could survive there with no money coming in. The truth is—they don't.

I arranged to play golf in the pro shop near the hotel lobby, where I met Bekithemba Nyoni—a thirty-two-year-old Zimbabwean who runs the golf there. As I entered the shop, he sprang up from his seat, surprised to actually have a customer.

"Hello, sir! Do you wish to play golf?" he asked.

"I do," I replied.

"Very good, sir, I think you'll love our course! We're so happy you're here!" he exclaimed brightly. His good cheer and happiness to see me made me feel glad to have made the effort to visit. Zimbabweans would be the most welcoming people I encountered in my entire worldwide journey.

Bekithemba Nyoni became my buddy during my stay. We chatted several times a day about golf around the world and the current political climate in his country. He was well-educated and willing to talk about anything I threw at him. I told him how nice I found the hotel and how strange it was to be the only guest. He was thirty-two and had been at the club for the past ten years. "We used to be so busy; we barely had time to sleep. It was wonderful! But, not anymore," he said, shaking his head sadly.

He continued on, "We just need visitors like you. We sit around with nothing to do and it looks like we're lazy, but we're not. We love to help people. We just need more visitors."

I asked him about Mugabe. He lost his cheerfulness for a second with a blunt, gruff reply. "We're tired of this man. We pray to God for him to go."

I told him about my golfing trip around the world and asked him if he played.

"No, sir, not anymore. I would love to, but I can't afford golf clubs."

Though I was more than willing to pay to play golf, Bekithemba wouldn't hear of it. "Please, be my guest," he insisted. "Just write about us so people will visit," was all he'd add.

I promised I would. I got my clubs and headed out to the course.

Elephant Hills is one of the most unique golfing spots in the world—it is truly carved right out of the living jungle. The land, near the nourishing Zambezi River, is intensely flourishing there in Victoria Falls. Most every fairway is bordered by thick patches of dense, willowy trees and jungle bush. If you hit your ball into that jungle, don't go strolling in willy-nilly, or you could become something's lunch.

When designed by Player, the course was first built to the ungodly length of 8500 yards. That course was one of the longest and most difficult in the world. Even with today's space-age technology that allows even duffers to hit two-hundred-and-fifty-yard drives, 8500 yards of golf seems insane. Elephant Hills suffered rocket damage during the liberation wars of the 1980s, and the hotel was destroyed. The golfing grounds suffered damage as well. The hotel was rebuilt and the course was redesigned to a more manageable 6800 yards.

The great thing about golfing at Elephant Hills is the strange conversations that pop up golfing in the wilds. "Sir, aim between the bunker on the left and that pack of grazing warthogs," instructed Evans, my caddie, for my drive on the par-four first hole. By the way, one of the local rules states that warthog damage to the turf may be treated as "ground under repair"—you get a free drop if you end up in an area where they've been rooting around with their tusks. With several packs of warthogs on most every hole, there is plenty of opportunity to take advantage of that local rule—not that I ever relied on it! However, Evans told me if my ball landed in one of the thousands of hoofprints, or near one of the hundreds of giant termite mounds, my ball should be played as it lay with no relief. Jungle golf!

Bekithemba had said Evans was the best caddie at Elephant Hills. At around six feet tall and as skinny as a man can be, his tattered clothes hung from his bones like overalls on a scarecrow. I could tell he rarely had enough to eat. His eyes were bloodshot from illness of some kind. I didn't have the heart to ask him what his ailment was. He was glad to have a job for the day. I told him I was the lucky one to have him as a caddie. He beamed a full-wattage smile and said, right on cue, "Pleasure!" I asked him how often he works as a caddie at the club.

"We have fifty-five caddies here, sir. I work once every two weeks if I'm fortunate. We take turns."

Evans was educated and well-spoken, but I could tell his spirit was near breaking. Though cheerful and friendly, there was an air of sadness about him that broke my heart. Evans seemed the epitome of the lack of hope for the future of Zimbabwe. He laughed easily at my lame jokes and stories. His natural demeanor was kind, and he was very quick and bright. He erupted with glee when I hit a rare good shot or sank a putt. He'd pat my back and say, "Well done, sir!" No matter how hard I tried, I couldn't get those polite people to not call me "sir."

We discussed the terrible inflation that is rampant in Zimbabwe. Evans said that this had been the case for the past four years as things have gone from bad to worse. He said that if he lived in South Africa, for two hundred rand he could feed his family for thirty days, but in Zimbabwe two hundred rand buys food for only five days. "It's discouraging," he said. He continued on, "All we want here is a chance to feed our families." His pride was damaged since he couldn't care for his family as well as he would like. He said that he had a wife and a small baby who had been named "Precious," after an English missionary who had employed his mother when he was a boy. He told me his family eats once a day, if at all.

Evans was interesting company. He said that most Africans were named after animals and his surname of Tshuma means *bat*. As a stupid joke, I told him my surname of Wood meant *tree* and he thought that was the funniest thing he had ever heard. Zimbabweans are an easy crowd. He told me his favorite food was meat and rice, but usually meat is rare to find. Over the years, Evans said he'd eaten elephant, waterbuck, and warthog. His favorite of the three was warthog. He said that he goes to neighboring Botswana once a month to buy food for his family, but they won't accept Zimbabwean money. It's a terrible cycle.

Evans was indeed an excellent caddie, though far overqualified for the job of toting my small bag. On the ninth hole, his instruction for my drive was similar to that of the first hole: "Hit it near the large water buffalo." I had to ask, "Which one?" because there was a herd of fifteen hanging out by the 150-meter mark. They were just standing there, chatting about whatever it is that water buffalo chat about in the middle of the day. It's probably something like, "Boy, wasn't that warthog tasty last night! I know I shouldn't eat so much pork, but it *is* the other white meat!"

Elephant Hills teems with wild animals on every hole. Leaping impalas, cheeky monkeys, funny warthogs, graceful waterbucks, ugly mongoose, staring baboons, and god-knows-what-else lurking in the bush, all allowing you to play golf on their home turf. Zimbabwe can't afford the foreign currency to buy fertilizer for its constituents' needs—golf or farming—but not to worry at Elephant Hills: that land has all the nutrients that very regular mammals can provide. Looking down is mandatory if you don't want to step into the "natural hazards" throughout the excellent and fun-to-play course.

Oh, I forgot to mention the crocodiles that lurk in several water holes dispersed throughout the eighteen holes. There are BEWARE OF CROCODILE signs everywhere there, and as long as they leave me alone, I'll beware of them. On the course, I saw several hundred wild animals gallivanting about, but never saw one crocodile. I took that as a good thing.

That brings me to my next point: due to the lack of steadily incoming tourist dollars, the course is a bit run-down, but the novelty of playing amongst all the wildlife made for one of best golfing experiences of my life. It was like playing golf in a zoo with no cages. As I strolled down the flat fairways, I loved seeing the baboons helping their youngsters to scamper across the grounds as we neared. The impalas were delightful as they kicked up their hind legs, springing around like furry pogo sticks. Packs of warthogs knelt on their front legs as if praying to Mecca while eating the grass they had dug up with their sharp tusks near the greens. It was the most unique golf I've ever played in all the unique locales I've seen. It was wonderful.

As we strolled along, I asked Evans about his opinion of President Mugabe as well, and he said, "It's time he goes. Twenty-four years of this man is enough. He's a dictator. Give someone else a chance."

At the end of the eighteen, I gave Evans all the emergency cash that remained in my golf bag as a tip. It was way more than what he expected. He was overjoyed, as was I to see the big smile on his face.

"Thank you!" he said gratefully.

I smiled, and said, "Pleasure." And, it was.

20

Mena House Oberoi Golf Course

Giza, Egypt

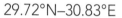

29.72°N–30.83°E

In *Dark Star Safari*, Paul Theroux's wonderful chronicle of an overland trip from Cairo to Cape Town, he states that tourists have made Egypt the destination of their traveling curiosity for over two thousand five hundred years. Ancient visiting Romans and Greeks, when not plundering Egyptian tombs for their riches, used Egypt as the Club Med of their time, coming just to frolic and cavort in the desert heat—away from prying eyes back home. In 48 BC, Julius Caesar romanced the Egyptian queen, Cleopatra, during a two-month tryst down the Nile. In the late 1700s, Napoleon unsuccessfully invaded Egypt in an attempt to steal away the land of the pharaohs from the Ottoman Empire. Mark Twain visited Cairo in 1867, telling of his exhilaration at seeing the Sphinx in his cheerful travel account, *Innocents Abroad*, exclaiming that the ancient wonder ". . . reveals to one something of what he shall feel when he shall stand in the presence of God."

As my taxi ride into Egypt from the airport wound through the quiet, early morning streets of Cairo after yet another dawn arrival

into a new country, I had to admit to being humbly thrilled—
frankly, amazed—to join that lofty club of travelers having visited
the "mother of the world."

The largest city in Africa, as well as the Middle East, one-
thousand-year-old Cairo was a concrete jungle before there was
concrete. The city is brown on brown as the landscape and most
every building is, at least, some tint of that drab hue. In essence,
the entire country of Egypt is one giant sand trap with a lateral
water hazard running right down its middle. Granted, that water
hazard is probably the most famous river in the world—the Nile—
and without its cooling influence and life-nourishing water, Egypt
would be virtually uninhabitable. Cairo's eighteen million residents are crammed as close to the world's longest river as they can
get—and still, the whole place looks like it could use a big, wet
gulp out of a full canteen.

The natives are a surprisingly friendly lot. "Welcome to Cairo!"
was a refrain I heard hundreds of times each day as I walked mile
after mile through the dusty streets, exploring the nooks and crannies of the old neighborhoods. Smiling merchants yelled out to me
as I walked past their shops, "Come have tea and rest from the sun."
As one of the few Westerners I saw my whole time there, I didn't
lack for attention. Several times a day while hoofing around Cairo
and exploring the city, I would acquire an unasked-for guide who
would walk along with me and inquire where I was going and what
I wanted to see. My new acquaintance would stick to me like a fly
to flypaper: I tried to lose them by walking fast or jogging across a
street to escape their spiel. Repeatedly I would tell them I was just
looking around and could manage on my own, but they would
keep up their shtick for block after block, trying to wear me down.

"What can I show you, my friend? Pyramids? Pretty girl? Fine
rugs? Camel ride?" they'd implore.

"I'm good on my own, thank you."

That was a catchphrase I'd repeat over and over, as the hucksters
wouldn't take no for an answer. Finally, I'd have to get a touch angry and tell my unwanted suitor to "beat it!" in a loud, threatening

voice. This ploy always worked immediately, as their resolve instantly crumbled like a house of cards in a gust of wind. Whenever rejected, the Egyptians would react like you'd just shot their dog. They'd sulk away with hurt feelings and sad faces like a jilted lover on the verge of tears. Though I had been charmed by their sensitivity, they didn't realize I wasn't some rube just off a plane from O'Hare. Egypt was the twentieth country on my trip. I had heard every type of sales pitch imaginable in the past ten months. To boot, I was "India certified," which is equivalent to a master's degree in "traveling in lands that want a piece of you and your wallet." A visitor still wet behind the ears with just a couple of passport stamps might have found Cairo overwhelming, with its filthy air, cars spewing exhaust, and the onslaught of humanity out and about; and it is, but this old metropolis was a pussycat compared to the madness and muck of India. After running the gauntlet in Delhi and Mumbai, everywhere else was as easy as miniature golf.

There weren't a lot of infidels, like me, walking the back alleys. I'm sure I looked as goofy as a Westerner could be to them, with my Bermuda shorts, golf visor, and bulging day pack. I spent happy days tramping innocently through the narrow streets and bazaars of old Cairo, some of which date back to the first century AD. I was such a novelty in some of those neighborhoods that little kids would dare a brave member of their gang to sneak up and touch me and then squeal with delight upon acting out that heroic deed. Perhaps it was my giddy mood at being at the crossroads of history, or maybe I was getting a touch bonkers from my long miles logged around the world, but mostly, I found all of this delightful rather than a bother. With Egyptians, there was always a hint of a smile or subtle wink of the eye as they enticed you to enter their shops or share a spot of tea, indicating that they were in on the joke—they knew that you knew they wanted a bit of your money.

Because of the brutal, ravaging desert heat and tight quarters of the narrow streets and alleys, everyone in Cairo is continually out on the sidewalks—chatting, selling fruit, eating, laughing, drinking tea, smoking water pipes, saying their daily prayers. This is a city where you better like your neighbors because you're going to be seeing quite a lot of them on a daily basis. I was continually met by cheerful smiles. After telling a happy-go-lucky fruit peddler that I was from Seattle, his cries followed me down his block, "Welcome, American! I love America! I hear of this place, Seattle! Bill Gates! Welcome to Cairo!"

After a couple of days spent getting familiar with the lay of the land, I finally went to see the sights that everyone goes to see when visiting Cairo. I had been savoring the prospect of seeing the Pyramids and hadn't wanted to just rush out to Giza immediately—I wanted to build up to them. Can you consider yourself a true world traveler without having seen the Pyramids? I don't think so. They have to be the most famous landmarks on earth.

No matter how much anticipation you muster up, they don't disappoint. My first glimpse was from several miles away as I rode in a smoke-spewing, gas-reeking taxi with tires as smooth as ice. The cab was going at least twice as fast as an automobile that ill-kept should be going. I was now well-versed on those harrowing rides. In my travels, I had learned that the more decrepit the vehicle, the faster the driver likes to go. Taxicabs of the world rarely have seat belts for passengers, although the drivers are usually as tightly fastened as John Glenn was in *Friendship* 7. We had driven the twenty minutes from downtown Cairo through the brown, urban sprawl toward the suburb of Giza. The land around Cairo is as flat as Iowa—you can see off into the biscuit-brown desert for miles and miles of nothing but tan, arid land. We had rounded a curve on the highway and presto! The Great Pyramids were suddenly looming grandly in front of me.

They were impressive from several miles away, but as you get closer, the Great Pyramids' dramatic thrust to their pointy tops in the cloudless, high desert sky makes you realize what a monumental undertaking their construction was. Each enormous brick came up past my shoulders. All I could think of was, *How in the hell did they do this?*

If you arrive early in the day, and are one of the first one hundred and fifty visitors, you can go inside the Great Pyramid for an extra 100 Egyptian pounds. I had figured what the heck, I'll take a peek. What they don't tell you is the reason that they only let in one hundred and fifty people, and only in the relative coolness of the morning: because the inside of the Great Pyramid is only slightly cooler than Hell. This is no cakewalk! To get to the main chamber (which turns out to be a small, featureless room with nothing in it), you crawl on all fours for sixty meters up a one-way chute at a 45-degree angle in what has to be the most claustrophobic passageway on earth. I had only crawled for a minute before the intense heat and close quarters started to make me panic. I desperately wanted to turn back and crawl out of this hellhole built for a king, but two factors kicked it.

For starters, there were now three people crawling up the passageway directly behind me, and I didn't want to look like the biggest wimp this side of Chad. Secondly, I am so cheap that I wanted to get my extra one hundred Egyptian pounds' worth even if I had to have a fear-induced heart attack to get it. Dripping with sweat and fright, I finally made it to the chamber. As I realized that all that climbing was for naught as there is next to nothing to see there, I waited for my pulse to slow down to two hundred beats per second. To get back down, you crawl the same way you came up. I wasn't keen on retracing that fear-producing route—especially since on the way back you have to go down butt first and can't see where you're going. I thought about just staying in the chamber for the rest of my life and telling visitors who made the climb that I was King Tut's great-great-great-great-great-great-great-great-great-great-great-great-great-great-great-great-great-great-grandson, but I figured the golf visor and shorts would give me away.

One of the more amazing aspects of seeing the imposing Great Pyramid of Giza and its trusty sidekick, the eerily serene Sphinx—which are no more than a well-hit eight-iron from each other—is a nine-hole golf course situated only a few hundred yards away from the timeless duo. How's that for convenience—the great wonders of the ancient world right next to the world's oldest game! For me, it just doesn't get better than that.

The Mena House Oberoi Golf Course is so close to the Great

Pyramid that it is almost a joke. The towering monument looms ominously over the flat, emerald oasis of fairways and greens. Though the links itself is ordinary at best, I found myself constantly marveling at the 4,500-year-old architectural feat to make sure I wasn't imagining all of this. A golfer is always told to "keep your head down," but that's not the easiest task there, as you find yourself continually peeking up at that miracle of Egyptian engineering in between chips and putts and drives. It has to be one of the more surreal venues for golf in the world.

There weren't any other golfers playing in the blazing midday heat of Cairo. "The sun was getting low" as Egyptians say, in what has to be the ultimate example of understatement, as the intense roast of summer arrives with gusto. There is a good reason why the surrounding land is biscuit-brown and hardened—it has been left too long in the oven through the millenniums. Mena House was, at least, a bit of flora in the surrounding sea of dust and sand. I set off as a single to play with my faithful caddie, Farouk, carrying my bag and talking a mile a minute as he waddled to the first tee with the satisfied gait of a desert penguin.

Farouk was short, squat, and forty-nine years old. He had a belly like Homer Simpson and spoke out of the side of his mouth like Buddy Hackett. For even more comic effect, Farouk had a hint of a Daffy Duck lisp. Had he been an actor, Farouk would have made a wonderful wisecracking neighbor in a sitcom. Perhaps it was the influence of having been inside the Great Pyramid that morning, but I blasted a soaring, long drive down the middle of the first fairway, hit a seven-iron to three feet from the cup, and sank an easy birdie putt. Farouk busted with pride on his golfing man as he said, with spittle flying, "We make a great team, you and me! After watching you swing, I know exactly what club to give you!"

And that's exactly what happened. On every hole, Farouk would hand me a club of his choosing. Before every swing, I would recheck to make sure the magnificent Pyramid was still there, and then hit one great shot after another—it was uncanny. I was a golfer I didn't know! After each beautiful shot, Farouk would remind me out of the corner of his mouth in his cartoonish cadence, "You and me make a great team, no!"

Other golfers hate to hear about the success of another golfer—nothing bores us more—but, nonetheless, here I go: I birdied five of the first six holes—something I had never even come close to doing before in all my years playing this crazy game. Was there truth to the belief in the power of the Pyramids? Was that the golfing secret I'd been searching for the world over? Was I destined to only play great under the silent gaze of an ancient wonder? If so, my choice for courses was going to be severely limited.

On the seventh hole, after gently setting down my golf bag, Farouk said, "Excuse me, sir, but I have to pray."

The beautiful Islamic call to prayers had just boomed its amplified wail out of the local mosque as the imam sang for the local faithful to begin the noon prayer. In Islam, the devoted pray together five times a day, starting at six in the morning and ending at ten in the evening. In Cairo, you might as well set your alarm for six in the morning because that's when you're going to be getting up as the call goes out from the many mosques dotting the city. I always found the daily call to prayers almost hypnotic; the wail travels through the narrow streets like the wafting aroma of freshly baked bread. One of my favorite things to do in Cairo became heading down to the banks of the Nile, which was only a few blocks from my hotel on the small river island of Zamalek, during these beautiful prayer calls and listen as the long, graceful songs from the various mosques of the city drifted out over the north-flowing Nile. The imams have beautiful, rich voices, and their calls converged on the old river as if you were turning up the dial of an ancient radio.

Farouk had laid down a towel he had brought for the occasion and went through the ritual as he bowed toward Mecca. Wanting more birdies, I faced northwest toward St. Andrews and put a prayer in to the Golf Gods for more great holes, but, alas, my plea went unheeded. The Golf Gods rarely take kindly to these earthly requests. Though I didn't birdie any more holes there at Mena

House, I continued to play solidly. Then, a strange thing happened. On the second nine of the day, on the thirteenth hole, Farouk suddenly said, "I have to go home now."

We had gotten along well. I was sure I hadn't offended him in any way. I guess he just needed to get back to his family and he had worked enough for that day. "That's cool, Farouk," I said. I certainly didn't mind carrying my own bag, which is the way I actually prefer to play golf. I gave him a tip for his services. Farouk smiled at the cash and said, "You must come visit my house for dinner and be a guest of my family." He didn't give me any way of reaching him to take him up on his kind offer—he just started his slow saunter back toward the khaki-colored clubhouse. Though the episode was baffling, perhaps it was just the Egyptian way. Grabbing my bag, I completed my round beneath the Pyramids in the setting desert sun.

After getting my golf fix taken care of, I spent a few more days sightseeing, since I wanted to see as much of Cairo that I could. I went to the wonderful Egyptian Museum of History, which houses the greatest collection of Egyptian antiquities in the world. After the museum, I walked several miles through the busy streets of Cairo up to the imposing dome and twin minarets of the Citadel, which looms on one of the few bluffs of Cairo and affords a view of the entire city from above. After a short climb, I looked out over the broad, flat city and realized that a curious fact of Cairo is that almost no building is completely finished being built. In Cairo, the building is either beyond grand and ornate, like the medieval Citadel, or in a state of what looks to be total disrepair. Most every building has girders sticking out of its top as well as raw framing on their unfinished roofs to build higher if need be. The whole city looks to be a one-thousand-year-old work in progress. There were thousands of such unfinished buildings spread across the horizon down to the Nile. Sooner or later, most Egyptians come to live in Cairo, and I guessed those buildings have the option to go higher at the ready as the population swells.

I have to say that I had been enjoying all of this touristy

sightseeing-type stuff immensely. Then, I made a fatal mistake. Walking back to my hotel in Zamalek from the Citadel, I decided to stop in an outdoor restaurant and eat a falafel. Falafels have long been one of my favorite things to eat. I had been passing scores of these wonderful-smelling eateries with their inviting aromas wafting out into the streets. All my walking had me famished and I was anxious to try one out.

Over the months, I had been following the orders of my doctor back in Seattle who had given me my travel shots. He had admonished me to never eat any kind of salad in locales where cleanliness was an issue. I had wisely followed his advice. Though I did get sick in India (it wasn't from any kind of salad); but then, I have yet to meet a visitor to that country who didn't suffer a terrible gastronomical malady. It just comes with the territory once you land in Delhi.

After picking out a restaurant packed with locals, a good sign (so I thought), I sat down and ate my falafel, which was wonderfully delicious. As I bit into the tasty fried chickpeas, I hadn't given a second thought to the small pieces of lettuce tucked inside the warm pita as well. Content and with a full belly, I had paid my bill and started the long, happy walk back to Zamalek. After only a couple of steps, all hell broke loose inside my gut. Something was desperately wrong! I began sweating like a madman. My head started pounding. I thought my insides were going to explode. Immediately knowing that I was in dire trouble and not wanting to pass out on a sidewalk in the middle of downtown Cairo, I quickly hired a cab back to my hotel. As I lay in the backseat to try and stop my world from spinning out of control, I knew that I was going to be at least as ill as I had been in India. Reaching my hotel, I stumbled into the bathroom of my room to splash cold water on my sweating face and looked in the mirror. The decrepit mummified corpse of Tutankhamen I'd seen on display at the Egyptian Museum looked healthier than I did at that moment. Weak, sick, and unable to move without becoming violently dizzy, I couldn't leave my hotel room for the next five days.

I had made plans to play golf at several other courses around Cairo, but I couldn't even hold a glass of water, let alone a golf club. It really wasn't a pretty scenario. I canceled all my plans for golf and tried to restore my health. My hoteliers tried to help me in every way they could, but I couldn't eat or drink anything without it coming up immediately. I was too weak to even get up and go see a doctor. I won't take you through all the gory details, but I was so ill I wondered if I would actually be able to continue north to Tromsö and complete my journey. I toyed with the idea of flying back to Seattle on the next plane out. Who knew a bit of lettuce could be so insidious?

While in Vietnam, a golf professional I'd met from the Vietnam Country Club, Howie Roberts, had called to his old club of Soma Bay on the Red Sea in Hurghada and arranged for me to visit. I had been trading e-mails with the general manager of the resort, Franz Kielnhofer, who had been expecting me. I called him and informed him of my dire physical condition. I also told him that I doubted I would be well enough to visit Soma Bay, as well as my sad thoughts that the remainder of my trip was in danger as well. Franz took control and told me to just get on a plane from Cairo to Hurghada for the one-hour flight. "We'll take care of you here," he said emphatically, and that was the end of that. That's exactly what I did.

If you need to convalesce in the Middle East, I couldn't recommend a better place than the Sheraton at Soma Bay on the azure-blue Red Sea near Hurghada. Only four hours by plane from central Europe, Soma Bay is a playpen for the well-heeled citizens of Germany. The hotel is a high-end, five-star destination resort with grand, giant columns at the entrance as you enter an oasis of luxury. The hotel is a modern take on the architecture of the pharaohs, but those ancient kings didn't reside in anything anywhere near this comfy. Sure, they had gold and riches, but we have air-conditioning and room service—we win hands-down. Plus our pillows are way better than those stone headrests they used to use. There are numerous restaurants and swimming pools with waterfalls and polite employees taking care of your every need—given my awful condition, it all seemed too good to be true. Franz got the hotel doctor to come to my room, where he examined me and gave me enough antibiotics to cure an elephant. The kind Mr. Kielnhofer, the savior of my quest, put me up in a beautiful suite with a view of the Red Sea, which is as grandly blue as the mountain-fed streams and lakes of New Zealand. It was a blue so deep and rich I was surprised all over again every time I gazed out my balcony to the sea. It almost seemed impossible for water to look so beautifully vibrant against that lifeless, desolate, brown land. Other than the emerald-green fairways of the Soma Bay Golf Course, just across the street from my lavish digs, there wasn't a blade of grass, or even a shrub, for as far as the eye could see.

Pretending to be a rich German industrialist, I rested in my comfortable room, ordering room service and watching American programs on the satellite television, and slowly came back to re-join the living. I got caught up on the latest news on CNN. I lay in bed and watched the finals of the French Open from Paris as well as the NBA play-offs. Room service brought me meals and after several days of healing and healthy food I was ready to go play golf along the Red Sea. Though not 100 percent, I was back in golfable action!

The Cascades Course at Soma Bay was designed by that globe-trotting South African Gary Player, and is one of the finest golf courses I have played in the world. Howie Roberts had told me over dinner in Saigon that the course there was his personal favorite in all his travels. It's not hard to see why. Many of the holes are dramatic as they play directly along the shores of the sparkling aqua-blue Red Sea. The water splashes right up to the greens on several holes abutting the vast blue expanse. The combination of the lush green fairways and the hypnotic blue water set against the backdrop of the cloudless, high desert sky makes for a mes-merizing golfing scene.

The course would have been difficult to play without wind, but that's not likely to happen. The wind blows strongly, steadily in-land off the sea and slaps your golf ball around in midair as if it were a Nerf ball. From the back tees, from which I always insist on playing, despite my periodic lapses in skill, the course measured almost 6900 yards. The gusting wind must have added another thousand yards to the total. I spent quality time running down my golf visor, which kept blowing off my noggin and pinwheeling down the fairways with every strong gust. After several days in bed I needed the extra exercise, anyway.

For some unknown reason, my good golf play under the gaze of the Great Pyramids continued. Still a bit woozy and weak from my illness, I nonetheless smacked a big drive down the first fairway and again hit my second shot within a few feet of the flag on the 425-yard first hole and made another birdie. I also birdied the wonderful sixth hole—a short par-four that runs parallel to the Red Sea, which lapped up against a rocky seawall protecting the course. The hole played directly into the industrial-strength headwind that blew in from the Sinai across the sea, but my ball flew straight and true as if it had a mind of its own and wasn't about to let any ineptitude on my part impede its goal of landing near the hole. Golf is a strange game—sometimes, though rarely, the ball just seems to want to behave itself as a welcome change of pace. To play constant, good golf, I guess I'm going to have to move to Egypt, as my handful of rounds there were among the most consistent of my whole trip. However, I don't think my intestines were going to allow me to put that kind of pressure on them on a long-term basis.

My strength improved as the antibiotics waged their war on my intestinal trespassers. Back on my feet, I played the golf course several days in a row and managed to shoot in the low eighties each day, which, for me, was exceptional even without that considerable sea breeze that rivaled windy Scotland and Ireland. Again, my good play had no rhyme or reason, but I was more than willing to take the good, as I have always done with its more frequently occurring counterpoint.

The Cascades Golf Course, a glorious golfing oasis trapped between an ocean of grim desert to the west and the sparkling Red Sea to the east, was a marvelous place to play the crazy game. The fairways were as vibrantly green as the felt on a billiard table. If your ball isn't sitting on the well-tended grass, it's on the brown, hard, lifeless ground. That hardpan soil looked incapable of growing anything other than more dust. So it was all the more shocking to play on turf that green and bright.

The course's grounds superintendent, whom I met after my last round there, gave me a tour of the watering plant and explained in elaborate, technical detail the difficult procedure of growing grass on land this infertile. I had the feeling the excited agronomy expert didn't often get an audience for this particular dissertation. With great gusto, he explained how they desalinate the water in a series of chemical reactions, but I'd be lying if I said I understood a single word that he said as he explained the complicated, scientific process in perfect English. Hey, I was just a guy with ten golf clubs who was happy to be back upright, taking nourishment, and playing the game he loves in that ancient land, that desert land of pharaohs, pyramids, and wanderers, of Egypt.

21

Pannonia Golf and Country Club Budapest, Hungary

47.30°N–19.50°E

One of my goals had been to be trimmer, in better shape, for my upcoming birthday. Birthdays have that nagging way of forcing you to take an inventory of your body against the unrelenting ravages of time as gravity shows you who the real boss is. However, between the germ-infested cuisines of India and the food-rejecting qualities of the microbes in Egypt, I had become slimmer than I had been in twenty years, and was even approaching the magic number: my high school graduation weight. Had I flown directly from Cairo back to Delhi one last time, I think I have could have taken a serious run at getting down to my weight at birth as well. Jenny Craig doesn't hold a candle to the weight-reducing cuisine of India! Nonetheless, I was happy that my faded travel pants were loose and baggy and my stomach didn't look like it propped up just another corn-fed American eating Ho Hos for breakfast. Granted, I had met my objective the hard way, through intestinal maladies so harsh that I had wanted to die, but I will say that if you are having trouble losing those extra pounds, fly to Cairo and eat a falafel from a street café. Make sure you ask for more lettuce. That extra weight will fly off quicker than liposuction.

As my birthday neared, my final travel goal of Tromsö, Norway was also getting more and more within reach as I headed north above the Mediterranean. I could feel myself wanting to pick up the pace and travel faster as I neared the finish tape, like a racehorse wanting to get that midget with a whip off his back so he could lounge in the hay of the paddock. However, I wanted to visit Eastern Europe and see how the bourgeois game of golf had crept into that former Communist territory. Other than Norway, my itinerary was still unplanned after Egypt. I had hoped to try and get into Russia, if I could secure a visa, so I could play at the Moscow Country Club—the first golf course in the former Soviet Union. That seemed too big a scalp for my golfing conquest to pass up. A vague notion of going to Budapest had also been floating around my brain, but that was more for seeing that breeding ground for supermodels in person rather than for golf. I had done a Google search on my laptop from my hotel room in Hurghada (Egypt has free Internet connections for all its citizens as well as visitors) and discovered that Hungary had a handful of golf courses in and around Budapest. I added it to my itinerary. From there, I would try and obtain a visa for Russia in between golf and my quest for finding the modern-day equivalents of the Gabor sisters.

It was early evening; the airport shuttle I rode in stopped at a series of Budapest hotels, each looking more uncomfortable and dreary than the last. My fellow passengers—four different twosomes of baggy-clothed, stocking-cap-sporting backpackers from England—all seemed as casual and nonchalant as if they were merely taking a school-bus ride home. It was apparent to all of us travelers too cheap to hire a taxi, which my guidebook had warned were expensive, that none of us were staying at any five-star hotels. The driver was speeding along a main thoroughfare lined with dour, boxy buildings in the early night, Budapest looked grim and unfriendly.

I had booked a room via the Internet while in Egypt that had looked good on its Web site, with pictures of a stylish lobby containing comfortable chairs for reading and bright, cheerful rooms; but I arrived to find a run-down, grubby hotel with all the allure of a dirty dishrag. The hotel's faded brick facade bore a coating of dark, grimy soot and the small lobby, the opposite of stylish, was twenty-four-hour-pawnshop bright: the overhead florescent light gave off a harsh, dull glow that was only attractive to a horde of moths flittering nearby. It seemed like the perfect hotel for a "down-and-out thug" in a Quentin Tarantino movie.

Too tired to find a new hotel, I checked in and hoped the room be would be better than what I had seen so far. There was no elevator—my room was up on the fifth floor. I barely had the energy to drag my golf bag behind me as I trudged up each flight, in the dark—it seems the lightbulbs had all been stolen. The hallway light near my room was missing as well—it was so dark I had to get on my knees and find the keyhole by Braille. I entered my room, which smelled like someone had been curing meat in there recently. Exhausted, I locked my door and barricaded it with my golf bag just in case my burglary theory was true. Even though it was only eight in the evening, I fell sound asleep on top of the lumpy bed with my clothes still on.

Waking early the next morning after ten hours of coma-like sleep, I found myself in the exact same position in which I had fallen asleep. Surprisingly, I felt refreshed. It was Sunday morning and I knew that room wasn't going to do: I hadn't imagined the meat smell the night before—it was the aroma of a tin of Spam left out and open for a few months. Bright sunlight flooded my room as I drew back the filthy curtains, only to reveal that my room was even dirtier than I had imagined. The sun exposed all the wads of dust balls that littered the floor. I got cleaned up as best I could, mostly by dusting myself and my belongings off, and went out in search of new accommodations.

The "Hotel Hormel," as I had renamed my lodging, was only a few blocks from the Danube—the only thing that had been correct on their Web page. After five minutes of walking, I came to the famous Danube River. Just as I reached the banks, a large passenger ship was slowly motoring by. I imagined the passengers boarding the ship upstream in Vienna the night before, heading now to the warm waters of the Black Sea for fun in the East European sun. The river, which was no more than a few hundred yards across, wasn't physically impressive, as the greenish water hardly stirred, but it was hard to not be immediately taken with the castles and grand, ornate government buildings lining both sides of the waterway. A series of striking bridges spanning the Danube added to the storybook setting.

With Buda and the imposing Royal Palace dominating the high ground across the way to the west, and Pest holding the flatter east bank where I stood, the two halves combine to create Budapest. The city proved to be perfect for a hiker like me, as there was always an imposing building with spires or columns off in the distance to walk toward and explore.

Right smack in the middle of Europe, Hungary's history is that of a speed bump on a highway overrun by all the ambitious and better-armed neighboring roadsters—it's the bull's-eye of Europe. Hungary has had trouble coming at it from most every point of the compass. Because of this, Hungarians are extremely wary of outsiders, which, to be honest, I rather enjoyed. The prevailing attitude there is a muttered: "nobody-cares-what-the-hell-you-do, just leave-me-alone!" After being in country after country where peddlers constantly begged and pleaded for you to buy their wares, Hungarians are exactly the opposite—they would prefer it if you would just leave their store as quickly as you can with no questions asked so they don't have to do anything but smoke their cigarettes and look grim. You get better customer service as a prisoner in Guantanamo Bay than you receive at a shop or restaurant in Budapest.

Here's a prime example of that Budapestean attitude. After finding and moving to a wonderful hotel on a leafy side street—the Radio Inn—where I had a three-room suite for the same price as the Hotel Hormel, not to mention its perfect location near Budapest's grand city park and main arteries, I had gone into a bookstore to buy a travel guide for Russia. The store's solo salesperson was a young girl of around twenty-five with spiked black hair so perfectly projected from her skull that it looked like she was recently electrocuted, and a nose ring so big you could hang a hand towel through it. She didn't even glance up as I entered the small, cramped store. Finding a copy of the Russian guidebook, I asked her how much the book cost, since it wasn't marked with a price. After a huge, deep sigh, she gave me a look like I had just asked her to donate me one of her corneas.

"It's on book," she said in broken English as if I had taken all the life out of her with that one simple inquiry.

"Nope, not on this one," I replied.

"Perhaps another copy have price," she said as she made no movement whatsoever to go look and find out. I went and found another copy, but it wasn't marked either.

Showing her the different copy, I said, "No price on this one, either."

"Perhaps you come back when manager is here," she sighed in her monotone voice with a hint of disgust. She never even looked up at me. She looked tired, the poor thing. I decided to go find another bookstore while she took another drag off that Camel. I do hope I hadn't bothered her too much. I got to find out: in Budapest, she wasn't alone in her lack of charming social skills; the whole city couldn't care less about you and your petty tourist concerns.

And here's the real kicker: you actually put up with this treatment, at least from the women, because they are indeed astonishingly beautiful. A potential Miss Universe candidate served me a coffee in a sidewalk café near the ornate Opera House. A shoo-in winner for Miss World checked me in at the Radio Inn. The maid that cleaned my room daily was drop-dead-movie-star-beautiful— I continually asked for extra towels or shampoo whenever I saw her just to get another close-up of her ravishing looks.

One of the greatest secrets kept from the Western world until the iron curtain came down was the ravishing beauty of the women of the East. Growing up in America, every time we were shown a picture of an eastern bloc woman she always looked like Ed Asner in a babushka. What propaganda and misdirection that was! Budapest is a sod farm for supermodels. These amazing creatures are just out walking on the streets right with us normal folk— not just a few—thousands of them, all towering over everyone else with their willowy, amazing good looks. Shopgirls, waitresses, businesswomen, executives, hotel maids, bank clerks—pretty much every other woman you encounter could be on a Paris or Milan fashion runway. What the hell is going on there? Something in the water of the Danube?

In Eastern Europe, the funny thing is that the men, for the most part, look nothing like the opposite sex. The men tend to be five foot four, sweaty, overweight, and hairy, with the uni-brow. It's like some bizarre evolutional joke. It's my theory that communism wasn't about the equal distribution of wealth, it was used to keep these beautiful women from leaving. All the Communist men got together. "Comrades, we have problem! Our women are all tall and beautiful and we all look like Danny DeVito. What are we to do?" They hunch their shoulders, thinking hard as they rub their uni-brows. "I know! Let's build a giant wall around our countries! An iron curtain! That way they won't be able to leave us. And, besides, women love new curtains! Send the Ed Asner look-alike pictures to *National Geographic*. Let's keep this our state secret!" That was the real impetus behind communism. All that Karl Marx stuff about "class struggle" was a bunch of bull—it's all about fencing in those amazing women to keep them home.

As Hungary has shed the economic chains forced upon them from the old Soviet Union, golf is starting to make a bit of headway there. The game is new to that part of the world and is generally viewed, not unsurprisingly, as a pastime of the rich; but since now everyone wants to accumulate wealth and wherever wealth gathers, golf seems to follow, Hungarians are finally discovering the joy of whacking that little white ball into a hole. That's how

I met Attila Hegyi. Attila Hegyi is living the life of this new capitalism in Hungary. He's in his mid-thirties, rich, good-looking,
and claims to have dated the last six winners of the Miss Hungary
pageant. That seemed an even more impressive pursuit than my
quest to become a scratch handicap golfer, which, of course, is
about as likely as me dating a Miss Hungary.

Attila is the front man for a financial group that is trying to
cash in on the worldwide golf craze. He oversees the Birdland
Golf Resort, which was built near the Austrian border.

I called on Attila in downtown Budapest and was shown to his
second-floor office by what was the most stunning-looking secre-
tary in the history of executive assistants. As she closed the door,
I asked Attila how he ever got any work done with someone so
beautiful just outside his office.

"Oh, we're used to beautiful women in Budapest. It's no big
deal," he replied nonchalantly.

I couldn't disagree with him more. I had trouble keeping my
jaw from permanently dropping any time I tried to just walk down
the street.

Over coffee, we discussed the challenges of getting golf into
the collective psyche of Hungarians—so far the country hadn't
become excited with the game. Attila sighed, "It's an uphill struggle." He grinned steadfastly. "But we'll get there." Attila then said
he was driving the six hours to Birdland the following morning,
and if I liked, I could tag along for the ride and stay there for a few
days, playing golf out in the Hungarian countryside and seeing
for myself how the sport was doing in Hungary. I liked.

The next morning Attila picked me up at the Radio Inn where
I said good-bye to the supermodel working the front desk who
didn't even look up and acknowledge my departure. The next
thing I knew, we were gunning down the highway in his super-
charged BMW while he told me about his Miss Hungary girl-
friends. That had me more intrigued than golf! I asked him what
his secret was.

"If you have money and a nice car and aren't too bad-looking, it's rather easy to date them, actually," he sighed, as if the whole thing was a touch boring.

In order to keep my head from exploding with jealousy, I changed the conversation to the less sexually-charged subject of golf. Attila said that golf was too slow-paced to catch on in Hungary; the public loves soccer and sees golf as a boring alternative. Golf is quite a long way from taking off in Hungary; there are only six courses in the country, and only two were full eighteen-holers. Attila addressed this dilemma by saying, "We need a Hungarian Tiger Woods to get the people excited."

Unfortunately, golfing phenomena like Tiger Woods appear about as often as Haley's Comet comes around. I had the feeling that golf is going to be on the back burner there for a while. Actually, the Hungarians didn't seem all too excited about much of anything. If you can be blasé about dating a Miss Hungary, it's hard to get worked up about playing golf. But then, golf does get me worked up, and Hungary has two excellent locales to play the ancient game. The first was Birdland.

The Birdland Golf Resort is somewhat secluded. It seemed tucked away in the flat Hungarian countryside that reminded me of Minnesota's farmland prairies with their sprawling fields protected by groves of poplars planted as windbreaks. The hotel was brand new and still had that feel of just being built—the smell of fresh paint and new carpet were in the air, which was better than that Spam odor in my first hotel room back in the city. Birdland is near the resort town of Bük, which is known for its rejuvenating mineral spas, so there is hope that, in the future, visitors might like a bit of golf in between hot soaks. Because of the flatness of the landscape, the course didn't look like much from the vantage point of my second-floor hotel room. However, the excellent eighteen holes play through groves of spruce trees and around a series of reed-encircled ponds teeming with ducks and birds: the moniker *Birdland* fitting aptly. I was one of the only guests there during my three-day stay and pretty much had the golf course just to myself.

In the pro shop on the ground floor of the hotel, I met Tim

Andruss, the resident golf professional there. Tim hails from Pryor, Oklahoma and, along with his wife Patti, took a six-month contract to see what life was like in Hungary and whether he would enjoy being a golf professional abroad—another strange golfer in a strange golfing land. They had sold their house back in Oklahoma, packed their bags, and flew sight unseen to Hungary and into the world of East European golf. "What the heck, you only live once," Tim said.

So far they loved their new life in a strange land. I admired their adventurous spirit; they were my kind of people. Tim is around fifty and a fabulous golfer with a beautiful, athletic swing to die for. We played a couple of rounds together and he makes the game I so badly want to excel at look as easy as boiling water. He's laid-back and easygoing in his Southern way, and, without even trying, was hitting the ball thirty and forty yards past mine on his drives. Life is so unfair.

While playing, I asked Tim about the prospect of the capitalist sport of golf becoming widespread there in Hungary. He said in his syrupy drawl, "Well, finding golf here is like finding a diamond in a pig's butt. You don't expect to find it, but when you do, you're very pleasantly surprised." Tim was full of these little nuggets of wisdom. Up until that point near the Austrian-Hungarian border, I had traveled tens of thousands of miles through a couple of dozen countries, but that was the first time I had heard someone say "pig's butt" and "diamond" in the same sentence.

When I asked Tim what he found surprising about living in Hungary, he thought for a second and then drawled, "Well, you have to get used to wearing wet clothes sometimes. Hell, I don't think there is one single clothes dryer in the entire country." He shook his head and added, "You can forget about a dishwasher or garbage disposal too. It just ain't gonna happen, son." Tim said that the change of lifestyle was harder for his wife because there's only one grocery store in the small village they live in, so the food selection was limited. The town did have a pizza place and without it, as Tim exclaimed, "Hell, we'd both starve to death!"

Tim said he had heard about the job at Birdland from his son-in-law, Brent, who is the teaching professional at the Pannonia Golf and Country Club, which is about an hour outside Budapest. After a few days of golf and relaxation in the Hungarian countryside as well as a few shared pizzas with Tim, I hitched a ride back toward Budapest with a van carrying a group of five teenage golfers—taught by Tim—who were going to go play a match against a team coached by his son-in-law at Pannonia. The teenagers teased each other in Hungarian as we motored along. None of them spoke English. I think the only English words they knew were *Tiger Woods*.

After a few hours driving, we turned off the main highway and started driving through the back countryside as the road began winding though the farmland hillocks. The land soon became delightfully scenic as we passed field after field covered with happy multicolored wildflowers. This was the picturesque land on which the Pannonia Golf and Country Club resided. I have to say that I immediately adored the couse and its lovely surroundings.

The clubhouse sits back from the country lane down a gravel turnoff. The building is an old converted farm-style manor with high ceilings and solid oak doors and would be the ideal place to live in, especially with a great golf course right outside your back door. From the clubhouse you walk across a delightful patio with solid wooden tables and the perimeter is lined with blooming rosebushes. You continue your short walk around a grove of oaks and then the course is spread right before your eyes as the holes roam off to the horizon. The whole setup there at Pannonia was wonderfully appealing and I think a former Miss Hungary (if Attila would give one up) and I would be quite happy living out our lives together in the serene countryside.

The course plays over a series of rolling hills full of vibrant purple and crimson wildflowers alongside the fertile fairways. The course is rather links-ish in style, with mounds and hollows and dips in the terrain as the land meanders on the side of a broad hill. The holes stand out vibrantly against meadows of golden wheat that cover the surrounding farmland, their long sprouted shafts swaying in the gentle summer breeze. With their excellent greens perched up enticingly on the flatter parts of the hill, this is enchanting golfing land. I loved being out in the warm sun under the cloudless sky and the air sweetened by all the flowers as songbirds flitted around, chirping gaily. A rather carefree happiness settled into me as I hit my ball around the jolly course—the Hungarians might be slow in coming to the game but I wasn't. My only concern, which had been lurking in the back of my brain, was the fact that I was having quite a bit of trouble obtaining a Russian visa.

Before leaving Budapest to go to Birdland with Attila, I had had no luck with the officials at the Russian embassy who were every bit as rude as their counterparts at the Indian embassy had been in Bangkok. That's hard to equal. The Russian embassy was only a few blocks from my spacious hotel, so I visited there several days in a row with little success. Even though I patiently waited for them to open each morning and was always the first one to enter when the dour, well-armed guard unlocked the door, I had to fill out the lengthy visa application anew each visit, and then was made to wait and wait: no one was in a hurry to assist me getting in, anyway. Russia didn't seem all that crazy about excepting visitors.

After spending the mornings waiting in the colorless lobby and leafing through Russian magazines to kill the time, the Russian embassy official—a cheerless bureaucrat in a constant haze of cigarette smoke who wore the same drab brown suit each day—would hear my plea once again for a chance to visit his country and perhaps play their one golf course just outside Moscow. Each day, the dour gentleman would utter an unsmiling *"nyet!"* Nonetheless, I persisted for several days in a row hoping that my enthusiasm for the hope of visiting his homeland would win him over. After the fifth *"nyet!"* I was told not to come back—it wasn't going to happen. Disappointed, I was about to let the whole idea go, and just find a way to travel directly to Scandinavia and make my way to Tromsö.

I was about to give up on Russia completely when I walked past a travel agency with its windows covered in touristy pictures of

Red Square, St. Petersburg, and the Kremlin. A Russian travel agency! Hmm, I wonder if they might have any ideas on getting a visa for their country. I went into the office and explained my dilemma to the gorgeous miniskirted Russian lady behind the counter. She smiled seductively, winked at me, and purred in a sexy whisper so that only I could hear, "Anything can happen for a little extra cash, no?" *Baksheesh*, Eastern European–style!

It was remarkable what a little American money could accomplish when greased by the proper hands. I paid a bribe of a hundred dollars to the travel agency so they, in turn, could pay another bribe of another hundred dollars (paid by me) to that cheerless-chain-smoking-brown-suit-wearer at the Russian embassy who had told me not to return. Cold, hard, American greenbacks pried the iron curtain (kept around for decoration, I guess) wide open, and in three days I had my visa secured and in my poorer-by-the-second mitts. Packed and ready to travel, it was another glorious summer day in Budapest as me and my golf clubs boarded a train to Mother Russia.

22

Moscow Golf and Country Club Moscow, Russia

55.45°N–37.36°E

"I have never been kicked out of a country." Before trying to enter the Ukraine, that was a claim I could make with full assurance and complete accuracy.

At one in the morning on a cool, black June night, I was rudely ushered off a train and told that I would be unable to continue my journey across the Ukraine. I was traveling overland from Budapest to Moscow and had settled into my spacious sleeper berth for the two-day journey. As you know, I love train travel and, to me, there is nothing more perfect on earth than a comfortable sleeper cabin all to myself. I had been in heaven—travel-wise.

My wood-paneled cabin was roomy—the largest I had had in my journey—and I was looking forward to two days of leisurely travel. We had left Budapest at six-thirty on a glorious summer evening as the setting sun had bathed the city in a tinge of gold as we chugged out. I had settled right in. My luggage was stowed away and I had immediately closed my door and put my slippers and pajamas on. I was going to wallow in the comfort of my first-class berth and victory over the Russian visa office.

Having been warned there was no dining car on the train, I had spent that afternoon in Budapest wandering through food markets selecting the perfect foods to bring along: crisp apples, freshly baked bread, creamy cheese, olives, some delicious salami I had just discovered, and chocolate-covered biscuits for desert. For the following morning, I had a couple of almond croissants and some wonderfully fragrant green tea that I had bought in China and had been hoarding and saving for the perfect time such as this. I had bottled water, books, a new *Time* magazine, travel guides, maps, an unread *International Herald Tribune* newspaper that I had painfully avoided reading all day just so I could savor every word and do the crossword puzzle when I wasn't gazing out my window at the scenery once hidden from the West by the old iron curtain. I was more prepared than an Enron official in front of a grand jury.

All I had to do was relax, eat, read, and enjoy the train as it cruised into Russia through the green Eastern European countryside while I dreamed of playing golf at the Moscow Country Club. Life was grand! At least it was until the train stopped at the Ukraine border just after midnight. There was a loud knock on my cabin door and I opened it to find a Ukrainian immigration officer—a beautiful, blond woman of about twenty-five who looked like a young Madonna playing soldier in a World War II officer's uniform.

"Papers!" she roughly snarled as her face went from beautiful to evil quicker than an old lady can yell "bingo!" to win ten grand. I gave her my passport containing my new Russian visa that I was so proud of. Getting a Russian visa had been the most difficult document that I had to obtain on this journey. Getting a visa from the paranoid Chinese officials in Hong Kong or the rude Indian embassy in Bangkok was no picnic, but they were one-foot putts compared to Russia. The visa application itself required more information than I supplied when I got my home mortgage and was only slightly shorter than *War and Peace*. Plus, I had had to pay two expensive bribes.

"Where's your visa for the Ukraine?" the evil, uniformed Madonna barked.

I explained I was going to Moscow and was in transit through the Ukraine and hadn't realized I needed a visa just to cross the country. In all my trials and tribulations when obtaining the Russian visa, no one had told me that it was needed. I showed her my voucher for a prepaid Moscow hotel and told her I had no plans to stay in her country. I did want to say, "Yes, you caught me sneaking into the Ukraine! It has been my lifelong dream to denounce my American citizenship and to live in a country where I have to stand in line twelve hours just to get a new roll of see-through, scratchy toilet paper!"

I decided against this line of reasoning. I gave her my best puppy-dog smile and said, "Look, I'm sorry. I didn't know. I'm on my way to Russia."

My honest charm had about as much chance of working as Mike Tyson does of starring in *Hamlet*. "You must have a visa for the Ukraine! Pack your bags and be ready to leave the train at once!"

She now looked nothing like Madonna to me, but did begin to bear a striking resemblance to Sean Penn in a blond wig and military outfit. She stomped away, and I started packing. It was the start of a very long night.

It was now one in the morning. It was dark and it was cold. Budapest had been glowing and warm with a pleasant summer breeze, but there at the poorly-lit Ukraine border it seemed exceptionally bleak and chilly and inhospitable. Told to leave my delicious food onboard, two armed soldiers directly led me off the train and into the spooky-looking border station. I struggled with my golf bag as I crossed the numerous railroad tracks between my train car and the station, but the brisk walking guards made no effort to help. They seemed pissed off that I had forced them into duty. Inside, I was told that I would be put on a train back to Budapest at six that morning.

The station was dirtier than any I had seen in India, and that's saying something! The floor was littered with cigarette butts and trash, with two inches of dust coating the whole filthy mess like grimy frosting. The windows were either broken or missing and what glass remained looked as if it had never been washed. Huge hunks of the ceiling were gone as if they had been torn away by either looters or a tornado, or both. Though there were portions of the station that were lit with harsh fluorescent lighting, they made me sit in the darkest corner of the large, drafty room. It was like being a prisoner and, in essence, I was. The wary guards never left my side—even when I had to go to the bathroom in a room that was so foul I thought I was going to get sick. Apparently, hygiene isn't high on the list of priorities in the Ukraine. It was as dreadful and unappealing as a place could be. I heard the whistle of my train blow and my comfy first-class berth, complete with a tin of chocolate-covered biscuits, went on to Moscow without me.

Honestly a bit too scared to fall asleep as I didn't care for the continual menacing stares the soldiers gave me and my golf bag, I stayed up all night. The officials at the Ukraine border had tried to get me to pay for the ticket to Budapest, but I told them firmly: "*nyet!*" I figured they wanted to get rid of me as much as I wanted rid of them, so I refused to cough up any money and it seemed to have made no difference. I boarded the train and promised myself I'd never visit the Ukraine—unless I hear of some great golf course near Kiev on a future adventure in this part of the world. Once in Budapest, I hurriedly bought an airline ticket at a travel agency near the train station, took an extremely expensive taxi ride to the airport, and flew to Moscow directly over the useless, foul Ukraine.

My hard-fought visa had only been approved for five days of visiting in Russia and the foul-up at the Ukrainian border had cost me a day. It was going to be a whirlwind trip through the capital of the world's largest country.

Though grumpy at first, Muscovites warm up when engaged a bit and are friendly, for big-city folk, in a New York City sort of manner. The Ukraine visa incident was merely a hiccup and I was, nevertheless, thrilled to be in Russia. How often does one get to Russia anyway? I was met by a driver at the airport who chauffeured me to my hotel just off downtown Moscow. I checked in and hit the streets immediately as I wanted to see all I could see on my limited visa.

I visited all the big tourist's sights right off the bat: the Kremlin,

Red Square, Saint Basil's Cathedral, and Lenin's Tomb. At an expensive Western-style hotel just off Red Square, I bought a ticket for the opera that night at the Bolshoi Theater and saw Tchaikovsky's *Queen of Spades.* I gussied up in my black sweater and sat in one of the gilded boxes on the mezzanine. It was a wonderful tale of greed and gambling and tragic love, and though it was belted out in Russian, I could easily follow the story—it was a great show. Then, as full of culture as a golf maniac could be, I walked out into the Moscow evening after the opera. The magnificent Bolshoi Theater sits directly across the street from Red Square, and it was still light out at half past ten as the buzzing crowd filtered out of the theater. Moscow sits high on the globe, almost level with Juneau, Alaska. My final destination of Tromsö would be brighter still—the sun never sets that time of year.

Seeking golf Russian-style, I had called ahead the following morning and made arrangements to play at the Moscow Country Club, but no one at my hotel had any clue how I was to get a cab to take me there. Moscow had, of the countries I had visited, by far the fewest number of people who spoke English and, to brighten my prospects, Muscovites usually made little effort to take the time to try and decipher any of the small number of Russian words I tried in vain to utter. No one had any clue on where the Moscow Country Club seemed to be.

The best advice I got from the cranky front-desk clerk was to go out the front door of the hotel, stand alongside the busy street and someone would stop and give me a ride. You quickly learn that every car in Russia is a potential taxi. Everybody needs a few extra rubles. You stand on the side of the road and hold your hand out. Cars immediately stop to see if you're headed in a similar direction where they're going and if a price can be negotiated.

After a few minutes a car stopped and I showed the driver my golf clubs and the name of the Moscow Country Club that I had copied and written in Russian on a piece of paper. He didn't speak English but he nodded his head yes and held up five fingers meaning five hundred rubles, which was around seventeen dollars. I was a touch apprehensive to just get into a strange car that wasn't a licensed cab, but I thought, *what the hell*, and got in. When in Russia, do as the Russians do.

The Moscow Country Club is twenty-five miles north of the town center in the Nakhabino parkland, but my driver didn't seem to know that geographical tidbit. We had been driving for around forty-five minutes through the outer ring of Moscow when it finally dawned on me that the driver had no clue where the golf course was. At stoplights, he would roll down his window and ask other drivers for directions, but it must have been a state secret because no one seemed to know. Golf isn't exactly booming there as the only eighteen-hole course serving Russia's one hundred thirty million–plus people is, in fact, the Moscow Country Club.

My driver was getting more and more frustrated and though I couldn't translate exactly what he was saying, I was positive he was starting to swear more and more violently in his native tongue. He wasn't happy about how giving me a ride was turning out. Finally, after another thirty minutes of driving around the suburbs of Moscow and asking several other motorists at stoplights, he found another motorist who knew where the club was. He wasn't happy to hear its location. All of a sudden his English improved dramatically. "Five hundred more rubles!" he shouted as he pounded the steering wheel in anger.

I told him emphatically the only Russian word I had down pat: *"nyet!"*

He started swearing at me in a rush of saliva-spewing Russian expletives and I stuck up for Western travelers everywhere as I did the same right back to him in English. I was India trained! East met West in a war of curses. Luckily, I hadn't paid him yet and had my small golf bag across my lap, so I quickly got out of the car and he sped off in a flurry of squealing tires and profanity.

Now a pro at this game of Moscow hitchhiking, I stuck my hand out for another ride as if I hitchhiked this way every day of my life. Several cars immediately stopped, but no one had a clue where the golf course was when I showed them the piece of paper.

I'm sure I had probably left out a few Russian letters as I copied the name down from a magazine. Finally, a polite, young English-speaking student stopped and said he knew where the course was and that he'd take me there for two hundred rubles. It sounded like a good deal to me. I hopped in.

My driver was named Mikeal. He said he was twenty-two and a student at a local university. He said his dream in life was to one day go to California and meet Pamela Anderson in person as if that prospect was as normal as going to Grauman's Chinese Theater.

The golf course was well out of the city and we drove for twenty minutes down the evergreen-lined back roads. The forests were lush with growth, but had the uniform look of a giant tree farm that had been growing wild for the past twenty years. The rows of trees looked military and orderly as if standing at attention for inspection by a drill sergeant. We arrived at the gate to the golf course. I paid Mikeal his rubles, thanking him, and excitedly went to see what golf was like in Russia.

The Moscow Country Club is the first and, as I've said, only eighteen-hole golf course in Russia. Built in 1994 and designed by—you guessed it—the esteemed and experienced Robert Trent Jones, Jr., the course took a decade to become a reality as Russia grappled with the idea of a game so closely identified with capitalism on socialist soil. As golf took root around the globe while the British Empire expanded in the second half of the nineteenth century, the game did become a pastime of the wealthy, which belied its democratic roots in Scotland.

Golf is the last frontier, sports-wise, for the athletics-loving Russians. Personally, I loathe the fat cat, golf cart–riding, expensive-cigar–smoking exclusivity that, unfortunately, the game has come to signify in many parts of the world and I don't blame anyone for their timid embrace of this bourgeois time-killer. To me, golf is a refreshing walk in beautiful natural vistas with simple rules of honor started by common folk in the Kingdom of Fife. If I had my way, it would be free for all who want to play. I'm the Karl Marx of golf.

The Moscow Country Club was a complete surprise with its natural beauty and design. It was the finest course I had played since South Africa. The course is championship caliber, a full-on true test of golfing skill, and far grander than I would ever have dreamed existed in the former cold war archenemy of my home country. Actually, I probably shouldn't have been all that surprised because most any course designed by the gifted Robert Trent Jones, Jr. is special. On my trip, I had played a couple of magnificent courses that were his creations—the dramatic Wild Coast on the east coast of South Africa, wonderful Spring City in Kunming, and enchanting Santiburi in Chiang Rai. Mr. Jones has a full passport.

Like his famous father for whom he's named and from whom he learned his craft, Jones has traveled the globe to build his unique golfing playgrounds. He has more than two hundred designs on six continents. Simply to play on one of his courses is to see that it's obvious he is a lover of the game's honest roots, as the holes he creates seem an integral part of the landscape and never forced. His father was famous for designing courses that would challenge golfers of all abilities, as the layouts allow a mediocre golfer to make bogies and a couple of pars to brighten the day, but birdies have to be earned by expertise and execution. For me, the mark of a great golf-course design is one that allows for pleasure as well as skill and most golf-course designers would do well to keep up with the Jones family.

The Moscow Country Club is built into a swath of Russian forest with thick groves of birch and towering evergreens sharing the peaceful setting with pretty ponds and streams. The gently rolling land teems with wild birds and as I strolled down the fairways chasing my ball I had to keep reminding myself I was playing golf in Russia and not some excellent parkland course in Minnesota or Canada. The course seemed a million miles away from the clamor and din of cement-laden Moscow. The only sound in the Russian countryside was the croaking of frogs and chirping of birds. It's a lovely spot.

Like most courses I have visited over the previous months both before and since I was in golf-mad South Africa, the place was empty. Before teeing it up, I had chatted briefly with the gregarious golf professional, Igor Ivashin, who looks like he's Ernie Els's Russian twin brother. Like many Russian men, I noticed Igor was burly, with broad shoulders and looked as strong as an ox—Russian men look as sturdy as their buildings. He said he had gotten into golf after playing professional hockey as a teenager. Ice hockey is a huge sport there, as the long, cold winters are much more conducive to ice-skating than playing outdoor sports. Barely five months a year are warm enough for golf.

Igor arranged for me to play with a twelve-year-old local golfing wonder named Misha Morozov. Misha's parents are divorced and he lives with his dad during the summer in Moscow. During the school year he lives in Budapest with his mother. His home course is the Pannonia Golf Club. Misha is lively and bright and speaks three languages fluently, including English. Though already an excellent golfer at his tender age, Misha has the necessary skill and maturity to become a great golfer—he possesses that calm demeanor of a winner. If he wasn't such a sweet and engaging kid, I would have been extremely jealous of his seemingly bright golfing future.

Unlike most twelve-year-olds I've met who you can't get to open up and talk, Misha was the opposite; he rarely shuts up and loves to ask question after question. He asked me all about my trip and where I'd been in the world in between hitting one gorgeous golf shot after another. He asked me what kind of golf balls I used and about my clubs and had me describe my home course in Seattle. He's small for his age, but the ball didn't know that: it soared well past mine as he pounded his drives with the graceful ease of a professional. The minute his ball left the clubface and soared toward the pin he was asking another question about life in America. Misha was a delight.

We played and chatted as a light mist started to fall. The day was gray and cloudy and rain had seemed a probability. On the par-three eighth, my ball landed in the bunker. I bladed my sand shot and the ball shot off into the woods. Embarrassed, I told Misha that I had been having trouble with my sand game. He plopped his ball into the same bunker where mine had been and said this is the easiest shot in golf and promptly re-created the exact same shot I'd just screwed up and hit the ball to within a foot of the hole. "See, it's easy!" he gushed with delight.

After the round I bought Misha a hamburger in the clubhouse and he became a twelve-year-old kid again rather than an excellent golfer I envied. Before I left to go back to my hotel, he insisted that he show me the nest of a baby bird that was lodged behind the ball machine of the practice range. He seemed more delighted in seeing the baby bird than he had been hitting one great golf shot after another on the course. His youthful glee and nonchalant zest for life made me wish I were twelve again.

Me, I was far from twelve and the next day added another year to my sum total of time on the earth. It was my birthday and also my last day in Moscow. I had purchased an overnight train ticket to Helsinki that would be leaving that evening at eleven—this time not crossing through countries with surprise visa checks.

After a birthday dinner of sushi as I ogled at Russian supermodels, I went back to my hotel and packed my golf bag for the final leg of my adventure to the top of the golfing world. I had packed and unpacked my bag so often I could probably do it in my sleep. For the first time in many months I wondered what it would be like not to live out of a suitcase and hand-wash clothes in a bathroom sink. On the plus side, I now realized how few things I actually needed for survival on a day-to-day basis. I had gone around the world with only a few shirts and two pair of pants and one sweater.

My train was leaving from the Leningradsky train station, which I had painstakingly written down on a piece of paper with all the correct, bizarre letters of the Russian alphabet. I paid my hotel bill and dragged my golf travel bag out to the curb in front of the hotel and stuck out my hand for a ride to the depot—I had become a wily veteran of Moscow hitchhiking. I knew the drill.

My hand had only lingered outstretched in the cool night air of

Moscow for two minutes before a car screeched to a halt at my feet offering a ride. The gentleman who stopped was named Vladimir. The top button of his white dress shirt was undone and the knot on his blue business tie was loosened. He looked to be heading home after a long day at the office. Knowing how the system worked, I showed him two hundred rubles and a piece of paper bearing the name of my designation.

He nodded and said curtly, "ya." Off we sped to the Leningrad-sky terminal and my train ride, to Finland.

23

Tromsö Golf Club
Tromsö, Norway

69.68°N–18.92°E

Punctual to the minute, the train left exactly at eleven and we slowly rolled out of Moscow. A sea of soft blue still lingered in the northern night sky with a canary yellow sunset off on the horizon. Daylight looked as if it would finally tire out and knock off shop around midnight. My pajamas were on and I tucked myself snugly in bed, gazing out my open window as I tried to get every last glimpse of Russia that I could. We wheeled through the suburbs of endless no-frills high-rise apartment buildings, in which the vast majority of Muscovites live. I never once saw a single-dwelling home during my time in Russia.

In half an hour we were in the forests of western Russia and chugging speedily en route to St. Petersburg. I would be sound asleep as we passed through that historic city and would have to see it during another adventure when I had more than five days on a visa. The gentle swaying of the car rocked me to sleep as I fell into the peaceful slumber of someone who wasn't under any sort of time constraints. Having already done the bulk of the heavy lifting of my trip around the world, I would get to Tromsö in due course. As I neared the finish line, I felt myself relaxing more and more.

The next morning, I awoke to a gentle knocking on my door

from the smiling conductor, who presented me with a hot cup of tea. Sipping the sweet brew as I sat up in bed, I assumed we were at the Finnish border by the flurry of official-looking types scurrying alongside the train. We were stopped alongside a frigid-looking lake with its gunmetal gray water forming small whitecaps in the gusty wind. It looked chilly and wet outside as rain was falling from low inky clouds hovering just above the groves of evergreens dotting the landscape. My papers were in order and the immigration officer barely looked up as he stamped my passport and moved on down the car. No rude ushering off the train would happen there.

Starting up once again, we railed past more chilly-looking lakes and brown farmhouses as neat and tidy as any in rural Wisconsin or Minnesota. Finland immediately gave me a feeling of home— that long-ago home in the Midwest I'd found. We arrived at the main train station of Helsinki and the city continued to put me at ease right from the get-go. There was immediate order and efficiency and signs in English. It had been a long slog of difficult countries—China, India, Nepal, Zimbabwe, Egypt, Turkey, Hungary, the impenetrable Ukraine, and Russia. It's not that I hadn't enjoyed those stops on my journey; in fact, I had enjoyed them immensely. Even my physical hardships in the Andes and India and Egypt now occupied a warmer spot in my memory the farther away I got. However, that last half of my journey had all been in countries where one had to be continually wary and on guard. Simple communication could be difficult. A misstep with cuisine or Ukrainians, potentially deadly.

The awful intestinal sickness I'd suffered in Egypt hadn't helped, either, as the unpleasant effects of that lone falafel had lingered for weeks afterwards. Whatever microbe that had been hitchhiking on those evil shards of lettuce still lurked menacingly in my body. It will be eons before I will again have the courage to eat another falafel or a plate of Indian curry—the smell I associate with a possible gastronomical meltdown from those foods still lingers in my taste buds and nose. A lifelong lover of curry, I now avoid Indian restaurants the way Dracula avoids the sun.

Intestinal worries aside, there in Finland, the pressure was off. Good healthy food would be easy to find and tickets for travel would be a snap to obtain. I could figure out how to get a decent haircut and clothes laundered and catch up with my notes and correspondence home. There wouldn't be the rude butting-in-line as in China or the malaria worries of Southeast Asia or the heat and mayhem of India. I had never realized in all my forty-eight years how much I craved order. Finland and spic-and-span Singapore are the Felix Ungers of countries and both the epitome of civic tidiness.

Suddenly, I wasn't in a hurry to finish my journey anymore. I decided to lay low right there for a spell and relax in Helsinki. The truth is, I just didn't want my trip to end. I loved being out in the world and seeing how others go about the course of their lives. I was in no hurry to get back to answering machines and monthly bills, nor did I relish hopping back on the treadmill of life in the U.S. with worries about retirement plans and soaring insurance costs. I had enjoyed not worrying about the maintenance of a car or complaining about the increased rates of my cable television bill. The windfall from the selling of my condo was now seriously depleted; the idea of having to find ways to replenish my coffers wasn't attractive either. Nor did I want responsibilities or the expectations of others. I merely wanted to be out in the world traveling with my golf clubs with new lands to explore and exotic courses to play. My old life was dead and gone, but I didn't mourn. May it rest in peace.

Before falling asleep on the train the previous evening, rather than count sheep as we chugged out of Moscow, I had counted the number of rounds of golf I had played on my trip and realized with a start that the Moscow Country Club round with young Misha had been my seventy-ninth round. That serendipity made me giggle: I initially had toyed with the idea of naming my book-to-be *Around the World in 80 Rounds* as a tribute to Jules Verne's classic travel tale, all the way back in Seattle planning this trip. I had correctly figured that playing golf every third or fourth day over twelve months would come out somewhere near the number eighty. That idea hadn't entered my mind for many months as I had merely tried to navigate the country and course directly in front of me while trying to find golf and keep myself out of trouble in those strange lands. Perhaps, the Golf Gods had indeed been guiding me! My final round in Tromsö would be number eighty. Sometimes, life works out.

In Helsinki, I found a hotel highly recommended by my Finnish guidebook on a quiet street not too far from the train station. I checked in and immediately went in search of a bookstore to get my hands on a copy of *Around the World in Eighty Days.* The ominous sky was jam-packed with black rain clouds. As a Seattleite well-versed in rain, I knew it was going to pour for days on end. Rather than bring gloom, I loved that it made me feel like I was back in the Pacific Northwest. Luckily, there was a bookstore across the street from my hotel. I sprinted out into the wet to go buy the book.

My hotel was modest, but comfortable. I had a cushioned chair and lamp perfect for reading. Most everything built in Finland is made with function in mind; things such as chairs can be comfortable, but only just. The Scandinavian idea is to be happy, but not too happy. My well-developed Seattle nose for rain had indeed been correct; there was clouds and drizzle for the rest of the week. So, I bought food and provisions and happily camped out in my room and reread *Around the World in Eighty Days* with child-like pleasure.

I had read the book as a teenager, but I was curious to reread it anew after seeing much of the world that Verne had written about but never actually saw firsthand. He had penned his timeless classic from the comfort of his London home without ever actually traveling completely around the world. Verne, like me, had forsaken law school against the wishes of his parents. While I had packed my bags and headed to Los Angeles to learn how to become a stand-up comedian, Verne went to Paris and learned the art of writing. He, of course, succeeded grandly.

After achieving both literary and financial success, Verne bought a sailboat and did a bit of traveling, some of which was very adventurous, including a sea voyage across the Atlantic to North America for a weeklong stay on our eastern shores. Verne had also sailed from England to the Mediterranean, but never went farther east than Italy. He had the debonair adventurer of his imagination, Phileas Fogg, travel to more exotic lands in his stead. In Fogg's race to circumnavigate the globe in eighty days and thus win a wager on which his personal fortune rested, Fogg and his faithful sidekick, Passepartout, saw Egypt, the Red Sea, India, Singapore, Hong Kong, and San Francisco—all lands and locales Verne knew only through secondhand accounts and his imagination.

Actually, even Fogg saw very little of these lands himself, as he rarely took interest in sightseeing or the customs of the inhabitants in those exotic stops. Fogg took his English club life with him as if he awoke daily to the chimes of Big Ben. He continually played cards in the lounges of trains and steamers or in the lobby of his accommodations just as he did daily in his London gentleman's club. British to the core, Fogg didn't care to sample local cuisines or interact with the locals—mentally he never ventured outside his daily habits of England. He merely wanted to win his bet and go around the world in eighty days.

I loved the book all over again—it's charming and funny, but Verne had taken the easy way out. To gather his material, he didn't personally have to cross the Andes at fifteen thousand feet on a dirt road or suffer delays on a train in Malaysia or have to take malaria pills with the awful, violent dreams that accompany the medication. Verne wrote about India, but was never personally harassed by the greedy merchants or given incorrect change when taking a *tuk-tuk*. He surely never housed with a chicken in a crowded train compartment shared by a squabbling Indian family and their deadbeat, poultry-wielding, yogi for a son. He didn't have to spend days never leaving his hotel room in Cairo too sick to even crawl downstairs for tea. His was the travel of his imagination and while I greatly admire his wonderfully humorous creativity, I'll say it again: Verne took the easy path around the world.

After several days of constant downpour and my reading finished, the rain finally cleared and Helsinki's citizens got back to
enjoying their pleasant summer weather. Helsinki is a city of spacious streets and flowery gardens and well-used parks. People were
out jogging off their layer of winter insulation or strolling with
baby carriages through the leafy spaces.

Helsinki was so much to my liking I ended up spending two enjoyable weeks there just walking around and seeing where a new
street might lead. The city seemed ideal in its livability and other
cities of the world would be well-served to use it as a model—
Helsinki is orderly, functional, and well-designed. Coffee shops
and cafés abound, the *International Herald Tribune* easy to obtain, and
the public transportation was first-rate. For a traveler like me, it was
Eden.

There were several golf courses in and around Helsinki; Scandinavia has become golf-mad in the past decade. However, I chose
not to play so as not to spoil my eightieth round-to-be in Tromsö.
After reading Jules Verne, *eighty* was ever prominent in my mind
and playing *eighty* rounds exactly became sacred to my quest.

Eighty had other personal significance to me as well. Breaking
eighty for the first time in a round of golf had been the biggest
thrill of my golfing life. It had occurred at the excellent Brookside Golf Course on the grounds of the Rose Bowl in Pasadena
when I had lived in southern California during my stand-up
comedy years. Though I knew I was playing well on that sunny
autumn day in the San Fernando Valley, I wasn't the one in my
foursome keeping score. To my great shock, I found myself *only*
three over par after fifteen holes. Was breaking *eighty* finally going to happen?

Up until then, I had shot eighty exactly on the nose probably
forty times or so. However, I had always choked as I tried in vain
to finish in those magical *seventies*. Something perilous would always occur; I'd hit my ball out of bounds on the seventeenth hole
or blade a sand wedge thirty yards over the eighteenth green up
against the clubhouse and thus ruin my score and chance to finish

in the *seventies*. I felt snakebit and had started to think I would always be just another *eighties* golfer.

At tree-lined Brookside, near the base of the San Gabriel Mountains, it seemed my goal would finally happen as being only three over par after fifteen holes with just three more holes to navigate gave me at least a bit of a margin for error. I needed that margin! Oh, how I wish I could say I ended the round like a champion while making three straight pars coming into the clubhouse in a blaze of glory, but that wasn't the case. As with my futile attempts in the past, I came in low and hot and leaking oil with my wings on fire like the *Memphis Belle* trying to land back in England after getting pounded by antiaircraft fire from the Germans. I made two awful double bogeys in a row on sixteen and seventeen, but somehow I calmed my shaky nerves, righted the rudder for the landing, and parred the last for a seventy-nine. I had finally broken *eighty*! I was so relieved and happy you would have thought I had just won an Academy Award and a Nobel Prize on the same day—drinks in the clubhouse were gladly on me! *Eighty* is a special number in my golfing life.

Using Helsinki as my base camp to rest up, I was acclimating myself before my final ascent to the top of the golfing world. Granted, I wouldn't need an ice ax or crampons, but that last northern hike was my personal assault up my version of the north face of Everest without oxygen or a Sherpa or even an able assistant like Passepartout. It was just me and my ten clubs with the summit of the Tromsö Golf Club beckoning me to journey north. Reaching the pinnacle, I didn't even have to worry about planting a flag to signify the meeting of my goal once there—they already had eighteen of their own planted in the holes on the greens and awaiting me. It was time to head to Tromsö.

The day I left Helsinki, the bad weather came back with a vengeance. Intense precipitation and cold wind hammered Helsinki with a fury. The watery gusts were so harsh that using an umbrella was pointless. Pedestrians huddled in storefront doorways before again venturing out in brief fits and starts to brave the elements as they went about their chores and errands. I was soaked to the gills after my short jaunt to the main railway station to buy my ticket north to Lapland's Rovaniemi.

My train was an overnighter heading due north. That particular train is known as the "Santa Claus Express," as the route ends in Rovaniemi—the capital and commercial center of Finland's north-ernmost province of Lapland. Rovaniemi straddles the Artic Circle. From there I would catch a bus to Tromsö through northern Norway, which sits atop Scandinavia like the lid on a mason jar. That overland route between the two countries is only open during the summer months, as the severe winter makes the roads through the mountains of northern Norway impassable.

The compartment I had been assigned on the train was again comfortable and well laid-out, but I didn't expect anything less from the Finns. The train left the splendid station exactly on time at 7:26 in the evening as rain continued to moisturize the lush green countryside. The green grass looked like it had had all the moisturizing it could handle. That downpour was overkill. We passed sports fields flooded with standing water. Helsinki's suburban parks within eyeshot of the tracks were as wet as they could be. The foliage was nothing but green and more green and the city could just as easily have been known by Seattle's nickname, the "Emerald City."

The next morning the rain had cleared as we pulled into Rovaniemi under a dull, gray sky. The streets of Rovaniemi were deserted on that Sunday morn—very few of the town's citizens were out and about. The absence of people seemed odd, as if there weren't enough summer months to unthaw after the long winter, so people just stayed indoors near the hearth. Rovaniemi has a top-of-the-world feel with a frosting of bleakness to it. It wasn't appealing in its physical beauty—the town looked as plain and nondescript as brown butcher's paper. Rovaniemi was mostly a stopover for those wanting to head even further north on the globe. I was a member of that club. I killed a couple of hours at the train station waiting for my bus's departure to Tromsö. There seemed little reason to sightsee. After being in the great cities of the world like Melbourne, Buenos Aires, or Cape Town, a lackluster town on the Arctic Circle was hard to get excited over.

My bus arrived around noon. I boarded quickly for the eight-hour ride to Tromsö. There was symmetry to my trip: the tour bus was a replica of the one I had boarded in Punta Arenas for the final leg to Ushuaia and the bottom of South America. Unlike that journey, these roads were paved and my bones wouldn't be rattled as they had been for those twelve hours of torture in Tierra del Fuego.

We motored steadily along toward the Norwegian border. The terrain of northwestern Finland was windswept and flat, similar to lonely Patagonia with the same scrubland of muted purple and brown brush. It was inhospitable, desolate land. We passed frigid-looking lakes and icy streams. Every so often a single A-framed home would present itself just off the desolate road. I had never thought about why A-framed homes were built the way they were, but it was plain to see in this terrain that the steep roofs wouldn't allow snow to pile up and that had to be a major concern this far north on the globe. Why had that simple architectural design fact never entered my mind before in all my years? I guess I had been too busy thinking about golf.

We entered Norway and the scenery changed dramatically. Jagged, snowcapped peaks towered up into the puffy white clouds. Waterfalls free-fell hundreds of feet down the steep slopes and fed the magically blue fjords and waterways on both sides of the road. At the base of the peaks, broad green pastures spread all the way to the water's edge and looked as idyllic as pastures could possibly look. The windy two-lane road had to navigate the outline of the fjords and it was easy to understand why there was no train route through that section of the world—it would have been fantastically difficult to engineer rail tracks through the wild topography. The scenery was spectacularly beautiful as the color contrasts of the snowcapped glacier peaks, the intensely deep-blue inlets, and the emerald green fields were only broken up periodically by a picture-book farmhouse with smoke billowing out of its chimney. Nature seems to do its best work in places that are still difficult to get to. Northern Norway was magical land.

Our bus was behind schedule and we entered Tromsö at ten-thirty that evening in broad daylight—it might as well have been noon, it was so bright out. The harbor city looks appealing and only gets more so as you cross the arched bridge spanning Tromsö's picturesque harbor that leads to the charming town center. Tromsö is such a physically beautiful town set against the dramatic backdrop of peaks and sea that from the moment your eyes first catch a glimpse, you know you've ventured to one of the great secret locales on earth.

Tromsö, at a latitude of 69 degrees north, has both the northernmost university and the northernmost golf course in the world—a delightful combination in my humble view.

Tromsö revels in the midnight sun. The narrow lanes have street musicians playing classical music interspersed with polka-sounding tunes. Smiling Norwegians and tourists are on a constant pub crawl as Tromsö has more pubs per capita than any other town in Norway. Side-by-side houses gaily painted canary yellow and periwinkle blue dot the hillside, which looks out over the island's harbor and the thriving pedestrian-only town center. Months ago in Seattle, I had conjured up an image of an austere, windswept outpost, not a merry, prosperous burg; which is what Tromsö actually is. It was the perfect place to end to my quest. Surprisingly, Tromsö was the most delightful town I found in my journey.

I found it impossible to sleep with the sun shining as brilliantly in the middle of the night as it does at high noon, so I went out wandering around the town in the wee hours. I wasn't alone—Tromsö's streets are lively no matter what the time of day. Norwegians basically stay awake all summer and then hibernate like bears in the winter, as they sleep when they have month after month of no sunlight at all. I had never been in the midnight sun before, and experienced the strange event of having to go back to my hotel room to get my sunglasses for my late-night stroll at two in the morning.

After two days of enjoyable sightseeing and people-watching in the bustling village, it was time for my final round of golf—big number eighty. I hadn't wanted to just rush out to the golf course upon arrival until I had savored the town a bit. No "city course" like the wonderful St. Andrews, the Tromsö Golf Club is well out of town—roughly twenty-five miles. With no buses making that trip, I had tried in vain to rent a car as they are actually cheaper than hiring a taxi—which would have been another seventy-dollar fare like I had suffered in Budapest (Norway was far and away the most expensive country I visited). There were only ten cars for hire in the entire town, and they were all rented, as Tromsö was full of tourists enjoying its end-of-summer charms. I guessed I was going to have to hitchhike to go play golf as I had done in Moscow.

I called out to the golf course and explained the lack of rental cars and inquired if they might have any ideas for transportation. A cheerful lady told me a local resident was coming to play golf that afternoon and could give me a lift. Sounded great to me.

Lars Erstad, my ride and soon-to-be golfing pal, is the owner of a local computer software company. He was taking the afternoon off for a round of golf—that right there made him my kind of guy. Tromsö is the sort of place where folks don't let work get in the way of life's enjoyment. Lars picked me up in front of my hotel. We drove off into the Norwegian countryside to go play the ancient game at the top of the golfing world.

Golf is relatively new to Norway, but they are taking to it with gusto. The Tromsö Golf Course, only open for two years, already sported over seven hundred members! It's a good, solid course with no pretensions—just a friendly, fun, and welcoming spot to play that wonderful game. Golf is best when inclusive, and the Tromsö Golf Club was certainly that—they accept all comers. Playing round number eighty at a truly *public* golf course was the fittingest way for me to end my journey. I would have been greatly disappointed if I had found a snobby rich man's club at the top of the world, even if it had offered foot massage. I had come full circle.

That was the lovely setting for my final round of golf as Lars and I played happily along through the groves of evergreens and poplars flanking the fairways. The Tromsö Golf Club is surrounded by the same awesome peaks I saw on the bus ride into town. The setting is blissfully peaceful as the course serenely resides in a long, narrow valley well away from anything but glorious nature in her full regalia. The sound of my shots echoed along the steep mountainsides, the reverberation carried north toward the nearby fjord. The Tromsö Golf Club was eerily reminiscent of the Ushuaia Golf Club in its majestic setting—both are horse-shoed by magnificent, sheer-sided mountains. It was gratifying to learn those two extreme courses of the world were encapsulated within nature's wonder. It seemed fitting.

Lars loves the game and, despite having only played for a couple of years, was hitting the ball well. We had a spirited match while marching along, chatting and whacking our shots as we came to our respective placement. A fellow golf nut, Lars became a new golfing friend in a new golfing locale. What's better than that?

He described how, in Norway, all prospective golfers have to take a class on the rules and etiquette of the game before they are allowed out on the course. Is there any wonder why Norway perennially is named the number-one country of the world to live in? That simple instruction should be mandatory everywhere in the golfing world as the game thrives when played with courtesy and manners. Norway seems to do things right.

Just to see what he'd say, I asked Lars why Norway is always ranked so high as a place to live in the world. He thought for a second and said, "I think it's the fact we have free national health care for all. It takes a lot of pressure off our society when people know they don't have to worry about becoming ill or disabled. In Norway, we take care of each other." There you go.

Finally, we came to my final hole of the adventure—a 200-yard par-three with the green sitting directly in back of the charming one-story wooden clubhouse. It was funny, but I was extremely nervous: I wanted my final tee-shot to be memorable and pure, not some ugly miss-hit clanking weakly shy of the green as I'd done hundreds of times during my travels. Nor did I want to come in again like the *Memphis Belle.*

Please, Golf Gods, if you're there, let this be a good shot!

Slowly, I lined up the final full shot. I took a deep breath. I then struck my four-iron, at least, near the sweet spot. For once, I hadn't choked! The ball soared like a rocket through the pristine Norwegian air. Holding my follow-through as if posing for the cover of a golf magazine, I watched the shot climb against the backdrop of jagged peaks off in the distance. I hoped the ball would never come down so I could just keep watching its flight forever. A well-hit golf ball is a rare and beautiful thing to witness. When you're the one who hit it, and when you're standing at the top of the world when you did, life is good.

The ball flew directly over the flag and came to rest twelve feet behind the hole. I walked up the last fairway with tears in my eyes. The trip had been my own journey—one I had just made up while daydreaming back in Seattle as I had wondered where the world's southernmost and northernmost golf courses were on the globe. I loved that I had acted on my silly idea—life is short. Hiding my tears from Lars, I sized up my putt and with nervous, shaky hands hit a mediocre putt that never had a chance of going in. Alas, the birdie-two wasn't to be as I missed by a couple of inches to the right of the hole. The Golf Gods wanted me to know they were still in charge—they'll hand out a good shot once in a while, but rarely two in a row. The Golf Gods prefer their flock of worshippers nice and humble as we golfers try to conquer this untamable game. However, a tap-in par on my final hole—I'll take it every time. Par is a good score anywhere in the world; as now I know.

A sense of euphoria washed over me as I picked my ball out of the cup. I had played golf and made new friends in twenty-two countries and on every continent except Antarctica. I had seen the Pyramids, the Taj Mahal, Victoria Falls, Ayer's Rock, the Nile, Alice Springs, Patagonia, the Zambezi, the Danube, the Atacama Desert, Moscow, Istanbul, Buenos Aires, La Paz, Stewart Island, Melbourne, Cape Town, China, Mumbai, Bangkok, Hanoi. Golf in exotic lands, different foods, friendships, challenges, gaining new experiences, overcoming fears—like Phileas Fogg settling back into life in London after circumnavigating the planet, I'll add my own words to those of Jules Verne: And for golf, who would not go round the world for less?

It was a sun-drenched Thursday evening in Tromsö as I put the flag back in the cup for the final time on my around-the-world golfing quest. Lars and I shook hands at the end of our round as golfers have done for hundred of years after holing out at the last. Friendships made on the first-tee, good manners, courtesy while competing—it's what makes the ancient game of the Scottish shepherds from the Kingdom of Fife great to this very day.

The next morning, I was catching a flight back to Seattle via Oslo and Amsterdam. If all the flights left on time, I'd be home to play golf on Saturday morning with my buddies back for our normal weekly game. It'll be great to see them. I have stories to tell.

Acknowledgments

I wish to thank all the people in my travels who pointed me and my ten clubs in the right direction. Especially, Ted McDougall, Dermot Whelan, Doug Harradine, Andrew Whiley, Ross Murray, Russell Squires, Peter Cassidy, and Irish in New Zealand; Mark Duder, Phil Carr, Jim Grehan, Graham Ware, and Wayne Crook in Australia; Mark Lawrie in Buenos Aires; Peter Goh in Singapore; Roger Foo and Peter Andraes in Thailand; K.K. Cheong and Richard Ang in Laos; Robert Bicknell and Howie Roberts in Vietnam; Patrick Lim, Francis Poon, Arthur Yeo, George Shay, and Lau Tong Chye in China; Jeremy Lindquist, John Terry-Lloyd, and John Commins in South Africa; Eduardo Payovich in Uruguay; Igor Ivashin and Nick Taylor in Moscow; Lars Erstad in Tromsö; and Franz Kielnhofer in Egypt for his kindness to a sick traveling stranger.

Special thanks to: Sarah Hernandez for her grammatical expertise and encouragement; my agent, Jane Dystal, for believing in my project; and Daniela Rapp for her wisdom in shaping the manuscript.

To my Seattle golf pals: Larry H., Larry B., Tom, Jim, JZ, Dr. Jerry, and Bill B. (in absentia in Arizona).

Finally, to my family: Georgiana, Patrick, Alfredo, Emily, and Sofia, with love.